Nikon D800:
From
Snapshots to
Great Shots

Jeff Revell

Peachpit
Press

Nikon D800: From Snapshots to Great Shots
Jeff Revell

Peachpit Press
1249 Eighth Street
Berkeley, CA 94710
510/524-2178
510/524-2221 (fax)

Find us on the Web at www.peachpit.com
To report errors, please send a note to errata@peachpit.com
Peachpit Press is a division of Pearson Education.

Project Editor: Valerie Witte
Production Editor: Katerina Malone
Copyeditor: Scout Festa
Proofreader: Erin Heath
Composition: WolfsonDesign
Indexer: Valerie Haynes Perry
Cover Image: Jeff Revell
Cover Design: Aren Straiger
Interior Design: Riezebos Holzbaur Design Group
Back Cover Author Photo: Scott Kelby

ISBN-13: 978-0-321-84074-5
ISBN–10:   0-321-84074-7

9 8 7 6 5 4 3 2 1

Printed and bound in the United States of America

DEDICATION

For my truly awesome family.

ACKNOWLEDGMENTS

It's funny how people tend to think that once you start writing books about cameras, the manufacturers will start dropping new production models at your feet. The truth is that I get my cameras the same way you do, by plunking down my credit card and placing an order. Yes, that's right, I buy my cameras like everyone else. Normally this is not a problem when it comes to writing my books, because the manufacturers usually have plenty of cameras in the market for the initial release. But that wasn't the case with the D800.

When the D800 was announced, I was already convinced that I was going to buy the camera, regardless of whether I wrote a book for it. I placed my order the day after the camera was announced and then waited the couple of months for the first shipments to arrive. In the meantime, my publisher and I decided that we definitely wanted to move forward with a book for this exciting new camera, so everything was moving ahead as normal. The only problem was that I had not anticipated the level of excitement that this new 36MP body would create in the marketplace. As the first shipments started to hit the shores, it became quite evident that there just weren't enough bodies to go around.

I was a little concerned at first but didn't give it too much thought, because I had ordered so early in the process. But the days turned into weeks, and I still didn't have a camera to work with, and there's only so much prepping you can do by reading the owner's manual. After a couple of months, I got a little panicky and thought I might have to spend an extra thousand dollars to buy one from one of the profiteers selling bodies on the Internet. But that's when my friends at Adorama stepped in. To be specific, my buddy Jeff Snyder, who works in the Adorama Professional department, got a hold of me and told me that he would try his best to help me find a camera. After many phone calls and emails, he was able to locate one for me and I finally had my D800.

So here's the thing—I didn't pay Adorama one extra cent for my camera. I didn't make any special deals with them. Jeff just knew that I was a professional photographer who had a desperate need to get my hands on a piece of gear and he jumped in to help. This, my friends, is the hallmark of dedication, professionalism, and passion for the industry. With that I offer a huge thank you to Adorama, Adorama Professional, and my friend Jeff Snyder for coming through in my hour of desperation. You guys are THE BEST!

Contents

Introduction

Walk into any bookseller and you will see countless books on the subject of photography. Look a little further and you will locate the camera-specific books. It is this divide between the camera-specific and instructional photography books that inspired me to write this book. I was seeing a lot of books that were just sort of missing the mark—especially when it came to combining actual photographic instruction with the use of a specific brand and model of camera. So with that, I set about to write the Snapshots to Great Shots camera series, not as a rehash of the owner's manual but as a resource to teach photography with the wonderful technology present in the D800. I have put together a short Q&A to help you get a better understanding of just what it is that you can expect from this book.

Q: IS EVERY CAMERA FEATURE GOING TO BE COVERED?

A: Nope, just the ones I felt you need to know about in order to start taking great photos. Believe it or not, you already own a great resource that covers every feature of your camera: the owner's manual. Writing a book that just repeats this information would have been a waste of my time and your money. What I did want to write about was how to harness certain camera features to the benefit of your photography. As you read through the book, you will also see callouts that point you to specific pages in your owner's manual that are related to the topic being discussed. For example, in Chapter 6, "Say Cheese!," I discuss the use of the AE-L button, but there is more information available on this feature in the manual. I cover the function as it applies to our specific needs, but I also give you the page numbers in the manual to explore it even further.

Q: SO IF I ALREADY OWN THE MANUAL, WHY DO I NEED THIS BOOK?

A: The manual does a pretty good job of telling you how to use a feature or turn it on in the menus, but it doesn't necessarily tell you *why* or *when* you should use it. If you really want to improve your photography, you need to know the whys and whens to put all of those great camera features to use at the right time. To that extent, the manual just isn't going to cut it. It is, however, a great resource on the camera's features, and it is for that reason that I treat it like a companion to this book. You already own it, so why not get something of value from it?

Q: WHAT CAN I EXPECT TO LEARN FROM THIS BOOK?

A: Hopefully, you will learn how to take great photographs. My goal, and the reason the book is laid out the way it is, is to guide you through the basics of photography as they relate to different situations and scenarios. By using the features of your D800 and this book, you will learn about aperture, shutter speed, ISO, lens selection, depth of field, and many other photographic concepts. You will also find plenty of full-page photos that include captions, shooting data, and callouts so you can see how all of the photography fundamentals come together to make great images. All the while, you will be learning how your camera works and how to apply its functions and features to your photography.

Q: WHAT ARE THE ASSIGNMENTS ALL ABOUT?

A: At the end of the chapters, you will find shooting assignments, where I give you some suggestions as to how you can apply the lessons of the chapter to help reinforce everything you just learned. Let's face it—using the camera is much more fun than reading about it, so the assignments are a way of taking a little break after each chapter and having some fun.

Q: SHOULD I READ THE BOOK STRAIGHT THROUGH OR CAN I SKIP AROUND FROM CHAPTER TO CHAPTER?

A: Here's the easy answer: yes and no. No, because the first four chapters give you the basic information that you need to know about your camera. These are the building blocks for using the camera. After that, yes, you can move around the book as you see fit because those chapters are written to stand on their own as guides to specific types of photography or shooting situations. So you can bounce from portraits to shooting landscapes and then maybe to a little action photography. It's all about your needs and how you want to address them. Or you can read it straight through. The choice is up to you.

Q: IS THERE A CHAPTER DEVOTED TO VIDEO?

A: One of the reasons you bought the D800 was probably its ability to capture video. I have written one chapter at the end of the book that covers some basic video setup information, but I really wanted the focus of this book to center around the photographic capabilities and possibilities. The truth is, even though your camera has full video capabilities, it would take an entire book to cover all the aspects of shooting quality movies with your D800 (luckily there is already a Snapshots to Great Shots book that covers DSLR video). The chapter I have included should be enough to get you started and help you explore some of the advantages of shooting video with your D800.

Q: IS THERE ANYTHING ELSE I SHOULD KNOW BEFORE GETTING STARTED?

A: In order to keep the book short and focused, I had to be selective about what I included in each chapter. The problem is that there is a little more information that might come in handy after you've gone through all the chapters. So as an added value for you, I have written a bonus chapter (called "Pimp My Ride") that is full of information on photo accessories that will help you make better photographs. You will find my recommendations for things like filters, tripods, and much more. To access the bonus chapter, just log in or join Peachpit.com (it's free), then enter the book's ISBN. After you register the book, a link to the bonus chapter will be listed on your Account page under Registered Products.

Q: IS THAT IT?

A: One last thought before you dive into the first chapter. My goal in writing this book has been to give you a resource that you can turn to for creating great photographs with your Nikon D800. Take some time to learn the basics and then put them to use. Photography, like most things, takes time to master and requires practice. I have been a photographer for 30 years and I'm still learning. Always remember, it's not the camera that makes beautiful photographs—it's the person using it. Have fun, make mistakes, and then learn from them. In no time, I'm sure you will transition from a person who takes snapshots to a photographer who makes great shots.

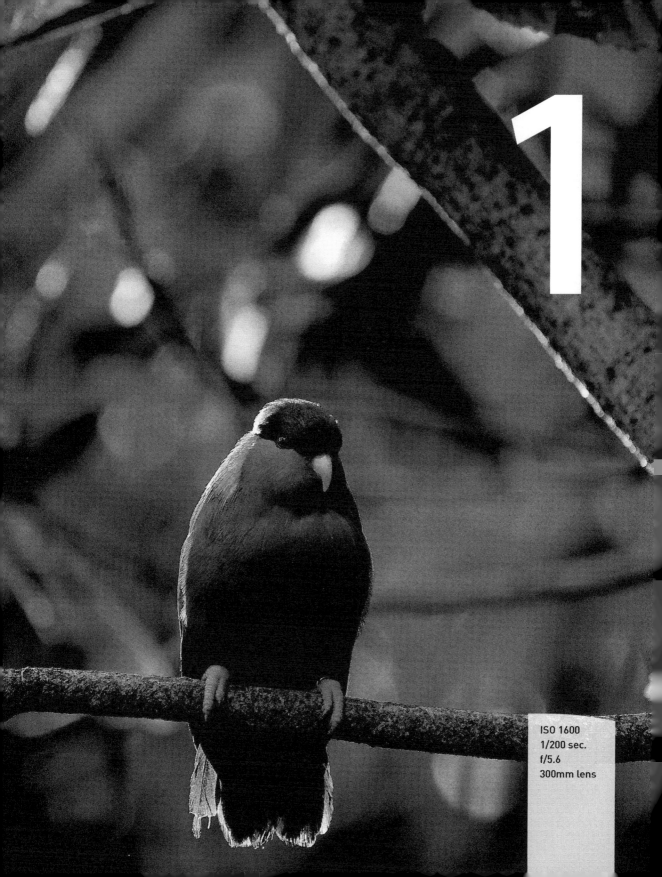

1

ISO 1600
1/200 sec.
f/5.6
300mm lens

The D800
Top Ten List

TEN TIPS TO MAKE YOUR SHOOTING MORE PRODUCTIVE RIGHT OUT OF THE BOX

Whenever I get a new camera, I am always anxious to jump right in and start cranking off exposures. What I really should be doing is sitting down with my instruction manual to learn how to use all of the camera features, but what fun is that? After all, we all know that instruction manuals are for propping up that short leg on the family room table, right?

Of course, this behavior always leads me to frustration in the end—there are always issues that would have been easily addressed had I known about them before I started shooting. Maybe if I had a Top Ten list of things to know, I could be more productive without having to spend countless hours with the manual. So this is where we begin.

The following list will get you up and running without suffering many of the "gotchas" that come from not being at least somewhat familiar with your new camera. So let's take a look at the top ten things you should know before you start taking pictures with your Nikon D800.

PORING OVER THE CAMERA

CAMERA FRONT

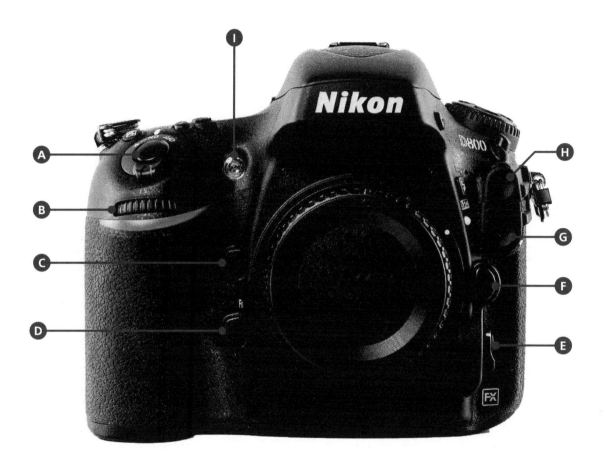

A Shutter Release Button
B Sub-Command Dial
C Depth-of-Field Preview Button
D Function Button
E AF Mode Selector

F Lens Release Button
G 10-Pin Remote Terminal
H Flash Sync Terminal
I AF-Assist/Red-Eye Reduction Lamp

CAMERA BACK

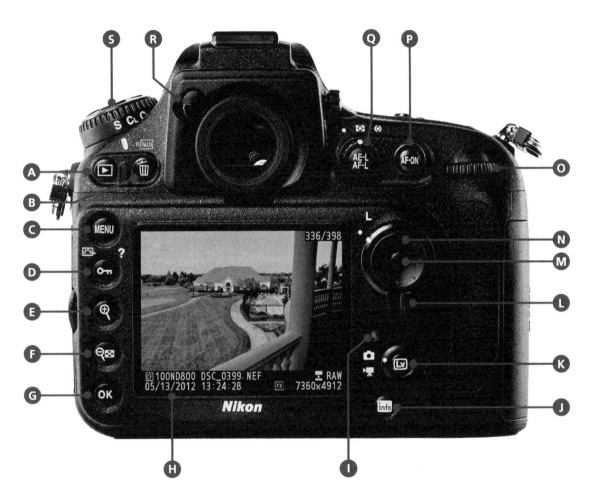

A Image Playback Button	H Monitor	O Main Command Dial
B Delete Image Button	I Ambiant Brightness Sensor	P AF-On Button
C Menu Button	J Info Button	Q Meter Selector Dial/AE-L/AF-L Button
D Protect/Picture Control/Help Button	K Live View Button	R Eyepiece Shutter Lever
E Playback Zoom In	L Focus Selector Lock	S Release Mode Dial
F Thumbnail/Playback Zoom Out	M Multi-Selector Button	
G OK Button	N Multi-Selector	

CAMERA TOP

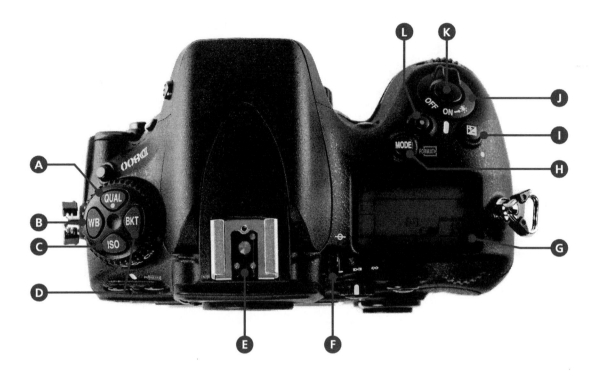

A	Quality Button	G	Control Panel
B	White Balance Button	H	Mode Button
C	ISO Button	I	Exposure Compensation Button
D	Bracketing Button	J	On/Off Switch
E	Accessory Shoe	K	Shutter Release Button
F	Diopter Adjustment Knob	L	Move Record Button

1. CHARGE YOUR BATTERY

I know that this will be one of the hardest things for you to do, because you really want to start shooting, but a little patience will pay off later.

When you first open your camera and slide the battery into the battery slot, you will be pleased to find that there is probably juice in the battery and you can start shooting right away. What you should really be doing is getting out the battery charger and giving that power cell a full charge. Not only will this give you more time to shoot, but it will also start the battery off on the right foot. No matter what claims the manufacturers make about battery life and charging memory, I always find I get better life and performance when I charge my batteries fully and then use them right down to the point where they have nothing left to give. To check your battery level, put the battery in the camera, turn the camera on, and look for the battery indicator in the lower-right section of the top LCD screen. You can also see the battery level by pressing the Info button on the back of the camera and then locating the battery meter on the rear preview screen to the right side of the display (**Figure 1.1**).

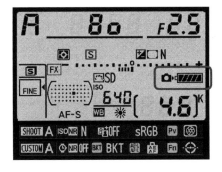

FIGURE 1.1
The LCD screen shows the current state of your battery.

KEEPING A BACKUP BATTERY

If I were to suggest just one accessory that you should buy for your camera, it would probably be a second battery. Nothing is worse than being out in the field and having your camera die. Keeping a fully charged battery in your bag will give you the confidence that you can keep on shooting without fail. Not only is this a great strategy to extend your shooting time, but alternating between batteries will help lengthen their lives. No matter what the manufacturers say, batteries do have a life, and using them half as much will only lengthen their usefulness. You could also consider getting the MB-D12 battery grip, which lets you use an additional battery in your camera.

2. TURN ON IMAGE REVIEW

One of the things that really surprised me when I first began shooting with the D800 was that the playback for reviewing images was turned off. I am used to seeing my images on the rear LCD screen after capturing a shot, so this is one of the first things that needed addressing. When turning the review on, I adjusted the default review time (the time that the monitor stays on after capturing a shot). It's also a good idea to check the auto-off durations for features like the menu screen. It can be very frustrating when you are trying to learn about the camera and its features and you have to keep pressing the Menu or Info button to bring the screen back to life. This is also the case when reviewing images on the screen after taking a picture. I don't know about you, but the default time of 4 seconds to review a shot seems very short. The answer to this problem is to increase the timer settings to longer durations. The D800 has five settings for the Monitor off delay function: Playback, Menus, Information display, Image review, and Live view. All of these can be found in the Custom Setting menu under item c4 in the Timers/AE Lock section. The image review feature can be turned on in the Playback menu. After turning on the image review, I like to set my image review to 20 seconds and the information display to 1 minute. I also change the Menus setting to 5 minutes. This might seem long, but I always end up turning it off before the end of the 5 minutes. It's just nice to have it on when I need it for a little longer.

TURNING ON IMAGE REVIEW

1. Press the Menu button and navigate to the Playback menu.
2. Select the Image review item, and press OK (**A**).
3. Highlight On, and press OK a final time to lock in your change (**B**).

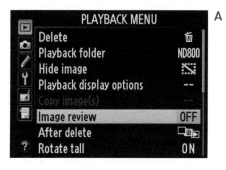
A

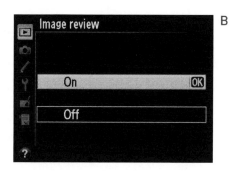
B

SETTING THE AUTO-OFF TIMERS

1. Press the Menu button and navigate to the Custom Setting menu (the pencil icon).

2. Select the item labeled c Timers/AE lock, and press OK (**A**).

3. Use the Multi-selector to scroll down to c4 Monitor off delay, and press OK (**B**).

4. Select the items that need changing, such as image review, and press OK (**C**).

5. Highlight the desired time duration for the feature you want to adjust, and then press the OK button to lock in the change and return to the previous screen (**D**).

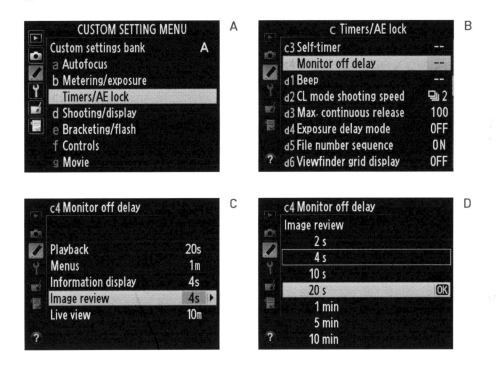

Once you have changed all of the settings, press the Menu or shutter button to exit the menu screen and go back to shooting mode.

3. SET YOUR JPEG IMAGE QUALITY

Your new D800 has a number of image quality settings to choose from, and you can adjust them according to your needs. Most people shoot with the JPEG option because it allows them to capture a large number of photos on their memory cards. The problem is that unless you understand what JPEG is, you might be degrading the quality of your images without realizing it.

The JPEG (Joint Photographic Experts Group) format has been around since about 1994 and was developed as a method of reducing large file sizes while retaining the original image information. (Technically, JPEG isn't even a file format—it's a mathematical equation for reducing image file sizes—but to keep things simple, we'll just refer to it as a file format.) The problem with JPEG is that, in order to reduce file size, it has to throw away some of the information. This is referred to as "lossy compression." This is important to understand, because while you can fit more images on your memory card by choosing a lower-quality JPEG setting, you will also be reducing the quality of your image. This effect becomes more apparent as you enlarge your pictures.

The JPEG file format also has one other characteristic: to apply the compression to the image before final storage on your memory card, the camera first applies all of the image processing. Image processing involves such factors as sharpening, color adjustment, contrast adjustment, noise reduction, and so on. Many photographers now prefer to use the RAW file format to get greater control over the image processing. We will take a closer look at this in Chapter 2, "First Things First," but for now let's just make sure that we are using the best-quality JPEG possible.

The D800 has nine settings for the JPEG format. There are three settings each for the Large, Medium, and Small image size settings. The three settings (Basic, Normal, and Fine) represent more or less image compression based on your choice. The Large, Medium, and Small settings determine the actual physical size of your image in pixels. Let's work with the highest-quality setting possible. After all, our goal is to make big, beautiful photographs, so why start the process with a lower-quality image?

SETTING THE IMAGE QUALITY

1. Press the Info button on the back of the camera to display all of the settings.
2. Press and hold the QUAL button (on top of the camera to the left of the view-finder) to activate the cursor in the information screen.

3. Use the Main Command dial to select the Fine quality setting (**A**).

4. To adjust the image size, rotate the Sub-command dial (**B**).

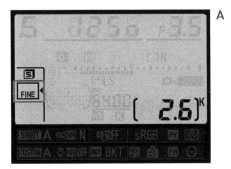

A

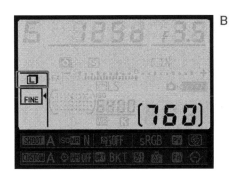

B

As you will see when scrolling through the quality settings, the higher the quality, the fewer pictures you will be able to fit on your card. If you have an 8 GB memory card, the quality setting we have selected will allow you to shoot about 360 photographs before you fill up your card. Always try to choose quality over quantity. Your pictures will be better for it.

Manual Callout

For a complete chart that shows the image quality settings with the number of possible shots for each setting, turn to page 436 in your user manual. Note that the settings we chose are for the FX (full frame) format.

4. DISABLE THE SLOT EMPTY RELEASE LOCK

This is one of the features that you may never pay attention to. That is, until it bites you right in the fanny. The short of it is that the camera is set up to take a picture even if there is no memory card in the slot. Why would anyone want this feature? Well, if you are trying to sell the camera and have it on display, it's nice to have the camera actually take pictures and display them on the rear LCD screen just as if there were a card in it—that way, you don't have to worry about anyone taking off with the card.

The problem for the rest of us is that if we don't turn this feature off and forget to check, we might assume that there is a card and start shooting. Of course every image that is captured without a card will be thrown out with each new click of the shutter or when the camera is turned off. To their credit, Nikon does display a nice red Demo notation in the upper-left corner of the image, but believe me when I tell you that sooner or later this feature will come back to haunt you. The easiest way to safeguard yourself is to just have the camera be locked when there is no card in either of the two memory card slots.

TURNING ON THE DISABLE FUNCTION

1. Press the Menu button and locate the Custom Setting menu.

2. Highlight f Controls, and press OK (**A**).

3. Scroll down to item f11 Slot empty release lock, and press OK (**B**).

4. Highlight LOCK Release locked, and press OK (**C**).

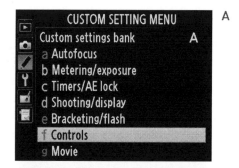

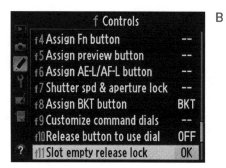

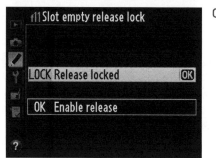

Now when you press the shutter release button without a card in the camera, you will find that the camera does nothing. This should be your cue to dig that memory card out of your camera bag.

5. ADJUST THE VIEWFINDER DIOPTER

If you wear glasses or your eyes are just getting older, you might have trouble looking through the viewfinder. Actually, you will be able to see through the viewfinder, but what you see might not look like it is in crisp focus. This may not be a huge problem when you are using autofocus, but if you are trying to manually focus your lens, you will find that your images look a bit soft. To remedy this, use the diopter adjustment control (located to the right of the viewfinder) to adjust things for your vision. There is no "correct" setting for this adjustment, so you will have to dial it in yourself. It's easy if you know this little trick.

1. Pull out the diopter adjustment control knob, turn on the camera, and look through the viewfinder (if you normally wear glasses, you should have them on).

2. Turn the knob forward or backward until the digital readout in the viewfinder looks sharp.

3. Push in the knob to lock in your changes.

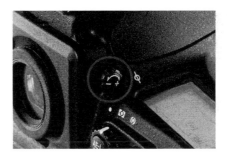

That's all there is to it. You're now ready to start shooting with a clearer view.

6. SET THE CORRECT WHITE BALANCE

White balance correction is the process of rendering accurate colors in your final image. Most people don't even notice that light has different color characteristics, because the human eye automatically adjusts to changes in color temperature—so quickly in fact that everything looks correct in a matter of milliseconds.

When color film ruled the world, photographers would select which film to use depending on what their light source was going to be. The most common film was balanced for daylight, but you could also buy film that was color balanced for tungsten light sources. Most other lighting situations had to be handled by using color filters over the lens. This process was necessary for the photographer's final image to show the correct color balance of a scene.

Your camera has the ability to perform this same process automatically, but you can also choose to override it and set it manually. Guess which method we are going to use? That's right, once again your photography should be all about maintaining control over everything that influences your final image.

Luckily, you don't need to have a deep understanding of color temperatures to control your camera's white balance. The choices are given to you in terms that are easy to relate to and that will make things pretty simple. Your white balance choices are:

- **Auto:** The camera determines the best white balance setting and adjusts accordingly. Very useful in mixed lighting situations.

- **Incandescent:** Used for any occasion where you are using regular household-type bulbs for your light source. Tungsten is a very warm light source and will result in a yellow-orange cast if you don't correct for it.

- **Cool-White Fluorescent:** Used to get rid of the green-blue cast that can result from using regular fluorescent lights as your dominant light source. Some fluorescent lights are actually balanced for daylight, which would allow you to use the Daylight white balance setting.

- **Daylight:** Most often used for general daylight/sunlit shooting.

- **Flash:** Used whenever you're using the built-in flash or a flash on the hot shoe. You should select this white balance to adjust for the slightly cooler light that comes from using a flash. (The hot shoe is the small bracket that rests just above the eyepiece on the top of your camera. This bracket is used for attaching a more powerful flash to the camera; see Chapter 8, "Mood Lighting," for more information.)

- **Cloudy:** The choice for overcast or very cloudy days. This and the Shade setting will eliminate the blue color cast from your images.

- **Shade:** Used when working in shaded areas that are still using sunlight as the dominant light source.

- **Kelvin:** This setting works well when you know the actual Kelvin temperature (color) of the lights that you are working with.

- **Pre:** Indicates that you are using a customized white balance that is adjusted for a particular light source. This option can be adjusted using an existing photo you have taken or by taking a picture of something white or gray in the scene.

SETTING THE WHITE BALANCE

1. After turning on or waking the camera, press and hold the WB button located on the top of the camera, to the left side of the viewfinder.

2. Rotate the Main Command dial to change the white balance mode, which is visible on the top control panel LCD. You can also use the info screen to view the changes (**A**).

3. If you want to use the Kelvin setting, rotate the Main Command dial to set the white balance to Kelvin and then use the Sub-command dial to set the desired temperature setting (**B**).

4. Once everything is set, just release the WB button and start shooting.

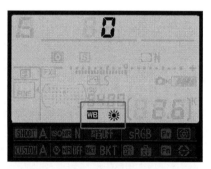

A

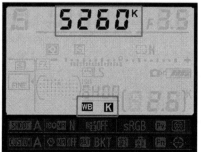

B

WHITE BALANCE AND THE TEMPERATURE OF COLOR

When you select white balances in your camera, you will notice that underneath several of the choices is a number—e.g., 5200K, 7000K, or 3200K. These numbers refer to the Kelvin temperature of the colors in the visible spectrum. The visible spectrum is the range of light that the human eye can see (think of a rainbow or the color bands that come out of a spectrum). The visible spectrum of light has been placed into a scale called the Kelvin temperature scale, which identifies the thermodynamic temperature of a given color of light. Put simply, reds and yellows are "warm" and greens and blues are "cool." Even more confusing can be the actual temperature ratings. Warm temperatures are typically lower on the Kelvin scale, ranging from 3000 degrees to 5000 degrees, while cool temperatures run from 5500 degrees to around 10,000 degrees. Take a look at this for examples of Kelvin temperature properties.

KELVIN TEMPERATURE PROPERTIES

Flames	1700K–1900K	Daylight	5000K
Incandescent bulb	2800K–3300K	Camera flash	5500K
White fluorescent	4000K	Overcast sky	6000K
Moonlight	4000K	Open shade	7000K

The most important thing to remember here is how the color temperature of light affects the look of your images. If something is "warm," it will look reddish-yellow, and if something is "cool," it will have a bluish cast.

7. SET YOUR COLOR SPACE

The color space deals with how your images will ultimately be used. It is basically a set of instructions that tells your camera how to define the colors in your image and then output them to the device of your choice, be it your monitor or a printer. Your camera has a choice of two color spaces: sRGB and Adobe RGB.

The first choice, sRGB, was developed by Hewlett-Packard and Microsoft as a way of defining colors for the Internet. This space was created to deal with the way that computer monitors actually display images using red, green, and blue (RGB) colors.

Because there are no black pixels in your monitor, the color space uses a combination of these three colors to display all of the colors in your image.

In 1998, Adobe Systems developed a new color space, Adobe RGB, which was intended to encompass a wider range of colors than was obtainable using traditional cyan, magenta, yellow, and black colors (called CMYK) but doing so using the primary red, green, and blue colors. It uses a more widely defined palette of colors than the sRGB space and, therefore, looks better when printed.

A LITTLE COLOR THEORY

The visible spectrum of light is based on a principle called *additive color* and is based on three primary colors: red, green, and blue. When you add these colors together in equal parts, you get white light. By combining different amounts of them, you can achieve all the colors of the visible spectrum. This is a completely different process than printing, where cyan, magenta, and yellow colors are combined to create various colors. This method is called *subtractive color* and has to do with the reflective properties of pigments or inks as they are combined.

The choice you need to make when selecting your color space is based on whether you intend to use your photographs for prints or for online applications. The thing about selecting a color space is that it does not directly affect the color information of your images. It simply embeds the color space profile into the image file as instructions for your computer so that your output device (monitor or printer) can correctly interpret the colors.

SETTING THE COLOR SPACE

1. With the camera turned on, press the Menu button.

2. Using the Multi-selector, select the Shooting menu and then highlight the Color space option. Press the OK button (**A**).

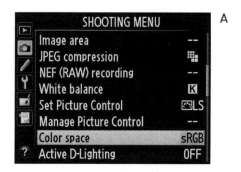

3. Highlight your desired color space, and press the OK button once again (**B**).

4. Press the Menu button or the shutter release button to return to shooting mode.

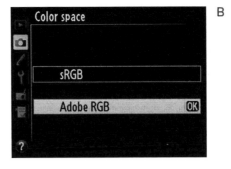

There will be no future indication of which space you have selected when you are looking at your pictures on the camera, so it's important to set this early and make changes if your output intentions change. If you forget which space you are currently using, press the Info button on the back of the camera and look for the color space in the bottom of the screen.

I typically use the Adobe RGB space when shooting because I like to print a lot of my images. If I decide to use them online, I use my image software application to change them to the sRGB color space. It is always better to go from a larger color space to a smaller one.

CHANGING SPACES

If you aren't sure about how you are going to be using your images, don't worry too much. Since the color space setting is not really affecting the color of the image, it can always be changed later by using a photo-processing program.

8. KNOW HOW TO OVERRIDE AUTOFOCUS

As good as the Nikon autofocus system is, there will be times when it just isn't doing the job for you. Many times this has to do with how you would like to compose a scene and where the actual point of focus should be. This can be especially true when you are using the camera on a tripod, where you can't pre-focus and then recompose before shooting. To take care of this problem, you will need to manually focus the lens. There are a multitude of lenses available for the D800, and they are not all the same when it comes to manual/autofocus control, so be sure to check the accompanying instruction manual for the lens.

Some lenses have a switch on the side for controlling the focus setting. You simply need to slide the switch at the base of the lens (located on the lens barrel near the body of the camera) from the M/A setting to the M setting (**Figure 1.2**). You can now turn the focus ring of the lens to set your focus, and the autofocus will not engage when you press the shutter release button. If your lens does not have a manual focus switch, you can use the focus mode selector switch located on the front of the camera just beneath the lens release button. Turn the switch from AF to M, and your lens will be all set for manual focusing.

We'll cover more manual focus situations in greater detail in future chapters.

FIGURE 1.2
To manually focus, slide the focus switch on the lens to the M position.

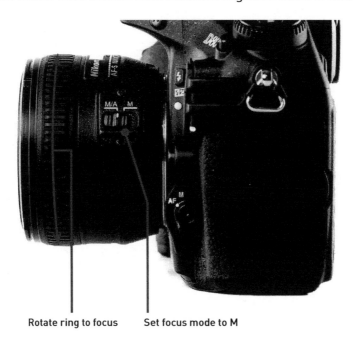

Rotate ring to focus   Set focus mode to M

9. REVIEW YOUR SHOTS

One of the greatest features of digital cameras is their ability to give instant feedback. By reviewing your images on the camera's LCD screen, you can instantly tell if you got your shot. This visual feedback allows you to make corrections on the fly and make certain that all of your adjustments are correct before moving on.

When you first press the shutter release button, your camera quickly processes your shot and then displays the image on the rear LCD display. The default setting for that display is only 4 seconds, which is why we changed the review times (as discussed earlier).

Since we have already adjusted the auto-off timer, let's check out some of the other visual information that will really help you when shooting.

There are two display modes that give you different amounts of information while reviewing your photos. The default view (**Figure 1.3**) simply displays your image along with the image file name, date, time, and image quality setting.

To get more visual feedback, press the Multi-selector up to display the second display mode, called Overview (**Figure 1.4**). This view mode not only displays the same information as the default view, but it also includes camera settings such as aperture, shutter speed, lens length, white balance, exposure compensation, shooting mode, ISO, white balance setting, picture control, quality setting, any compensation settings, the active color space, and the picture control. The other noticeable item will be the histogram, which gives you important feedback on the luminance values in your image.

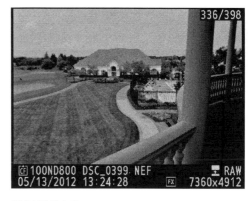

FIGURE 1.3
The default display mode on the D800.

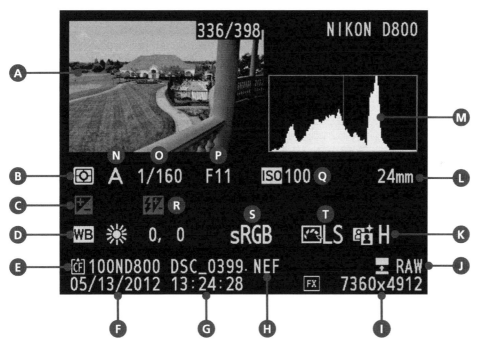

FIGURE 1.4
The Overview display mode gives you much more information.

A	Image Thumbnail	F	Date	K	Active D-Lighting	P	Aperture
B	Meter Setting	G	Time	L	Lens Length	Q	ISO
C	Exposure Compensation	H	File Name	M	Histogram	R	Flash Compensation
D	White Balance	I	Image Size	N	Camera Mode	S	Color Space
E	Folder Name	J	Quality Setting	O	Shutter Speed	T	Picture Control

Because the image thumbnail is so small, you probably won't want to use this display option as your default review setting, but if you are trying to figure out what settings you used or you want to review the histogram (see the sidebar "The Value of the Histogram"), you now have all of this great information available.

There are other display options available, but they must be turned on using the camera menu. These options can be found in the Playback menu under Playback display options (**Figure 1.5**). With this menu option you can add display modes such as None (image only), Highlights, RGB histograms (**Figure 1.6**), Shooting data (**Figure 1.7**), and Focus point. To add these items to your display, highlight them in the menu, add a checkmark by pressing right on the Multi-selector (**Figure 1.8**), and then go back to the Done option at the top and press the OK button (**Figure 1.9**). This last step is really important, because if you exit out before pressing OK on Done, your changes will not be locked in. Once you are done adding display options, you can review them by pressing the image review button and continually pressing up on the Multi-selector to cycle through the views.

I don't use the RGB histogram and Shooting data settings, because they don't offer me any visual information that I find critical during a photo session. I do, however, always have the Highlights option turned on so that I can make sure I am not clipping any information from my image highlights. (Check out the "How I Shoot" section of Chapter 4, "The Professional Modes," for more information about the Highlights display view and how to use it to improve your image quality.)

DELETING IMAGES

Deleting or erasing images is a fairly simple process that is covered on pages 44 and 234 of your manual. To quickly get you on your way, simply press the Image Playback button and use the Multi-selector to find the picture that you want to delete. Then press the Delete (trash can) button located on the back of the camera to the right of the Playback button. When you see the confirmation screen, simply press the Delete button once again to complete the process.

Caution: Once you have deleted an image, it is gone for good. Make sure you don't want it anymore before you drop it in the trash.

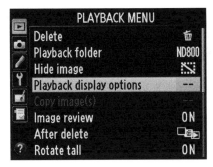

FIGURE 1.5
Select Playback display options.

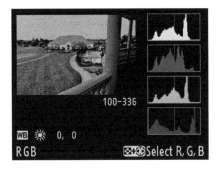

FIGURE 1.6
The RGB histogram display mode.

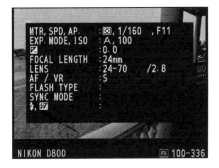

FIGURE 1.7
The Shooting data display mode.

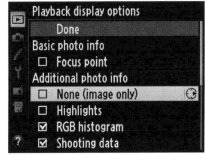

FIGURE 1.8
Add a checkmark to add an option to the display views.

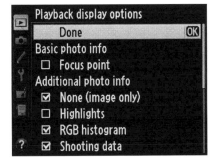

FIGURE 1.9
You must highlight the Done option and press OK to lock in the changes.

THE VALUE OF THE HISTOGRAM

Simply put, histograms are two-dimensional representations of your images in graph form. There are two histograms that you should be concerned with: luminance and color. Luminance is referred to in your manual as "brightness" and is most valuable when evaluating your exposures. In **Figure 1.10**, you see what looks like a mountain range. The graph represents the entire tonal range that your camera can capture, from the whitest whites to the blackest blacks. The left side represents black; the right side represents white. The heights of the peaks represent the number of pixels that contain those luminance levels (a tall peak in the middle means your image contains a large amount of medium-bright pixels). Looking at this figure, it is hard to determine where all of the ranges of light and dark areas are and how much of each I have. I can see that the largest peak of the graph is in the middle and trails off as it reaches the edges. In most cases, you would look for this type of histogram, indicating that you captured the entire range of tones, from dark to light, in your image. Knowing that is fine—but here is where the information really gets useful.

A histogram that has a spike or peak riding up the far left or right side of the graph means that you are clipping detail from your image. In essence, you are trying to record values that are either too dark or too light for your sensor to accurately record. This is usually an indication of over- or underexposure. It also means that you need to correct your exposure so that the important details will not record as solid black or white pixels (which is what happens when clipping occurs). There are times, however, when some clipping is acceptable. If you are photographing a scene where the sun will be in the frame, you can expect to get some clipping, because the sun is just too bright to hold any detail. Likewise, if you are shooting something that has true blacks in it—think coal in a mineshaft at midnight—there are most certainly going to be some true blacks with no detail in your shot.

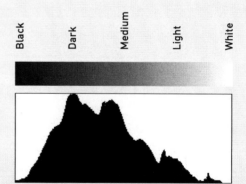

FIGURE 1.10
This is a typical histogram, where the dark to light tones run from left to right. The black to white gradient above the graph demonstrates where the tones lie on the graph and would not appear above your camera's histogram display.

The main goal is to ensure that you aren't clipping any "important" visual information, and that is achieved by keeping an eye on your histogram. Take a look at **Figure 1.11**. The histogram displayed on the image shows a heavy skew toward the left, with almost no part of the mountain touching the right side. This is a good example of what an underexposed image histogram looks like. Compare that to **Figure 1.12**, the histogram for the same image correctly exposed. Notice that even though there are two distinct peaks on the graph, there is an even distribution across the entire histogram.

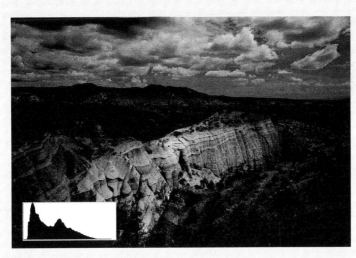

FIGURE 1.11
This image is about two stops underexposed. Notice that the histogram is skewed to the left.

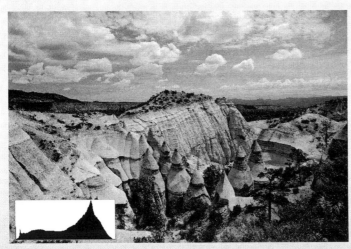

FIGURE 1.12
This histogram reflects a correctly exposed image.

10. HOLD YOUR CAMERA FOR PROPER SHOOTING

I can't begin to tell you how many times I've seen photographers holding their cameras in a fashion that is either unstable or just plain uncomfortable-looking. Much of this probably comes from holding point-and-shoot cameras. There is a huge difference between point-and-shoots and DSLR cameras, and learning the correct way to hold one now will result in great images later. The purpose of practicing correct shooting form is to provide the most stable platform possible for your camera (besides using a tripod, of course).

DSLR cameras are made to favor the right-handed individual, so properly holding the camera begins with grasping the camera body with the right hand. You will quickly find that most of the important camera controls are within easy reach of your thumb and forefinger. Next create a stable base for your camera to rest on by placing the camera body on the up-facing palm of your left hand (**Figure 1.13**). Now you can curl your fingers around the lens barrel to quickly zoom or manually focus the lens.

Now that you know where to put your hands, let's talk about what to do with the rest of your body parts. By using the underhand grip, your elbows will be drawn closer to your body. Concentrate on pulling them in close to your body to stabilize your shooting position, and try to maintain proper upright posture. Leaning forward at the waist can fatigue your back, neck, and arms. You can really ruin a day of shooting with a

FIGURE 1.13
The proper way to hold your camera to ensure sharp, blur-free images. (Photos by Matthew Revell)

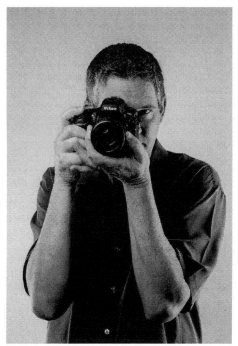
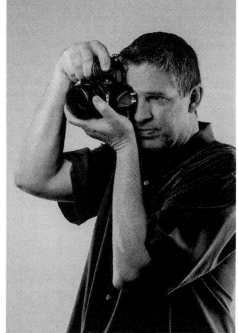

sore back, so make sure you stand erect with your elbows in. Finally, place your left foot in front of your right foot, and face your subject in a slightly wide stance. By combining all of these techniques, you will give yourself the best chance of eliminating self-imposed camera shake (or hand shake) in your images, resulting in much sharper photographs.

Chapter 1 Assignments

Let's begin our shooting assignments by setting up and using all of the elements of the Top Ten list. Even though I have yet to cover the professional shooting modes, you should set your camera to the P (Program) mode. This will allow you to interact with the various settings and menus that have been covered thus far.

Basic camera setup

Charge your battery to 100% to get it started on a life of dependable service. Next, using your newfound knowledge, set up your camera to address the following: image quality, diopter, and color space.

Selecting the proper white balance

Take your camera outside into a daylight environment and photograph the same scene using different white balance settings. You can use the Program (P) mode right now, since we haven't covered any of the other modes. Pay close attention to how each WB setting affects the overall color cast of your images. Next, try moving inside and repeat the exercise while shooting in a tungsten lighting environment. Finally, find a fluorescent light source and repeat one more time.

Evaluating your pictures with the LCD display

Set up your image display properties and then review some of your previous assignment images using the different display modes. Review your shooting information for each image and take a look at the histograms to see how the content of your photo affects the shape of the histograms.

Discovering the manual focus mode

Change your focus mode from autofocus to manual focus and practice a little manual focus photography. Get familiar with where the focus ring is and how to use it to achieve sharp images.

Get a grip: proper camera holding

This final assignment is something that you should practice every time you shoot: proper grip and stance for shooting with your camera. Use the described technique and then shoot a series of images. Try comparing it with improper techniques to compare the stability of the grip and stance.

Share your results with the book's Flickr group!

Join the group here: www.flickr.com/groups/d800fromsnapshotstogreatshots

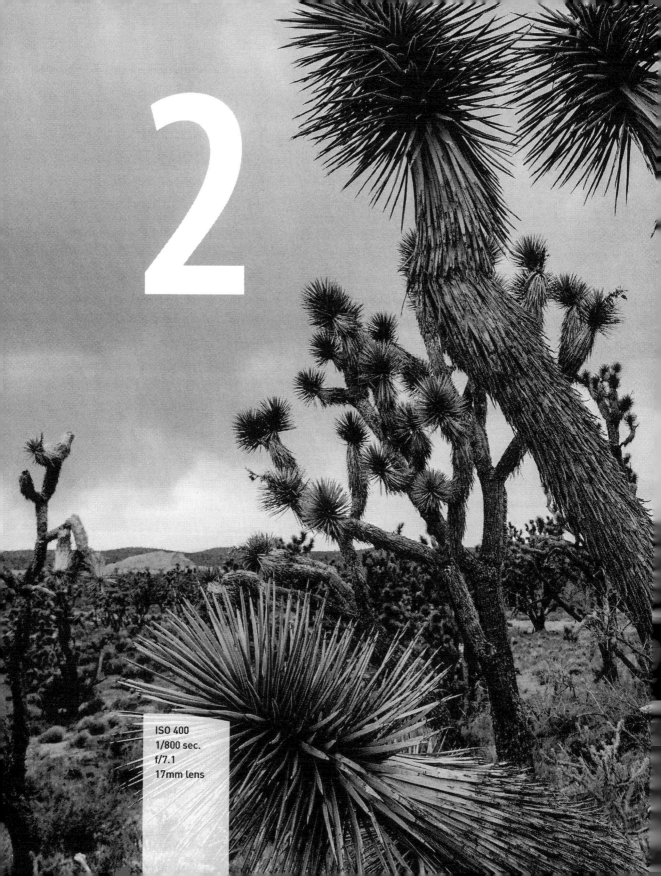

2

ISO 400
1/800 sec.
f/7.1
17mm lens

First Things First

A FEW THINGS TO KNOW AND DO BEFORE YOU BEGIN TAKING PICTURES

Now that we've covered the top ten tasks to get you up and shooting, we should probably take care of some other important details. You must become familiar with certain features of your camera before you can take full advantage of it. Additionally, we will take some steps to prepare the camera and memory card for use. So to get things moving, let's start off with something that you will definitely need before you can take a single picture: a memory card.

PORING OVER THE PICTURE

Every spring the Washington DC area is blessed with a wonderful gift from Japan that creates some amazing photo opportunities: the cherry trees surrounding the Tidal Basin. The funny thing is that, until this year, I had never had an opportunity to get any good shots. This year I made a real effort to get down to the city while they were in bloom and was rewarded with some great shots and some wonderful memories.

The use of a telephoto lens allowed me to crop in tight and fill the frame with blossoms.

A large aperture helped to blur the background.

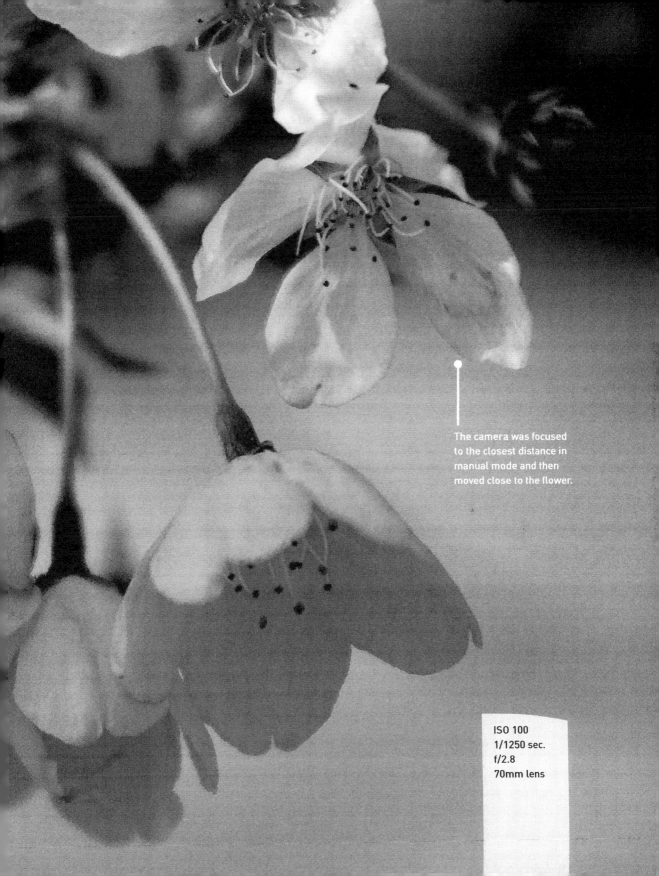

The camera was focused to the closest distance in manual mode and then moved close to the flower.

ISO 100
1/1250 sec.
f/2.8
70mm lens

PORING OVER THE PICTURE

Great Falls park is one of my favorite local shooting spots. The waterfalls always seem to offer something new each time I go, and the abundance of wildlife is always inspiring. I also know that if the water is running fast there's a good chance the kayakers will be out in force. This day was no exception, which is why I was glad to have my 70-300mm zoom so I could capture some of the action.

A fast shutter speed froze all the water drops in mid-air.

ISO 100
1/1000 sec.
f/4
280mm lens

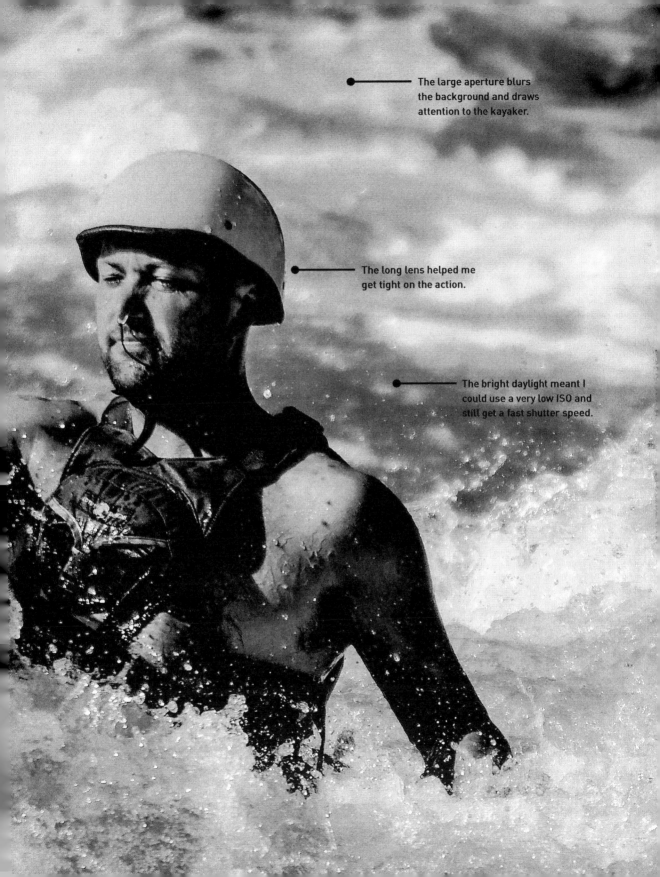

The large aperture blurs the background and draws attention to the kayaker.

The long lens helped me get tight on the action.

The bright daylight meant I could use a very low ISO and still get a fast shutter speed.

CHOOSING THE RIGHT MEMORY CARD

Memory cards are the digital film that stores all the shots you take until you move them to a computer. The cards come in all shapes and sizes, and they are critical for capturing all of your photos. It is important not to skimp when it comes to selecting your memory cards. The D800 has two memory slots that accept two types of cards: Secure Digital (SD) and Compact Flash (CF) (**Figure 2.1**).

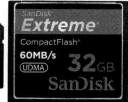

FIGURE 2.1
Make sure you select a card that has enough capacity to handle your photography needs.

If you have been using a point-and-shoot camera, chances are that you may already own an SD media card. Which brand of card you use is completely up to you, but here is some advice about choosing your memory card:

Manual Callout

Nikon has a complete list of approved SD and CF cards in the user's manual. Look at the charts on pages 434–435 to see their recommendations.

- Size matters—at least in memory cards. At 36.3 megapixels, the D800 will require a lot of storage space, especially if you shoot in the RAW or RAW+JPEG mode (more on this later in the chapter). You should definitely consider using a card with a storage capacity of at least 8 GB, if not 16 GB.

- Consider buying High Capacity (SDHC) cards. These cards are generally much faster, both when writing images to the card as well as when transferring them to your computer. If you are planning on shooting video, you can gain a boost in performance just by using an SDHC card with a class rating of at least 6. The higher the class rating of the SD card, the faster the write speed is.

- Buy more than one card. If you have already purchased a memory card, consider getting another. You can quickly ruin your day of shooting by filling your card and then having to either erase shots or choose a lower-quality image format so that you can keep on shooting. With the cost of memory cards what it is, keeping a spare just makes good sense.

FORMATTING YOUR MEMORY CARD

Now that you have your card, let's talk about formatting for a minute. When you purchase any new memory card, you can pop it into your camera and start shooting right away—and everything will probably work as it should. However, what you should do first is format the card in the camera. This process allows the camera to set up the card to record images from your camera. Just as a computer hard drive must be formatted, formatting your card ensures that it is properly initialized. The card may work in the camera without first being formatted, but chances of failure down the road are much higher.

As a general practice, I always format new cards or cards that have been used in different cameras. I also reformat cards after I have downloaded my images and want to start a new shooting session. Note that you should always format your card in the camera, not your computer. Using the computer to format a card could render the card useless. You should also pay attention to the card manufacturer's recommendations in respect to moisture, humidity, and proper handling procedures. It sounds a little cliché, but when it comes to protecting your images, every little bit helps.

Most people make the mistake of thinking that the process of formatting the memory card is equivalent to erasing it. Not so. The truth is that when you format the card, all you are doing is changing the file management information on the card. Think of it as removing the table of contents from a book and replacing it with a blank page. All of the contents are still there, but you wouldn't know it by looking at the empty table of contents. The camera will see the card as completely empty, so you won't be losing any space, even if you have previously filled the card with images. Your camera will simply write the new image data over the previous data.

FORMATTING YOUR MEMORY CARD

1. Insert your memory card into the camera (**A**).

2. Press the Menu button and navigate to the Setup Menu screen.

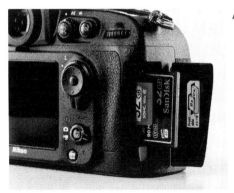

A

3. Use the Multi-selector on the back of the camera to highlight the Format memory card option, and press OK (**B**).

4. Select the memory slot that you want to format, SD or CF (**C**).

5. The next screen will show you a warning, letting you know that formatting the card will delete all images (**D**). Select Yes, and press the OK button.

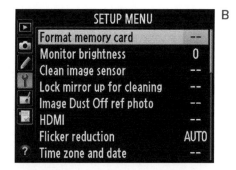

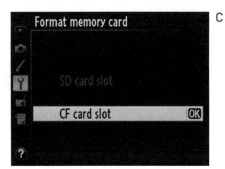

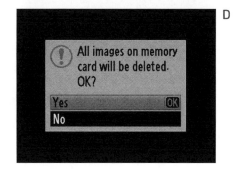

6. The card is now formatted and ready for use.

7. There is also a quick format method that you can use to bypass the menus. If you hold down the Delete and Mode buttons for more than 2 seconds, the camera will automatically format your card or cards.

UPDATING THE D800'S FIRMWARE

I know that you want to get shooting, but having the proper firmware can affect the way the camera operates. It can fix problems as well as improve operation, so you should probably check it sooner rather than later. Updating your camera's firmware is something that the manual completely omits, yet it can change the entire behavior of your camera's operating systems and functions. The firmware of your camera is the set of computer operating instructions that controls how your camera functions. Updating this firmware is a great way to not only fix little bugs but also gain access to new functionality. You will need to check out the information on the Nikon firmware update page (www.nikonusa.com/Service-And-Support/Download-Center.page) to see if a firmware update is available and how it will affect your camera, but it is always a good idea to be working with the most up-to-date firmware version available.

CHECKING THE CAMERA'S CURRENT FIRMWARE VERSION NUMBER

1. Press the Menu button and then navigate to the Setup menu.

2. Use the Multi-selector on the back of the camera to highlight the Firmware version option, and press OK (**A**).

3. Take note of the current version numbers (there are three of them), and then check the Nikon website to see if you are using the current versions (**B**).

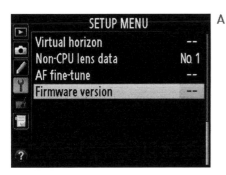 A

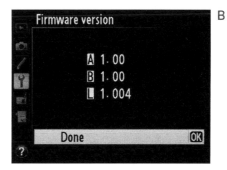 B

UPDATING THE FIRMWARE FROM YOUR MEMORY CARD

1. Download the firmware update file from the Nikon website. (You can find the file by going to the Download Center section of the Nikon camera site and locating the firmware update for your camera and computer operating system.)

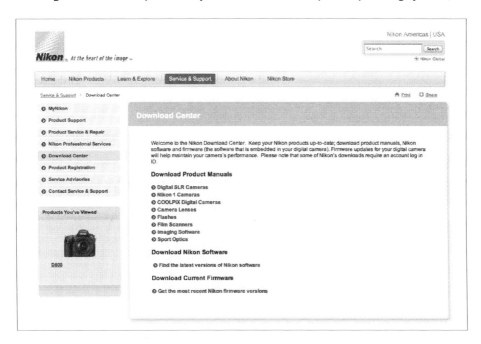

2. Once you have downloaded the firmware to your computer and extracted it, you will need to transfer it to your memory card. The card must be formatted in your camera prior to loading the firmware to it.

3. With a freshly charged camera battery, insert the card into the camera and turn it on.

4. Follow the instructions listed previously for locating your firmware version, and you will now be able to update your firmware using the files located on the memory card.

As of the writing of this book, there is one new firmware update available for the D800. After you check your camera firmware version and the Nikon site for updates, continue to check back periodically to see if any updates become available.

CLEANING THE SENSOR

Cleaning camera sensors used to be a nerve-racking process that required leaving the sensor exposed to scratching and even more dust. Now cleaning the sensor is pretty much an automatic function. Every time you turn the camera on and off, you can instruct the sensor in the camera to vibrate to remove any dust particles that might have landed on it.

There are five choices for cleaning in the camera setup menu: Clean at startup, Clean at shutdown, Clean at startup and shutdown, Cleaning off, and Clean now. I'm kind of obsessive when it comes to cleaning my sensor, so I like to have it set to clean when I turn the camera on and off.

The one cleaning function that you will need to use via this menu is the Clean now feature. This should be done every time you remove the lens from the camera body. That's because removing or changing a lens will leave the camera body open and susceptible to dust sneaking in. If you never change lenses, you shouldn't have too many dust problems. But the more often you change lenses, the more chances you are giving dust to enter the body. It's for this reason that I have added the Clean Now function to the custom My Menu list (see Chapter 11, "Advanced Techniques").

Every now and then, there will just be a dust spot that is impervious to the shaking of the Auto Cleaning feature. This will require manual cleaning of the sensor by raising the mirror and opening the camera shutter. When you activate this feature, it will move everything out of the way, giving you access to the sensor so that you can use a blower or other appropriate cleaning device to remove the stubborn dust speck. The camera will need to be turned off after cleaning to allow the mirror to reset.

If you choose to manually clean your sensor, use a device that has been made to clean sensors (not a cotton swab from your medicine cabinet). There are dozens of commercially available devices—such as brushes, swabs, and blowers—that will clean the sensor without damaging it. To keep the sensor clean, always store the camera with a body cap or lens attached.

The camera sensor is an electrically charged device. This means that when the camera is turned on, there is a current running through the sensor. This electric current can create static electricity, which will attract small dust particles to the sensor area. For this reason, it is always a good idea to turn off the camera prior to removing a lens. You should also consider having the lens mount facing down when changing lenses so that there is less opportunity for dust to fall into the inner workings of the camera.

USING THE CLEAN NOW FEATURE

1. Press the Menu button, then navigate to the Setup menu.

2. Use the Multi-selector on the back of the camera to highlight the Clean image sensor option, and press OK (**A**).

3. Highlight the Clean now option, and press the OK button (**B**). The camera will clean the sensor for about 2 seconds and then return to the menu.

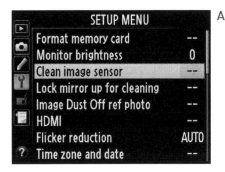
A

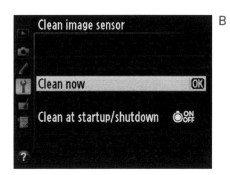
B

USING THE RIGHT FORMAT: RAW VS. JPEG

When shooting with your D800, you have a choice of image formats that your camera will use to store the pictures on the memory card. JPEG is probably the most familiar format to anyone who has been using a digital camera. I touched on this topic briefly in Chapter 1, so you already have a little background on what JPEG and RAW files are.

There is nothing wrong with JPEG if you are taking casual shots. JPEG files are ready to use right out of the camera. Why go through the process of adjusting RAW images of the kids opening presents when you are just going to email them to Grandma? Also, for journalists and sports photographers who are shooting nine frames per second and who need to transmit their images across the wire—again, JPEG is just fine. So what is wrong with JPEG? Absolutely nothing—unless you care about having complete creative control over all of your image data (as opposed to what a compression algorithm thinks is important).

As I mentioned in Chapter 1, JPEG is not actually an image format. It is a compression standard, and compression is where things go bad. When you have your camera set to JPEG—whether it is Fine, Normal, or Basic—you are telling the camera to process the image however it sees fit and then throw away enough image data to make it shrink into a smaller space. In doing so, you give up subtle image details that you will never get back in post-processing. That is an awfully simplified statement, but it's still fairly accurate.

SO WHAT DOES RAW HAVE TO OFFER?

First and foremost, RAW images are not compressed. Your camera does have a compressed RAW format, but it is lossless compression, which means there is no loss of actual image data. Note that RAW image files will require you to perform post-processing on your photographs. This is not only necessary—it is the reason that most photographers use it.

RAW images have a greater dynamic range than JPEG-processed images. This means that you can recover image detail in the highlights and shadows that just aren't available in JPEG-processed images.

There is more color information in a RAW image because it is a 14-bit image, which means it contains more color information than a JPEG, which is almost always an 8-bit image. More color information means more to work with and smoother changes between tones—kind of like the difference between performing surgery with a scalpel as opposed to a butcher's knife. They'll both get the job done, but one will do less damage.

Regarding sharpening, a RAW image offers more control because *you* are the one who is applying the sharpening according to the effect you want to achieve. Once again, JPEG processing applies a standard amount of sharpening that you cannot change after the fact. Once it is done, it's done.

IMAGE RESOLUTION

When discussing digital cameras, image resolution is often used to describe pixel resolution or the number of pixels used to make an image. This can be displayed as a dimension, such as 7360 x 4912. This is the physical number of pixels in width and height of the image sensor. Resolution can also be referred to in megapixels (MP), such as 36.3 MP. This number represents the number of total pixels on the sensor and is commonly used to describe the amount of image data that a digital camera can capture.

Finally, and most importantly, a RAW file is your negative. No matter what you do to it, you won't change it unless you save your file in a different format. This means that you can come back to that RAW file later and try different processing settings to achieve differing results and never harm the original image. By comparison, if you make a change to your JPEG and accidentally save the file, guess what? You have a new original file, and you will never get back to that first image. That alone should make you sit up and take notice.

ADVICE FOR NEW RAW SHOOTERS

Don't give up on shooting RAW just because it means more work. Hey, if it takes up more space on your card, buy more of them or larger ones. Will it take more time to download? Yes, but good things come to those who wait. Don't worry about needing to purchase expensive software to work with your RAW files; you already own a program that will allow you to work with your RAW files. Nikon's ViewNX software comes bundled in the box with your camera and gives you the ability to work directly on the RAW files and then output the enhanced results.

My recommendation is to shoot in JPEG mode while you are using this book. This will allow you to quickly review your images and study the effects of future lessons. Once you have become comfortable with all of the camera features, you should switch to shooting in RAW mode so that you can start gaining more creative control over your image processing. After all, you took the photograph—shouldn't you be the one to decide how it looks in the end?

SHOOTING DUAL FORMATS

Your camera has the added benefit of being able to write two files for each picture you take, one in RAW and one in JPEG. This can be useful if you need a quick version to email but want a higher-quality version for more advanced processing. If you have a RAW+JPEG setting selected, your camera will save your images in both formats on your card.

Note that using both formats requires more space on the memory card. I recommend that you use only one format or the other unless you have a specific need to shoot both.

SHOOTING IN RAW AND JPEG

1. Press and hold the QUAL button.
2. Use the Main Command dial to change the file type to RAW+JPEG (**A**).
3. Select one of the three RAW+JPEG settings: Fine, Normal, or Basic.
4. Use the Sub-command dial to change the size of the JPEG file (Large, Medium, or Small) (**B**).

 A

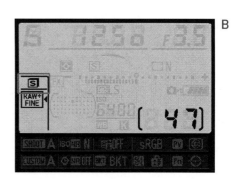 B

As you change the settings, you should see a change in the number of total images that you can capture before your card is full.

THE TIFF OPTION

While changing the file format, you might have noticed that there is one additional option that does not fall under RAW or JPEG: TIFF. TIFF (short for Tagged Image File Format) is an uncompressed file format that is processed in the camera like a JPEG file but is not compressed, so there is no loss of image data. It is also a very large file, even larger than the RAW format. You can also create different sizes of TIFF files that include large, medium, and small options. I don't use the TIFF option, but it's nice to know it's there if you need it.

LENSES AND FOCAL LENGTHS

If you ask most professional photographers what they believe to be their most critical piece of photographic equipment, they would undoubtedly tell you that it is their lens. The technology and engineering that goes into your camera is a marvel, but it isn't worth a darn if it can't get the light from the outside onto the sensor. The D800, as a digital single lens reflex (DSLR) camera, uses the lens for a multitude of tasks, from focusing on a subject to metering a scene to delivering and focusing the light onto the camera sensor. The lens is also responsible for the amount of the scene that will be captured (the frame). With all of this riding on the lens, let's take a more in-depth look at the camera's eye on the world.

Lenses are composed of optical glass that is both concave and convex in shape. The alignment of the glass elements is designed to focus the light coming in from the front of the lens onto the camera sensor. The amount of light that enters the camera is also controlled by the lens, the size of the glass elements, and the aperture mechanism within the lens housing. The quality of the glass used in the lens will also have a direct effect on how well the lens can resolve details and the contrast of the image (the ability to deliver great highlights and shadows). Most lenses now routinely include things like the autofocus motor and, in some cases, a vibration reduction mechanism.

There is one other aspect of the camera lens that is often the first consideration of the photographer: lens length. Lenses are typically divided into three or four groups depending on the field of view they deliver.

Wide-angle lenses cover a field of view from around 110 degrees to about 60 degrees (**Figure 2.2**). There is also a tendency to get some distortion in your image when using extremely wide-angle lenses. This will be apparent toward the outer edges of the frame. As for which lenses would be considered wide angle, anything smaller than 50mm could be considered wide.

Wide-angle lenses can display a large depth of field, which allows you to keep the foreground and background in sharp focus. This makes them very useful for landscape photography. They also work well in tight spaces, such as indoors, where there isn't much elbow room available (**Figure 2.3**). They can also be handy for large group shots but, due to the amount of distortion, are not so great for close-up portrait work.

FIGURE 2.2
The 24mm lens setting provides a wide view of the scene but little detail of distant objects.

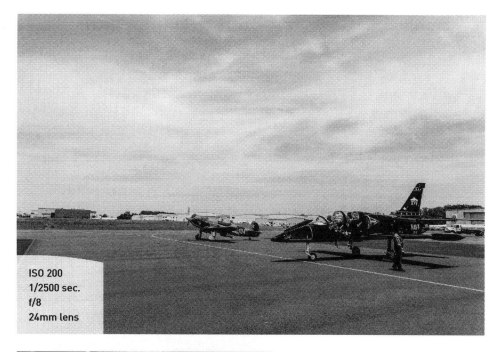

ISO 200
1/2500 sec.
f/8
24mm lens

FIGURE 2.3
When shooting in tight spaces, such as indoors, a nice wide-angle lens helps capture more of the scene.

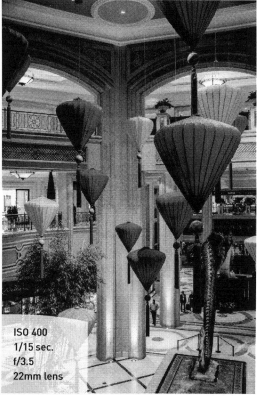

ISO 400
1/15 sec.
f/3.5
22mm lens

A *normal* lens has a field of view that is about 45 degrees and delivers approximately the same view as the human eye. The perspective is very natural and there is little distortion in objects. The normal lens for full-frame digital cameras is the 50mm lens (**Figure 2.4**).

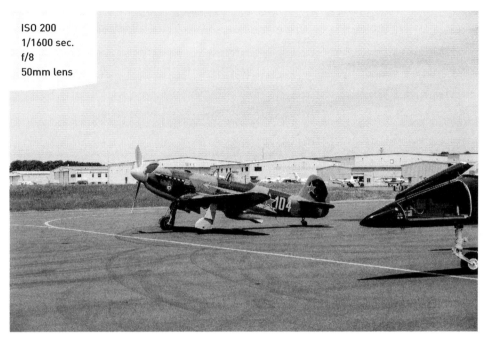

ISO 200
1/1600 sec.
f/8
50mm lens

FIGURE 2.4
Long considered the "normal" lens for 35mm photography, the 50mm does not offer the same angle as the human eye but objects seem about the same size in relation to each other.

Normal focal length lenses are useful for photographing people, architecture, and most other general photographic needs. They have very little distortion and offer a moderate range of depth of field (**Figure 2.5**).

Most longer focal length lenses are referred to as *telephoto* lenses. They can range in length from 135mm up to 800mm or longer and have a field of view that is about 35 degrees or smaller. These lenses have the ability to greatly magnify the scene, allowing you to capture details of distant objects, but the angle of view is greatly reduced (**Figure 2.6**). You will also find that you can achieve a much narrower depth of field. They also suffer from something called distance compression, which means they make objects at different distances appear to be much closer together than they really are.

FIGURE 2.5
The normal lens
worked well in
this image by
providing enough
coverage of this
concept car without
showing off the
surrounding area.

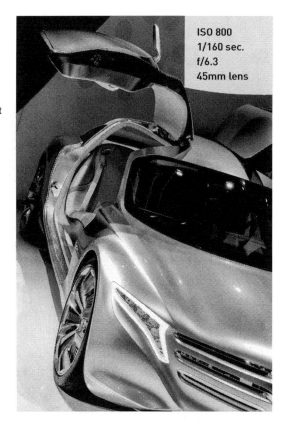

ISO 800
1/160 sec.
f/6.3
45mm lens

FIGURE 2.6
The telephoto
lens allowed me
to capture more
close-up detail of
the plane without
having to get physi-
cally closer.

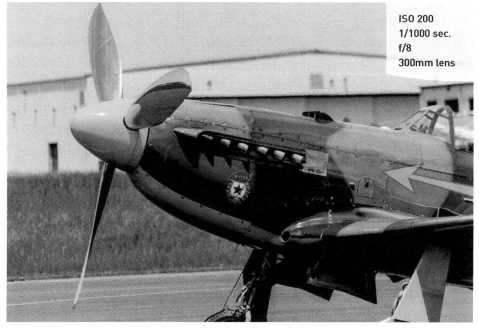

ISO 200
1/1000 sec.
f/8
300mm lens

Telephoto lenses are most useful for sports photography or any application where you just need to get closer to your subject (**Figure 2.7**).

A *zoom* lens is a great compromise to carrying a bunch of single focal-length lenses (also referred to as "prime" lenses). They can cover a wide range of focal lengths because of the configuration of their optics. However, because it takes more optical elements to capture a scene at different focal lengths, the light must pass through more glass on its way to the image sensor. The more glass, the lower the quality of the image sharpness. The other sacrifice that is made is in aperture. Zoom lenses typically have smaller maximum apertures than prime lenses, which means they cannot achieve a narrow depth of field or work in lower light levels without the assistance of vibration reduction, a tripod, or higher ISO settings. (We'll discuss all this in more detail in later chapters.)

Throughout the book, I will occasionally make reference to lenses that are wider or more telephoto than the lenses that you may own, because I have a multitude of lenses that I use for my photography. This doesn't mean that you have to run out and purchase more lenses. It just means that if you do this long enough, you are sure to accumulate additional lenses, which will expand your ability to be even more creative with your photography.

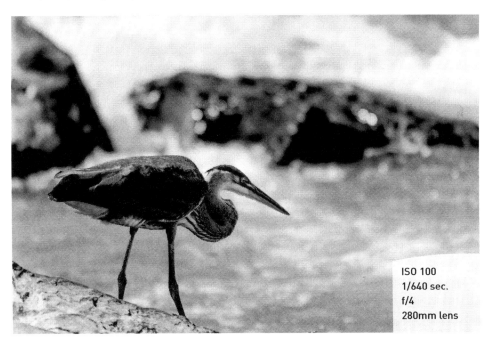

ISO 100
1/640 sec.
f/4
280mm lens

FIGURE 2.7
The long telephoto lens helped me isolate the heron from its background. There is also added separation because I used a large aperture to narrow the depth of field.

WHAT IS EXPOSURE?

In order for you to get the most out of this book, I need to briefly discuss the principles of exposure. Without this basic knowledge, it will be difficult for you to move forward in improving your photography. Granted, I could write an entire book on exposure and the photographic process—and many people have—but for our purposes I will just cover some of the basics. This will give you the essential tools to make educated decisions in determining how best to photograph a subject.

Exposure is the process whereby the light reflecting off a subject reflects through an opening in the camera lens for a defined period of time onto the camera sensor. The combination of the lens opening, shutter speed, and sensor sensitivity is used to achieve a proper exposure value (EV) for the scene. The EV is the sum of these components necessary to properly expose a scene. A relationship exists between these factors that is sometimes referred to as the "exposure triangle."

At each point of the triangle lies one of the factors of exposure:

- **ISO:** Determines the sensitivity of the camera sensor. ISO stands for the International Organization for Standardization, but the acronym is used as a term to describe the sensitivity of the camera sensor to light. The higher the sensitivity, the less light is required for a good exposure. These values are a carryover from the days of traditional color and black-and-white films.

- **Aperture:** Also referred to as the f-stop, this determines how much light passes through the lens at once.

- **Shutter Speed:** Controls the length of time that light is allowed to hit the sensor.

Here's how it works. The camera sensor has a level of sensitivity that is determined by the ISO setting. To get a proper exposure—not too much, not too little—the lens needs to adjust the aperture diaphragm (the size of the lens opening) to control the volume of light entering the camera. Then the shutter is opened for a relatively short period of time to allow the light to hit the sensor long enough for it to record on the sensor.

ISO numbers for the D800 start at 100 and then double in sensitivity as you double the number. So 400 is twice as sensitive as 200. The camera can be set to use 1/2- or 1/3-stop increments, but for ISO just remember that the base numbers double: 200, 400, 800, and so on. There are also a wide variety of shutter speeds that you can use. The speeds on the D800 range from as long as 30 seconds to as short as 1/8000 of a second. Typically, you will be working with a shutter speed range from around 1/30 of a second to about 1/2000, but these numbers will change depending on your circumstances and the effect that you are trying to achieve. The lens apertures will vary slightly depending on which lens you are using. This is because different lenses have different maximum apertures. The typical apertures that are at your disposal are f/4, f/5.6, f/8, f/11, f/16, and f/22.

When it comes to exposure, a change to any one of these factors requires changing one or more of the other two. This is referred to as reciprocal change. If you let more light in the lens by choosing a larger aperture opening, you will need to shorten the amount of time the shutter is open. If the shutter is allowed to stay open for a longer period of time, the aperture needs to be smaller to restrict the amount of light coming in.

HOW IS EXPOSURE CALCULATED?

We now know about the exposure triangle—ISO, shutter speed, and aperture—so it's time to put all three together to see how they relate to one another and how you can change them as needed.

STOP

You will hear the term *stop* thrown around all the time in photography. It relates back to the f-stop, which is a term used to describe the aperture of your lens. When you need to give some additional exposure, you might say that you are going to "add a stop." This doesn't just equate to the aperture; it could also be used to describe the shutter speed or even the ISO. So when your image is too light or dark or you have too much movement in your subject, you will probably be changing things by a "stop" or two.

When you point your camera at a scene, the light reflecting off your subject enters the lens and is allowed to pass through to the sensor for a period of time as dictated by the shutter speed. The amount and duration of the light needed for a proper exposure depends on how much light is being reflected and how sensitive the sensor is. To figure this out, your camera utilizes a built-in light meter that looks through the lens and measures the amount of light. That level is then calculated against the sensitivity of the ISO setting, and an exposure value is rendered. Here is the tricky part: there is no single way to achieve a perfect exposure, because the f-stop and shutter speed can be combined in different ways to allow the same amount of exposure. See, I told you it was tricky.

Here is a list of reciprocal settings that would all produce the same exposure result. Let's use the "sunny 16" rule, which states that when using f/16 on a sunny day, you can use a shutter speed that is roughly equal to the ISO setting to achieve a proper exposure. For simplification purposes, we will use an ISO of 100.

RECIPROCAL EXPOSURES: ISO 100

F-STOP	2.8	4	5.6	8	11	16	22
SHUTTER SPEED	1/4000	1/2000	1/1000	1/500	1/250	1/125	1/60

If you were to use any one of these combinations, they would each have the same result in terms of the exposure (i.e., how much light hits the camera's sensor). Also take note that every time we cut the f-stop in half, we reciprocated by doubling our shutter speed. For those of you wondering why f/8 is half of f/5.6, it's because those numbers are actually fractions based on the opening of the lens in relation to its focal length. This means that a lot of math goes into figuring out just what the total area of a lens opening is, so you just have to take it on faith that f/8 is half of f/5.6 but twice as much as f/11. A good way to remember which opening is larger is to think of your camera lens as a pipe that controls the flow of water. If you had a pipe that was 1/2" in diameter (f/2) and one that was 1/8" (f/8), which would allow more water to flow through? It would be the 1/2" pipe. The same idea works here with the camera f-stops; f/2 is a larger opening than f/4 or f/8 or f/16.

Now that we know this, we can start using this information to make intelligent choices in terms of shutter speed and f-stop. Let's bring the third element into this by changing our ISO by one stop, from 100 to 200.

RECIPROCAL EXPOSURES: ISO 200

F-STOP	2.8	4.0	5.6	8	11	16	22
SHUTTER SPEED	–	1/4000	1/2000	1/1000	1/500	1/250	1/125

Notice that, since we doubled the sensitivity of the sensor, we now require half as much exposure as before. We have also reduced our maximum aperture from f/2.8 to f/4 because the camera can't use a shutter speed that is faster than 1/4000 of a second.

So why not just use the exposure setting of f/16 at 1/250 of a second? Why bother with all of these reciprocal values when this one setting will give us a properly exposed image? The answer is that the f-stop and shutter speed also control two other important aspects of our image: motion and depth of field.

MOTION AND DEPTH OF FIELD

There are distinct characteristics that are related to changes in aperture and shutter speed. Shutter speed controls the length of time the light has to strike the sensor; consequently, it also controls the blurriness (or lack of blurriness) of the image. The less time light has to hit the sensor, the less time your subjects have to move around and become blurry. This can let you control things like freezing the motion of a fast-moving subject (**Figure 2.8**) or intentionally blurring subjects to give the feel of energy and motion (**Figure 2.9**).

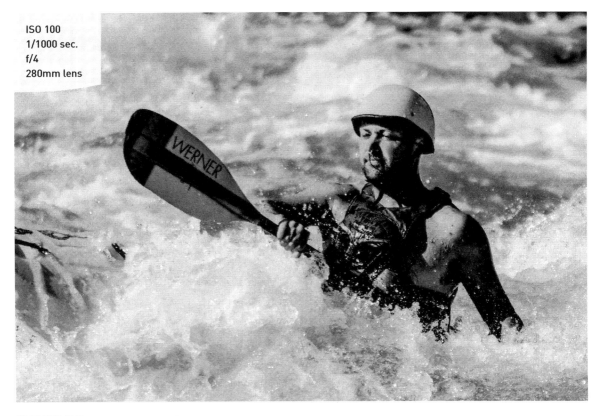

ISO 100
1/1000 sec.
f/4
280mm lens

FIGURE 2.8
A fast shutter speed was used to freeze the action as the kayaker worked his way through the rapids.

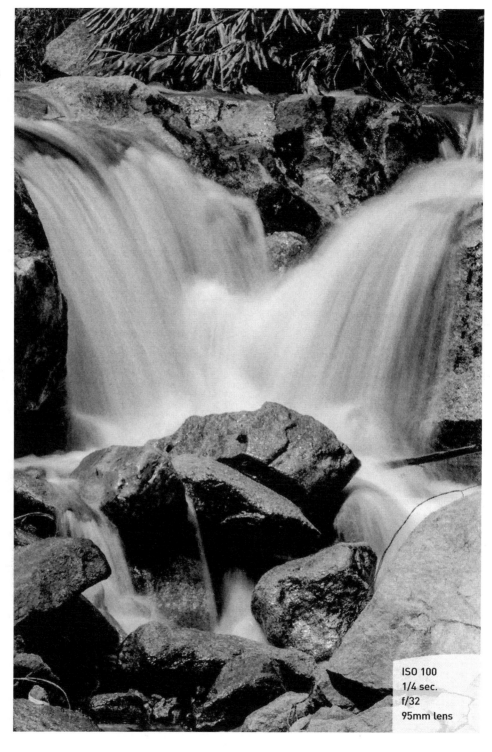

FIGURE 2.9
The slower shutter speed coupled with a neutral density filter shows the smooth flow of the water over the rocks.

ISO 100
1/4 sec.
f/32
95mm lens

The aperture controls the amount of light that comes through the lens, but also determines what areas of the image will be in focus. This is referred to as depth of field, and it is an extremely valuable creative tool. The smaller the opening (the larger the number, such as f/22), the greater the sharpness of objects from near to far (**Figure 2.10**). A large opening (or small number, like f/2.8) means more blurring of objects that are not at the same distance as the subject you are focusing on (**Figure 2.11**).

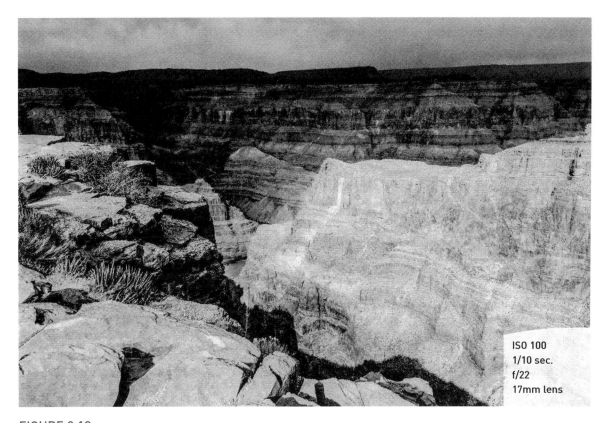

ISO 100
1/10 sec.
f/22
17mm lens

FIGURE 2.10
By using a small aperture, the area of sharp focus extends from a point that is near the camera all the way out to distant objects. In this instance, I wanted the rocks in the foreground as well as the distant ridges to be in focus. The use of a wide-angle lens added to the large depth of field.

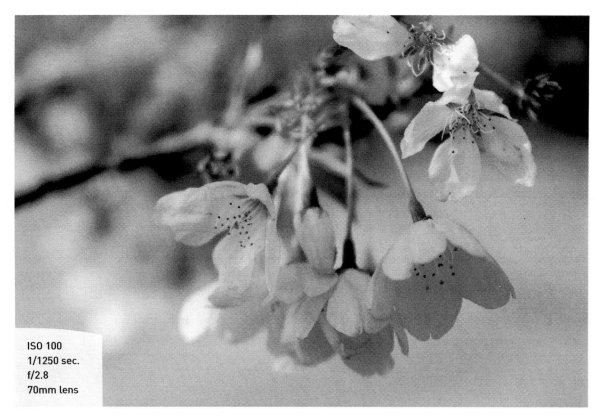

ISO 100
1/1250 sec.
f/2.8
70mm lens

FIGURE 2.11
Isolating a subject is accomplished by using a large aperture, which produces a narrow area of sharp focus.

As we further explore the features of the camera, we will learn not only how to utilize the elements of exposure to capture properly exposed photographs, but also how we can make adjustments to emphasize our subject. It is the manipulation of these elements—motion and focus—that will take your images to the next level.

Chapter 2 Assignments

Formatting your card

Even if you have already begun using your camera, make sure you are familiar with formatting the Secure Digital (SD) card. If you haven't done so already, follow the directions given earlier in the chapter and format as prescribed (make sure you save any images that you may have already taken). Then, perform the format function every time you have downloaded or saved your images, or use a new card.

Checking your firmware version

Using the most up-to-date version of the camera firmware will ensure that your camera is functioning properly. Use the menu to find your current firmware version, and then update as necessary using the steps listed in this chapter.

Cleaning your sensor

You probably noticed the sensor-cleaning message the first time you turned your camera on. Make sure you are familiar with the Clean Now command so you can perform this function every time you change a lens.

Exploring your image formats

I want you to become familiar with all of the camera features before using the RAW format, but take a little time to explore the format menu so you can see what options are available to you.

Exploring your lens

If you are using a zoom lens, spend a little time shooting with each focal length, from the widest to the longest. See just how much of an angle you can cover with your widest lens setting. How much magnification will you be able to get from the telephoto setting? Try shooting the same subject with a variety of focal lengths to note the differences in how the subject looks, and also the relationship between the subject and the other elements in the photo.

Share your results with the book's Flickr group!

Join the group here: www.flickr.com/groups/d800fromsnapshotstogreatshots

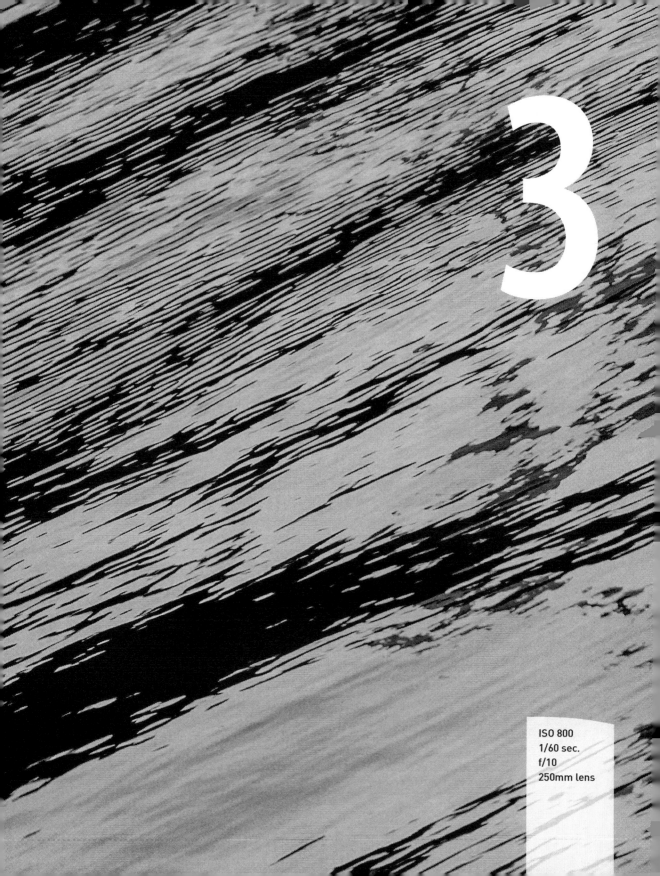

3

ISO 800
1/60 sec.
f/10
250mm lens

Running on Autopilot

LETTING THE CAMERA MAKE DECISIONS
USING AUTOMATIC FEATURES

Unlike many amateur DSLR cameras, the D800 does not have an assortment of automatic modes that you can turn to for shooting things like sports or portraits or close-ups. You have now left all that behind and must work with what I like to call "the professional modes." That being said, there are some features that you can use that will take away some of the heavy lifting and let you concentrate more on the image rather than the camera settings. Let's take a few minutes to see just what features we can set on autopilot.

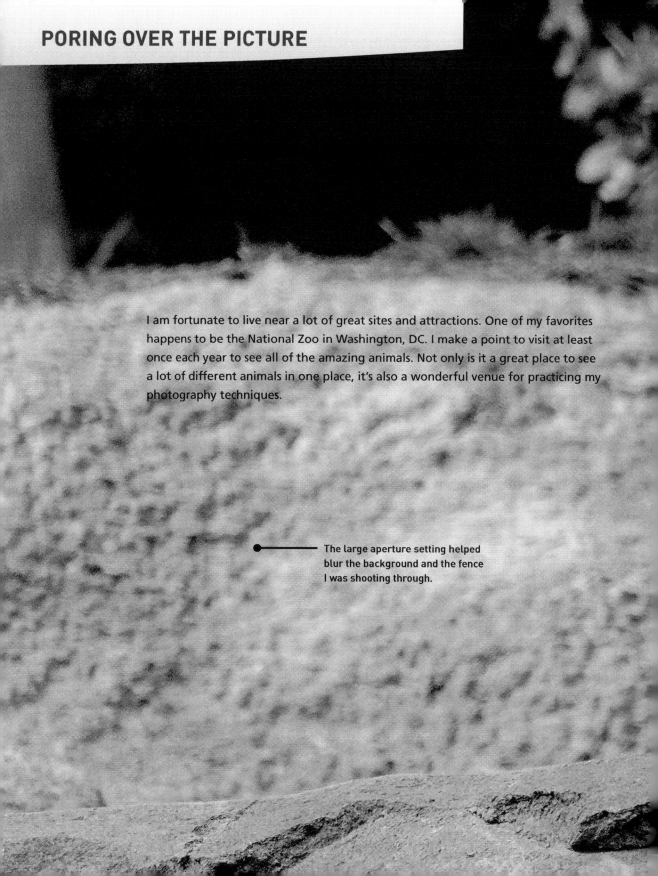

I am fortunate to live near a lot of great sites and attractions. One of my favorites happens to be the National Zoo in Washington, DC. I make a point to visit at least once each year to see all of the amazing animals. Not only is it a great place to see a lot of different animals in one place, it's also a wonderful venue for practicing my photography techniques.

The large aperture setting helped blur the background and the fence I was shooting through.

The dog was placed in the right side of the frame to add interest to the composition.

The white balance was set to Daylight.

ISO 1600
1/1600 sec.
f/5.6
300mm lens

The 300mm lens helped me get a tight shot from a distance.

City tours are a great way to find new photo locations while touring unfamiliar cities. This particular tour took me to a variety of locations that switched between indoor and outdoor venues. Since we were moving fast and I didn't have a lot of time to contemplate camera settings, I used the Auto ISO feature to help keep the ISO high enough to get good photos when moving from light to dark areas.

Auto ISO raised the ISO just high enough to allow for the camera settings I wanted to use.

Vibration reduction helped eliminate camera shake during the exposure.

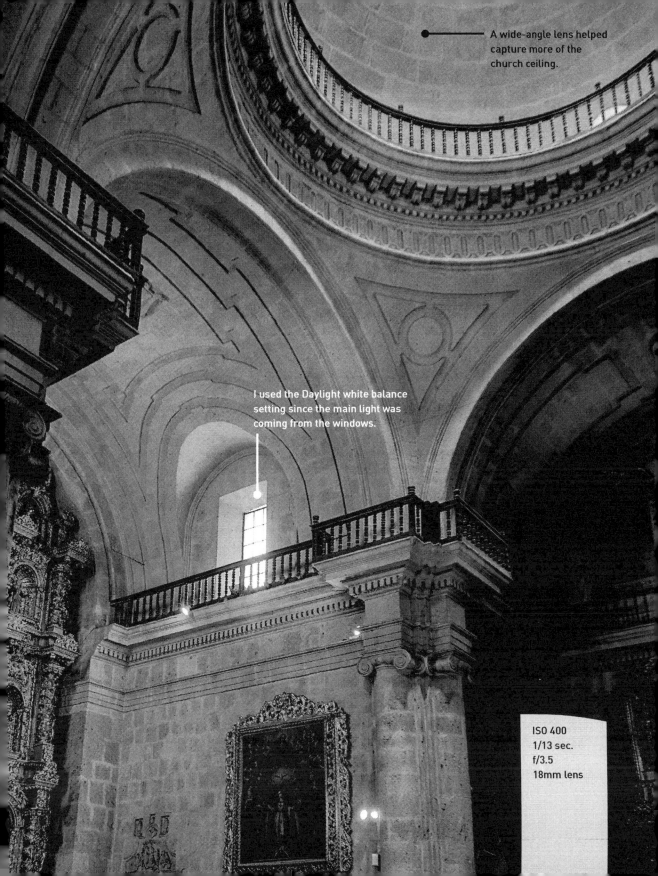

A wide-angle lens helped capture more of the church ceiling.

I used the Daylight white balance setting since the main light was coming from the windows.

ISO 400
1/13 sec.
f/3.5
18mm lens

PROGRAM MODE—CLOSE TO FULL AUTO

Some people might argue that Program mode is not an automatic mode, but with respect to apertures and shutter speeds, the camera is doing most of the thinking for you. First, let me say that it is very rare that I will use Program mode, because it just doesn't give as much control over the image-making process as the other professional modes. There are occasions, however, when it comes in handy, like when I am shooting in widely changing lighting conditions and don't have the time to think through all of my options, or when I'm not very concerned with having ultimate control of the scene. Think about taking pictures at a picnic outdoors in a partial shade/sun environment—you want great-looking pictures, but you're not looking for anything to hang in a museum. If that's the scenario, then Program mode might be just what you want.

WHEN TO USE PROGRAM (P) MODE

Sometimes photographers think that using Program mode is akin to cheating. It's letting the camera take control and make decisions. This may be true in some respects, but I like to think of Program mode as your free pass to being in the moment. It's not that you don't want to make decisions on aperture or shutter speed, but sometimes you just want to click and enjoy—and there's nothing wrong with that.

The other misconception about Program mode is that you are giving up creative control, which is absolutely not true. First of all, you will need to determine what ISO is right for your setting. This will really set the stage for the settings the camera will choose when determining exposure. Once you have the ISO set (see the sidebar on starting points for ISO selection), you can press the shutter release button halfway to let the camera select a working aperture and shutter speed. There is actually a pretty smart computer at work in your camera that is analyzing the scene and then picking through thousands of reference scenes to choose the best camera settings. When it comes to picking a proper exposure, it will be right much more than it is wrong. But here's the best part—if you don't like the settings, you can change them with a flick of your thumb so that the emphasis on the exposure is exactly where you want it.

So what do I mean by this? Well, the camera will select an exposure, but the Main Command dial allows you to shift the exposure to a reciprocal so you can have your choice of aperture or shutter speed, and the camera will adjust accordingly. For example, if I am outside taking pictures of my kids and the camera is offering an exposure of 1/125 of a second at f/11, I will probably get a good photo, but if my kids are running around, I might want to use a slightly faster shutter speed. By rotating the Main Command dial to the right, I can shift the shutter speed to a faster value, like 1/250, and the aperture will automatically shift to f/8 to compensate. Conversely, if there is a need for a smaller aperture for gaining more depth of field, I could roll that Main Command dial to the right to select a smaller aperture, and the shutter speed would increase in duration accordingly. Remember, your camera is using the internal meter to pick what it believes are suitable exposure values, but sometimes it doesn't know what it's looking at and how you want those values applied (**Figures 3.1** and **3.2**).

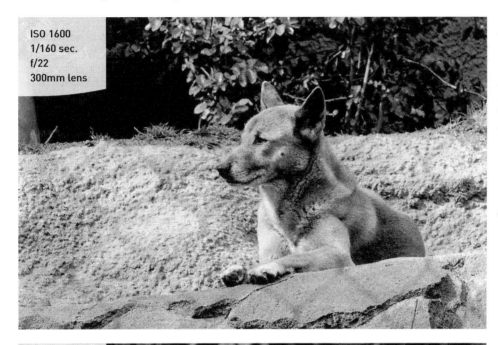

ISO 1600
1/160 sec.
f/22
300mm lens

FIGURE 3.1
This is my first shot using Program mode. The aperture setting is fairly small, and the fence in front of the animal is visible.

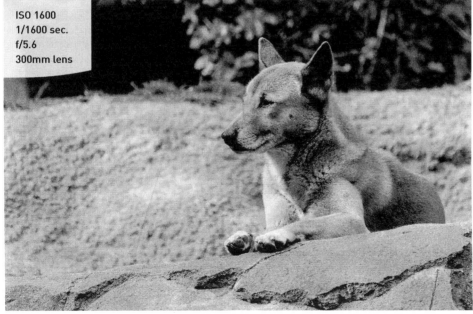

ISO 1600
1/1600 sec.
f/5.6
300mm lens

FIGURE 3.2
By shifting the exposure, I was able to use a faster shutter speed and larger aperture so that the fence was blurred out of view.

As you move forward in the book, you will notice a lot of similarities between the Program, Aperture Priority, and Shutter Priority modes and the way they function. The important thing is that you pick the right mode for your shooting situation.

STARTING POINTS FOR ISO SELECTION

There is a lot of discussion concerning ISO in this and other chapters, but it might be helpful if you know where your starting points should be for your ISO settings. The first thing you should always try to do is use the lowest possible ISO setting. That being said, here are good starting points for your ISO settings:

- 100: Bright sunny day

- 200: Hazy or outdoor shade on a sunny day

- 400: Indoor lighting at night or cloudy conditions outside

- 800: Late night, low-light conditions or sporting arenas at night

These are just suggestions, and your ISO selection will depend on a number of factors that will be discussed later in the book. You might have to push your ISO even higher as needed, but at least now you know where to start.

Let's set up the camera for Program mode and see how we can make all of this come together.

SETTING UP AND SHOOTING IN PROGRAM MODE

1. Turn your camera on. Turn the Main Command dial while holding down the Mode button until the letter **P** appears in the control panel.

2. Select your ISO by pressing and holding down the ISO button on the top of the camera.

3. Use the Main Command dial to select the desired ISO, which can be viewed in the control panel.

4. Point the camera at your subject, and then activate the camera meter by depressing the shutter button halfway.

5. View the exposure information in the bottom of the viewfinder or in the control panel on the top of the camera.

6. While the meter is activated, use your thumb to roll the Main Command dial left and right to see the changed exposure values.

7. Select the exposure that is right for you and start clicking. (Don't worry if you aren't sure what the right exposure is. We will start working on making the right choices for those great shots beginning with the next chapter, "Taking Control.")

If you use the Program shift, you will notice that a small star will appear above the letter **P** in the control panel and the rear info display if you rotate the Main Command dial. This star is an indication that you modified the exposure from the one that the camera chose. To go back to the default Program exposure, simply turn the dial until the star goes away or switch to a different mode and then back to Program mode again.

USING AUTO ISO

I am not a big fan of using Auto ISO settings, simply because the ISO setting can have a direct correlation to the quality of the image. If the ISO goes too high, there will undoubtedly be some noise introduced into the image. That being said, the D800 allows you to set up parameters so that you can get the benefit of some Auto ISO adjustments and still safeguard the quality of your image. You will need to set up these parameters in the menu; otherwise, the Auto ISO function will use the default values.

TURNING ON AUTO ISO

1. To turn on Auto ISO without setting custom parameters, press and hold down the ISO button.
2. Use the Main Command dial to set your desired low ISO (100 will give you the highest quality).
3. Rotate the Sub-command dial one click in either direction to turn on the Auto ISO function.
4. The Auto ISO designation will appear above the frame counter in the control panel as well as on the right side of the viewfinder display.

As you continue to shoot, the ISO will be continually adjusted as needed to maintain a good exposure. If you are using it in conjunction with Program mode, you should set some parameters so that your camera can operate in the best exposure environment.

AUTO ISO SENSITIVITY CONTROLS

Just because your camera can adjust the ISO doesn't mean that you want it to go crazy with the settings. It's a good idea to use the sensitivity controls to set limits for the ISO adjustment so that you can always get the best results. There are three control limits that you can set to maintain these limits. The first was done when you turned on Auto ISO. Whatever your current ISO setting is will be the bottom limit of the ISO range for Auto. That means if you have your ISO set for 400, the camera will not adjust it below that level (**Figure 3.3**). I like to keep mine at 100 in these circumstances because a lower ISO will only mean a cleaner image. The other settings are controlled in the camera menu and are the upper ISO limit and the minimum shutter speed.

FIGURE 3.3
Moving between bright outdoor and dark indoor conditions is a great time to set up and use the Auto ISO feature.

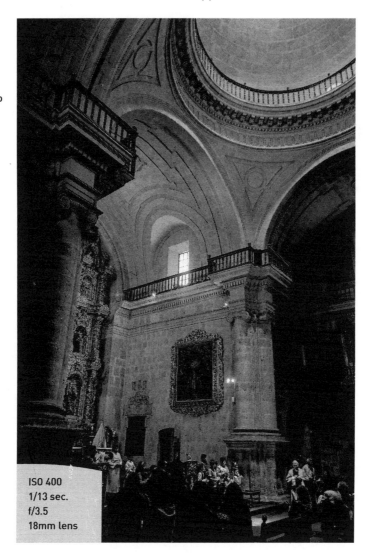

ISO 400
1/13 sec.
f/3.5
18mm lens

The upper limit sets a ceiling for how high your camera will set the ISO, so if you want to keep it leveled off at 3200, you just set that as the maximum sensitivity. If you want to ensure that you are always using a certain shutter speed or faster—for instance, if you are shooting action and don't want any blur—you can use the minimum shutter speed setting to choose a speed between 1 second and 1/4000 of a second. There is also an Auto setting for this option.

SETTING AUTO ISO SENSITIVITY CONTROLS

1. To set your control parameters, press the Menu button and navigate to the Shooting menu.

2. Locate the ISO sensitivity settings option, and press OK (**A**).

3. If Auto ISO was not already turned on, highlight the Auto ISO sensitivity control option, and press OK (**B**).

4. Select On and press OK to go back to the previous screen (**C**).

5. Highlight Maximum sensitivity, and press OK.

6. Select your desired ceiling for the ISO, and press OK (**D**).

7. Select the Minimum shutter speed selection, and press OK.

8. Select a shutter speed that you want to use as your slowest possible speed, and press OK (**E**).

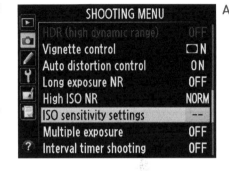

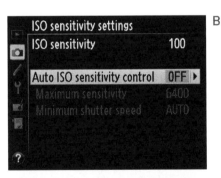

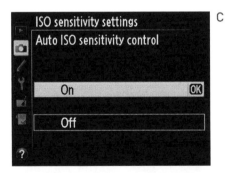

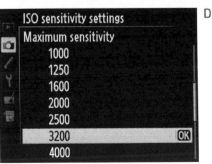

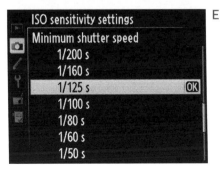

Press the Menu button twice to return to shooting mode and start taking photos. As you shoot, you may notice that the Auto ISO indicator will begin to blink. This is an indication that the camera has adjusted the ISO above your base setting.

AUTOFOCUS THE EASY WAY

The final consideration for automatic use of your D800 is which focus mode to use. If you really want to give up total control and be free from making any decisions, the Auto-Area AF mode is what you want. This mode will analyze all subjects within the 51 focus points and then locate what it believes to be the priority subject. It will then use the focus points covering that subject to establish the appropriate focus. So basically all you have to do is point and shoot. It's not a completely blind system as far as the photographer goes because it will highlight which focus points are being used so that you get an idea of what exactly it is basing its focus on. That way, as you shoot you have some idea what the camera believes the main subject to be.

This is perhaps my least favorite of all the focus modes because it takes all the control out of my hands and makes critical judgments on what should and should not be in focus. I can always fix an exposure problem using image processing software, but there's just no way to fix an out-of-focus photo. But if you feel the need to be free, here's how to set it up.

SETTING AUTO-AREA AF

1. Press and hold the AF-mode button located on the front of the camera just below the lens release button.

2. Set the focus mode to AF-S by rotating the Main Command dial and looking for the AF-S symbol in the control panel or rear info display (**Figure 3.4**).

3. While still holding in the AF-mode button, rotate the Sub-command dial until you see Auto in the display.

4. To activate the autofocus system, press the shutter release button halfway and look for the illuminated focus points in the viewfinder (**Figure 3.5**).

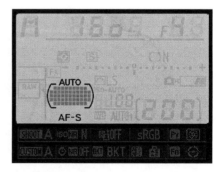

FIGURE 3.4
You can use the Info screen to view changes to the autofocus area.

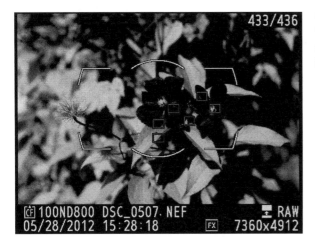

You can also use the Auto-Area AF mode in the continuous focusing mode (AF-C) if you are dealing with moving subjects.

With so many easy-to-use auto features, why would anyone ever want to use anything else? Well, the first thing that comes to my mind is control. It is the number one reason for using a DSLR camera. The ability to control every aspect of your photography will open up creative avenues that just aren't available with automatic settings. As we move forward through the next few chapters, we will explore many other techniques for focus and exposure that will give you much more control over the entire picture-making process. I'm not saying that full-auto features should never be used, but once you start shooting with the other camera modes, you may never want to go auto again.

Chapter 3 Assignments

These assignments will have you shooting with the various automatic features so that you can experience the advantages and disadvantages of using them in your daily photography.

Starting off with Program mode

Set your camera on Program mode and start shooting. Become familiar with the adjustments you can make to your exposure by turning the Main Command dial. Shoot in bright sun, deep shade, indoors—anywhere that you have different types and intensities of light. While you are shooting, make sure that you keep an eye on your ISO, and raise or lower it according to your environment.

Adding Auto ISO to the equation

Now that you have had some experience shooting in Program mode, go ahead and add the Auto ISO option. Hold the ISO button and rotate the Sub-command dial to turn it on. Now find some areas with contrasting brightness, like heavy shade and bright sun, and see how using the Auto ISO feature affects the settings in Program mode. You will hopefully notice that using the Auto ISO setting will limit the ability to shift exposure values because the ISO is constantly trying to maintain the established exposure values.

Focus on your subject

Handing off focus to the camera is something that is easy to do but may not always give you the results you want. It's important that you try the focus system in a variety of different situations so that you can anticipate how the camera will react to different types of subjects. Luckily there is some great feedback going on in the viewfinder in the form of illuminated focus points, so you can see what the camera believes the focal point of the picture is. Try shooting a lot of different subjects and see how the camera reacts. Shoot some landscape scenes where everything is off in the distance. Then shoot a subject that is close to the camera. Put the subject in the middle of the frame, and then try one with the subject off to the side. Pay attention to how the camera sees, and you will have a lot of success getting sharp images.

Putting it all together

Now that you have tried using the different automatic features individually, try using them all together for some fully automatic fun. This is as close to full auto as you will get.

Share your results with the book's Flickr group!

Join the group here: www.flickr.com/groups/d800fromsnapshotstogreatshots

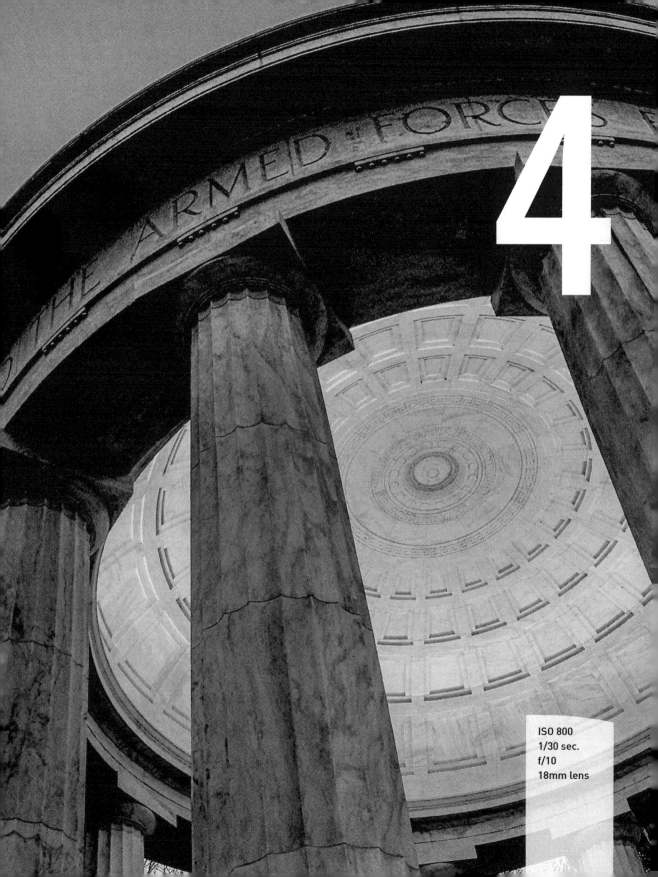

4

ISO 800
1/30 sec.
f/10
18mm lens

The Professional Modes

TAKING YOUR PHOTOGRAPHY TO THE NEXT LEVEL

Most professional photographers use a few select modes that offer the greatest amount of control over their photography. To anyone who has been involved with photography for any period of time, these modes are known as the backbones of photography. They allow you to influence two of the most important factors in taking great photographs—namely, *aperture* and *shutter speed*. To access these modes, you simply hold the Mode button and turn the Main Command dial to one of the letter-designated modes and begin shooting. But wouldn't it be nice to know exactly what those modes control and how to make them do our bidding? Well, if you really want to take that next step in controlling your photography, it is essential that you understand not only how to control these modes, but why you are controlling them. So let's switch over to the first of our professional modes: Shutter Priority.

PORING OVER THE PICTURE

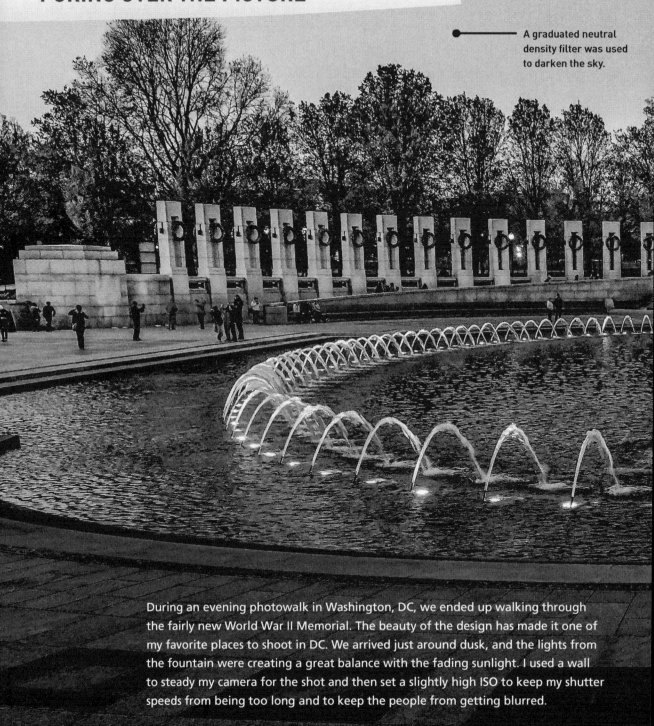

A graduated neutral density filter was used to darken the sky.

During an evening photowalk in Washington, DC, we ended up walking through the fairly new World War II Memorial. The beauty of the design has made it one of my favorite places to shoot in DC. We arrived just around dusk, and the lights from the fountain were creating a great balance with the fading sunlight. I used a wall to steady my camera for the shot and then set a slightly high ISO to keep my shutter speeds from being too long and to keep the people from getting blurred.

A slower shutter speed captured the movement of the water in the fountain.

I used a balanced composition, placing the fountain in the middle third of the scene.

The white balance was set to Auto to adjust for the different lighting in the scene.

ISO 800
1/6 sec.
f/10
18mm lens

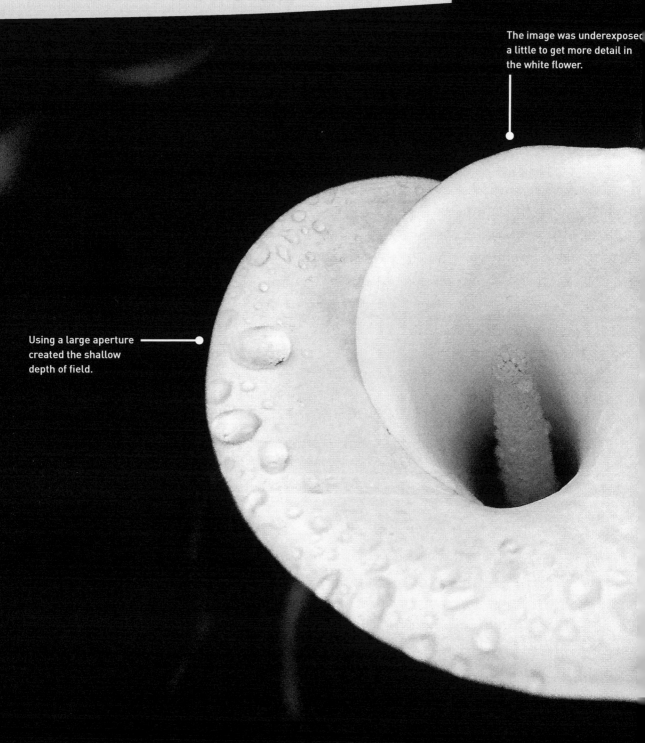

The image was underexposed a little to get more detail in the white flower.

Using a large aperture created the shallow depth of field.

I found this calla lily as I was coming out of my hotel room one morning in Peru. The morning dew had formed little drops on the flower, and the light was still soft and presented an excellent opportunity for a still life. I knew before I took the photo that I wanted to create a shallow depth of field to blur the background and get more emphasis on the flower.

The flower was placed off-center to increase visual interest.

A long focal length helped to keep the background blurred.

ISO 400
1/160 sec.
f/5.6
135mm lens

SHUTTER PRIORITY MODE (S)

S mode is what photographers commonly refer to as Shutter Priority. Just as the name implies, it is the mode that prioritizes or places major emphasis on the shutter speed above all other camera settings.

Just as with Program mode, Shutter Priority gives us more freedom to control certain aspects of our photography. In this case, we are talking about shutter speed. The selected shutter speed determines just how long you expose your camera's sensor to light. The longer it remains open, the more time your sensor has to gather light. The shutter speed also, to a large degree, determines how sharp your photographs are. This is different from the image being sharply in focus. One of the major influences on the sharpness of an image is just how much blurring is occurring based on camera shake and the subject's movement. Because a slower shutter speed means that light from your subject is hitting the sensor for a longer period of time, any movement by you or your subject will show up in your photos as blur.

SHUTTER SPEEDS

A *slow* shutter speed refers to leaving the shutter open for a long period of time—like 1/30 of a second or less. A *fast* shutter speed means that the shutter is open for a very short period of time—like 1/250 of a second or more.

WHEN TO USE SHUTTER PRIORITY MODE

- When working with fast-moving subjects where you want to freeze the action (**Figure 4.1**); much more on this in Chapter 5, "Moving Target."

- When you want to emphasize movement in your subject with motion blur (**Figure 4.2**).

- When you want to use a long exposure to gather light over a long period of time (**Figure 4.3**); more on this in Chapter 8, "Mood Lighting."

- When you want to create that silky-looking water in a waterfall (**Figure 4.4**).

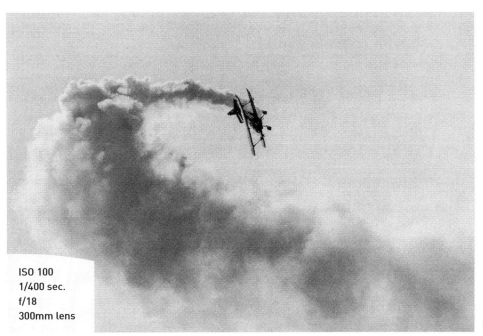

FIGURE 4.1
This shot was cre-
ated with a shutter
speed that was fast
enough to freeze
the action but not
the airplane's
propeller.

ISO 100
1/400 sec.
f/18
300mm lens

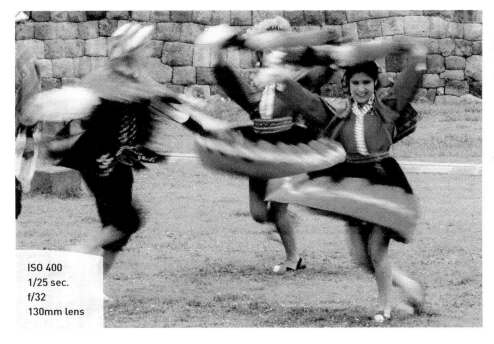

FIGURE 4.2
A slower shutter
speed was needed
to show the motion
of the dancers.

ISO 400
1/25 sec.
f/32
130mm lens

FIGURE 4.3
A slow shutter speed combined with a high ISO allowed me to capture this fountain at dusk.

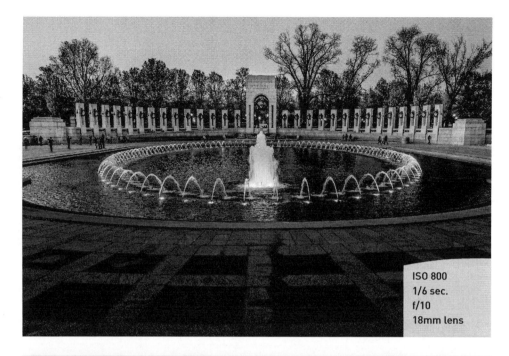

ISO 800
1/6 sec.
f/10
18mm lens

FIGURE 4.4
Increasing the length of the exposure time gives flowing water a silky look.

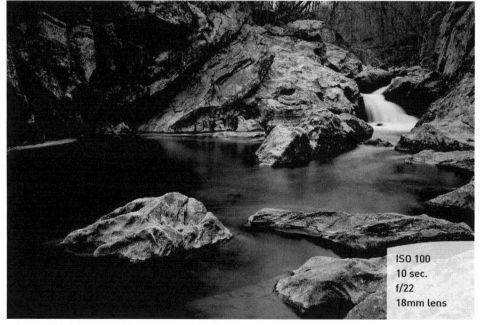

ISO 100
10 sec.
f/22
18mm lens

As you can see, the subject of your photo usually determines whether or not you will use Shutter Priority mode. It is important that you can visualize the result of using a particular shutter speed. The great thing about shooting with digital cameras is that you get instant feedback by viewing your shot on the rear LCD monitor. But what if your subject won't give you a do-over? Such is often the case when shooting sporting events. It's not like you can ask the quarterback to throw that touchdown pass again because your last shot was blurry from a slow shutter speed. This is why it's important to know what those speeds represent in terms of their capability to stop the action and deliver a blur-free shot.

First, let's examine just how much control you actually have over the shutter speeds. The D800 has a shutter speed range from 1/8000 of a second all the way down to 30 seconds. With that much latitude, you should have enough control to capture almost any subject. The other thing to think about is that Shutter Priority is considered a "semi-automatic" mode. This means that you are taking control over one aspect of the total exposure while the camera handles the other. In this instance, you are controlling the shutter speed and the camera is controlling the aperture. This is important, because there will be times that you want to use a particular shutter speed but your lens won't be able to accommodate your request.

For example, you might encounter this problem when shooting in low-light situations. If you are shooting a fast-moving subject that will blur at a shutter speed slower than 1/125 of a second and your lens's largest aperture is f/3.5, you might find that your aperture display in the viewfinder and the control panel will blink. This is your warning that there won't be enough light available for the shot—due to the limitations of the lens—so your picture will be underexposed. It does not, however, prevent you from taking the shot, so you need to be aware of the warning and the results.

Another case where you might run into this situation is when you are shooting moving water. To get that look of silky, flowing water, it's usually necessary to use a shutter speed of at least 1/15 of a second. If your waterfall is in full sunlight, you may see the aperture readout blink because the lens you are using only stops down to f/22 at its smallest opening. In this instance, your camera is warning you that you will be overexposing your image. There are workarounds for these problems, which we will discuss later (see Chapter 7, "Landscape Photography," for all the details), but it is important to know that there can be limitations when using the Shutter Priority mode.

SETTING UP AND SHOOTING IN SHUTTER PRIORITY MODE

1. Turn your camera on. Press and hold the Mode button while turning the Main Command dial until you see an **S** in the control panel.

2. Set your ISO by pressing the ISO button; select the appropriate setting by looking at the ISO readout on the control panel or by pressing the Info button on the back of the camera and looking at the info display on the rear LCD monitor (**Figure 4.5**).

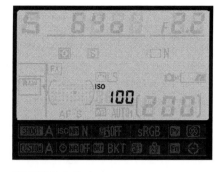

FIGURE 4.5
Set the appropriate ISO by holding down the ISO button.

3. Once your ISO is set, point the camera at your subject and then activate the camera meter by depressing the shutter button halfway.

4. View the exposure information in the bottom area of the viewfinder or in the control panel.

5. While the meter is activated, use your thumb to roll the Main Command dial left and right to see the changed exposure values. Roll the dial to the right for faster shutter speeds and to the left for slower speeds.

APERTURE PRIORITY MODE (A)

You wouldn't know it from its name, but Aperture Priority mode is one of the most useful and popular modes in DSLR photography. Aperture Priority is one of my personal favorite modes, and I believe that it will quickly become one of yours as well. Aperture Priority is also deemed a semi-automatic mode because it allows you to once again control one factor of exposure while the camera adjusts for another.

Why, you may ask, is this one of my favorite modes? It's because the aperture of your lens dictates depth of field. Depth of field, along with composition, is a major element in how you direct attention to what is important in your image. It is the controlling factor when determining how much of your image is sharp. If you want to isolate a subject from the background, such as when shooting a portrait, you can use a large aperture to keep the focus on your subject and make both the foreground and background blurry. If your emphasis is on keeping the entire scene sharply focused, such as with a landscape scene, then using a small aperture will render the greatest depth of field possible.

WHEN TO USE APERTURE PRIORITY MODE

- When shooting portraits or wildlife (**Figure 4.6**)

- When shooting most landscape photography (**Figure 4.7**)

- When shooting macro, or close-up, photography (**Figure 4.8**)

- When shooting architectural photography, which often benefits from a large depth of field (**Figure 4.9**)

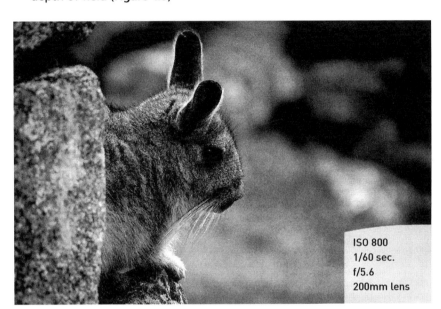

ISO 800
1/60 sec.
f/5.6
200mm lens

FIGURE 4.6
A large aperture and long lens helped to separate this little guy from the rocks in the background.

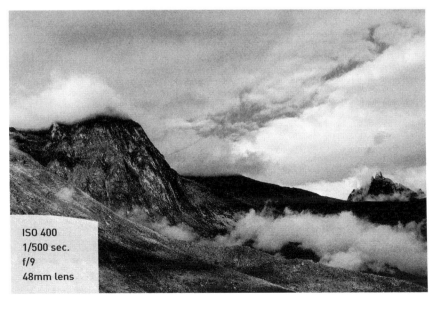

ISO 400
1/500 sec.
f/9
48mm lens

FIGURE 4.7
Using smaller apertures ensures that you will get sharp landscape shots.

FIGURE 4.8
The large aperture
helps focus atten-
tion on the water
drops on the flower.

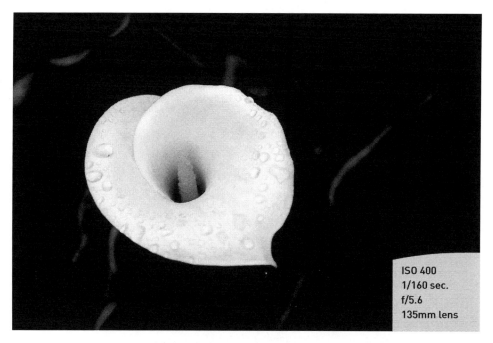

ISO 400
1/160 sec.
f/5.6
135mm lens

FIGURE 4.9
A large depth
of field ensures
sharpness from
near to far.

ISO 100
1/160 sec.
f/11
17mm lens

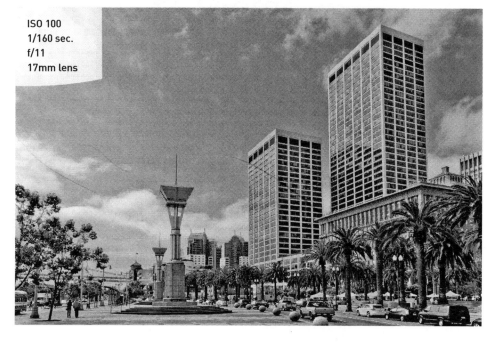

So we have established that Aperture Priority (A) mode is highly useful in controlling the depth of field in your image. But it's also pivotal in determining the limits of available light that you can shoot in. Different lenses have different maximum apertures. The larger the maximum aperture, or f-stop, the less light you need to achieve an acceptably sharp image. You will recall that, when in Shutter Priority mode, there is a limit at which you can hand-hold your camera without introducing movement or hand shake, which causes blurriness in the final picture. If your lens has a larger aperture, then you can let in more light all at once, which means that you can use faster shutter speeds. This is why lenses with large maximum apertures, such as f/1.4, are called "fast" lenses.

On the other hand, bright scenes require the use of a small aperture (such as f/16 or f/22), especially if you want to use a slower shutter speed. That small opening reduces the amount of incoming light, and this reduction of light requires that the shutter stay open longer.

F-STOPS AND APERTURE

When referring to the numeric value of your lens aperture, you will find it described as an *f-stop*. The f-stop is one of those old photography terms that, technically speaking, relates to the focal length of the lens (e.g., 200mm) divided by the effective aperture diameter. These measurements are defined as "stops" and work incrementally with your shutter speed to determine proper exposure. Older camera lenses used one-stop increments to assist in exposure adjustments, such as 1.4, 2, 2.8, 4, 5.6, 8, 11, 16, and 22. Each stop represents about half the amount of light entering the lens iris as the larger stop before it. Today, most lenses don't have f-stop markings, since all adjustments to this setting are performed via the camera's electronics. The stops are also now typically divided into 1/3-stop increments to allow much finer adjustments to exposures, as well as to match the incremental values of your camera's ISO settings, which are adjusted in 1/3-stop increments as well.

1. Turn your camera on. Press and hold the Mode button while turning the Main Command dial until you see an **A** in the control panel.

2. Set your ISO by pressing the ISO button; select the appropriate setting by looking at the ISO readout on the control panel or by pressing the Info button on the back of the camera and looking at the info display on the rear LCD monitor (**Figure 4.10**).

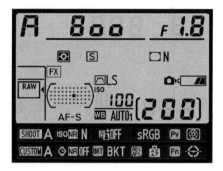

3. Once your ISO is set, point the camera at your subject and then activate the camera meter by depressing the shutter button halfway.

FIGURE 4.10
The info screen in Aperture Priority mode.

4. View the exposure information in the bottom area of the viewfinder or in the control panel.

5. While the meter is activated, use your index finger to roll the Sub-command dial left and right to see the changed exposure values. Roll the dial to the right for a smaller aperture (higher f-stop number) and to the left for a larger aperture (smaller f-stop number).

MANUAL MODE (M)

Once upon a time, long before digital cameras and program modes, there was manual mode. Only, in those days it wasn't called "manual mode," because there were no other modes. It was just photography. In fact, many photographers cut their teeth on completely manual cameras. Let's face it—if you want to learn the effects of aperture and shutter speed on your photography, there is no better way to learn than by setting these adjustments yourself. However, today, with the advancement of camera technology, many new photographers never give this mode a second thought. That's truly a shame, as it is not only an excellent way to learn your photography basics, it's also an essential tool to have in your photographic bag of tricks.

When you have your camera set to Manual (M) mode, the camera meter will give you a reading of the scene you are photographing, but it's your job to actually set both the f-stop (aperture) and the shutter speed to achieve a correct exposure. If you need a faster shutter speed, you will have to make the reciprocal change to your f-stop. Using any other mode, such as Shutter or Aperture Priority, would mean that you just have to worry about one of these changes, but Manual mode requires you to do it all yourself. This can be a little challenging at first, but after a while you will have a complete understanding of how each change affects your exposure, which will in turn improve the way that you use the other modes.

WHEN TO USE MANUAL MODE

- When learning how each exposure element interacts with the others (**Figure 4.11**)

- When your environment is fooling your light meter and you need to maintain a certain exposure setting (**Figure 4.12**)

- When shooting silhouetted subjects, which requires overriding the camera's meter readings (**Figure 4.13**)

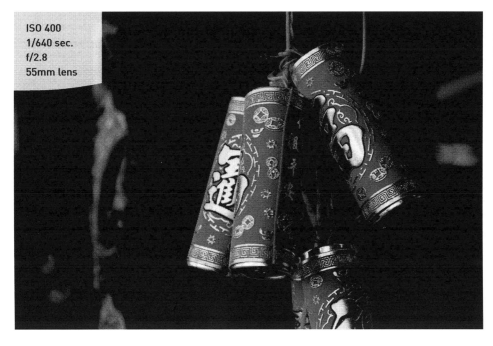

ISO 400
1/640 sec.
f/2.8
55mm lens

FIGURE 4.11
Capturing this image required the proper balance of ISO, aperture, and shutter speed.

FIGURE 4.12
Bright, sandy locations can fool the camera's meter and cause underexposure.

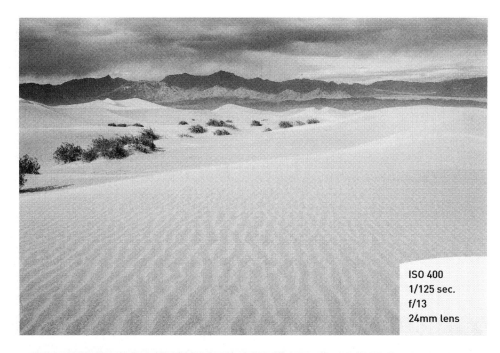

ISO 400
1/125 sec.
f/13
24mm lens

FIGURE 4.13
I purposely under-exposed this image to create more of a silhouette of the cactus and show off the needles.

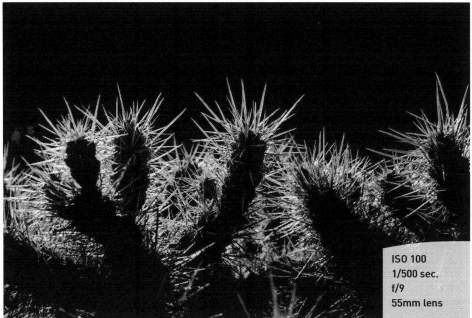

ISO 100
1/500 sec.
f/9
55mm lens

1. Turn your camera on. Press and hold the Mode button while turning the Main Command dial until you see an **M** in the control panel.

2. Set your ISO by pressing the ISO button; select the appropriate setting by looking at the ISO readout on the control panel or by pressing the Info button on the back of the camera and looking at the info display on the rear LCD monitor.

3. Point the camera at your subject and then activate the camera meter by depressing the shutter button halfway.

4. View the exposure information in the bottom area of the viewfinder or in the display panel on top of the camera.

5. While the meter is activated, use your index finger to roll the Main Command dial left and right to change your shutter speed value until the exposure mark is lined up with the zero mark. The exposure information is displayed in the viewfinder by a scale with marks that run from –2 to +2 stops (**Figure 4.14**). A proper exposure will line up with the taller mark in the middle. As the indicator moves to the left, it is a sign that you will be underexposing (not enough light on the sensor to provide adequate exposure). Move the indicator to the right and you will be providing more exposure than the camera meter calls for; this is overexposure.

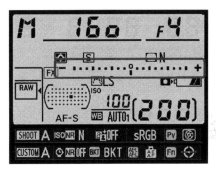

FIGURE 4.14
Use the over/under scale to find your exposure settings.

6. To set your exposure using the aperture, depress the shutter release button until the meter is activated. Then rotate the Sub-command dial to change the aperture. Rotate right for a smaller aperture (large f-stop number) and left for a larger aperture (small f-stop number).

HOW I SHOOT: A CLOSER LOOK AT THE CAMERA SETTINGS I USE

The great thing about working with a DSLR camera is that I can always feel confident that some things will remain unchanged from camera to camera. For me, these are the Aperture (A) and Shutter Priority (S) shooting modes. Although I like to think of myself as a generalist in terms of my photography, I do tend to lean heavily on the landscape and urban photography genres. Working in these areas means that I am almost always going to be concerned with my depth of field. Whether it's isolating my subject with a large aperture or trying to maximize the overall sharpness of a sweeping landscape, I am always keeping an eye on my aperture setting. If I do have a need to control the action, I use Shutter Priority, my fallback mode. It's not really a fallback; it's more like the right tool for the right job. If I am trying to create a silky waterfall effect, I can depend on Shutter Priority mode to provide that long shutter speed that will deliver. Maybe I am shooting a motocross jumper—I would definitely need the fast shutter speeds that will freeze the fast-moving action (**Figure 4.15**).

FIGURE 4.15
Freezing action like this requires some fast shutter speeds.

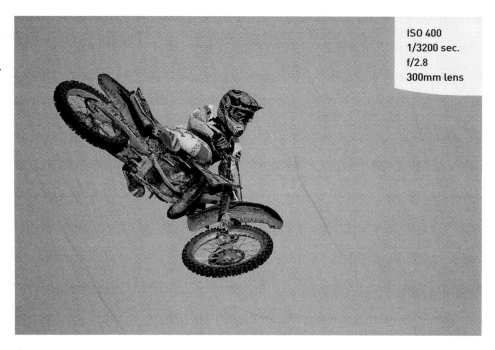

ISO 400
1/3200 sec.
f/2.8
300mm lens

While the other camera modes have their place, I think you will find that, like myself and most other working pros, you will use the Aperture Priority and Shutter Priority modes for 90 percent of your shooting.

The other concern that I have when I am setting up my camera is just how low I can keep my ISO. This is always a priority for me, because a low ISO will always give the cleanest image. I only raise the ISO as a last resort, because each increase in sensitivity is an opportunity for more digital noise to enter my image. To that end, I always have the High ISO Noise Reduction feature turned on.

To make quick changes while I shoot, I often use exposure compensation so that I can make small over- and underexposure changes. This is different than changing the aperture or shutter because it is more like fooling the camera meter into thinking the scene is brighter or darker than it actually is. To get to this function quickly, I simply press the Exposure Compensation button and then dial in the desired amount of compensation. Truth be told, I usually have this set to –1/3 so that there is just a tiny bit of underexposure in my image. This usually leads to better color saturation.

One of the reasons I change my exposure is to make corrections when I see the blink-ies in my rear LCD monitor. ("Blinkies" is not the real name for the highlight clipping warning, just the one most photographers use.) Blinkies are the warning signal that part of my image has been overexposed to the point that I no longer have any detail in the highlights. When the Highlight Alert feature is turned on, the display will flash between black and white whenever there is a potential of overexposing in the image. The black and white flashing will only appear in areas of the picture that are in danger of overexposure. To turn on this feature, go to the Playback menu and enable the feature as follows.

1. To set up the highlight warning for your camera, press the Menu button and then use the Multi-selector to access the Playback menu (**A**).

2. Use the Multi-selector to choose Playback display options (**B**), and press OK.

3. Move the Multi-selector down to the Highlights option (**C**), and then press the OK button to add a checkmark.

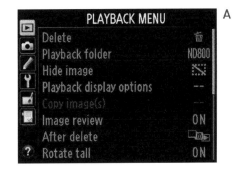

4. Now move back up to the Done heading, and press the OK button again to lock in your change.

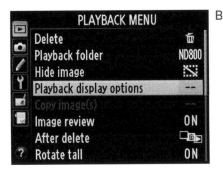
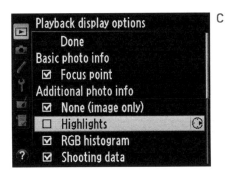

Once the highlight warning is turned on, I then use it to check my images on the LCD monitor (if the highlight warning display is not visible, press up on the Multi-selector until it is the selected mode). If I see an area that is blinking, I will usually use the exposure compensation feature to set an underexposed setting like –1/3 or –2/3 stop and take another photo, checking the result on the screen. I repeat this process until the warning is gone (**Figure 4.16**).

Sometimes the warning will blink no matter how much you adjust the exposure, because there is just no detail in the highlight, such as in an image of the sun. Use your best judgment to determine if the warning is alerting you to an area where you want to retain highlight detail. And remember, sometimes white is supposed to be white.

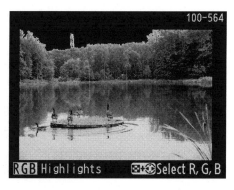

FIGURE 4.16
Enabling the Highlight Alert, or "blinkies," feature allows you to see when a part of your image is blown out.

As you work your way through the coming chapters, you will see other tips and tricks I use in my daily photography, but the most important tip I can give is to really understand the features of your camera so that you can leverage the technology in a knowledgeable way. This will ultimately result in better photographs.

Chapter 4 Assignments

This will be more of a mental challenge than anything else, but you should put a lot of work into these lesson assignments because the information covered in this chapter will define how you work with your camera from this point on. Granted, there may be times that you just want to grab some quick pictures and will resort to the Program mode, but to get serious with your photography, you will want to learn the professional modes inside and out.

Learning to control time with Shutter Priority mode

Find some moving subjects and then set your camera to S mode. Have someone ride a bike back and forth, or even try photographing cars as they go by. Start with a slow shutter speed of around 1/30 of a second, and then start shooting with faster and faster shutter speeds. Keep shooting until you can freeze the action. Now find something that isn't moving, like a flower, and work your way down from a fast shutter speed like 1/500 of a second. Don't brace the camera on a steady surface. Just try and shoot as slowly as possible, down to about 1/4 of a second. The point is to see how well you can hand-hold your camera before you start introducing hand-shake into the image, making it appear soft and somewhat unfocused.

Controlling depth of field with Aperture Priority mode

The name of the game with A mode is depth of field. Set up three items at varying distances from you. I would use chess pieces or something similar. Now focus on the middle item and set your camera to the largest aperture that your lens allows (remember, large aperture means a small number, like f/3.5). Now, while still focusing on the middle subject, start shooting with ever-smaller apertures until you are at the smallest f-stop for your lens. If you have a zoom lens, try doing this exercise with the lens at the widest and then the most telephoto settings. Now, try subjects that are farther away, like telephone poles, and shoot them in the same way. The idea is to get a feel for how each aperture setting affects your depth of field.

Giving and taking with Manual mode

Manual mode is not going to require a lot of work, but you should pay close attention to your results. Go outside on a sunny day and, using the camera in Manual mode, set your ISO to 100, your shutter speed to 1/125 of a second, and your aperture to f/16. Now press your shutter release button to get a meter reading. You should be pretty close to the zero mark. If not, make small adjustments to one of your settings until it hits that mark. Now is where the fun begins. Start moving your shutter speed slower, to 1/60, and then set your aperture to f/22. Now go the other way. Set your aperture on f/8 and your shutter speed to 1/500. Now review your images. If all went well, all the exposures should look the same. This is because you balanced the light with reciprocal changes to the aperture and shutter speed. Now go back to our original setting of 1/125 at f/16 and try just moving the shutter speed without changing the aperture. Just make 1/3-stop changes (1/125 to 1/100 to 1/80 to 1/60), and then review your images to see what a 1/3 stop of overexposure looks like. Then do the same thing going in the opposite way. It's hard to know if you want to over- or underexpose a scene until you have actually done it and seen the results.

With each of the assignments, make sure that you keep track of your modes and exposures so that you can compare them with the image. If you are using software to review your images, you should also be able to check the camera settings that are embedded within the images' metadata.

Share your results with the book's Flickr group!

Join the group here: www.flickr.com/groups/d800fromsnapshotstogreatshots

5

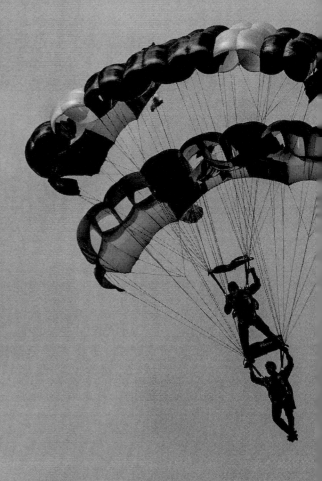

ISO 100
1/640 sec.
f/11
122mm lens

Moving Target

THE TRICKS TO SHOOTING SPORTS AND MORE

Now that you have learned about the professional modes, it's time to put your newfound knowledge to good use. Whether you are shooting the action at a professional sporting event or a child on a merry-go-round, this chapter will teach you techniques that will help you bring out the best in your photography when your subject is in motion.

The number one thing to know when trying to capture a moving target is that speed is king! I'm not talking about how fast your subject is moving, but rather how fast your shutter is opening and closing. Shutter speed is the key to freezing the moment in time—but also to conveying movement. It's all in how you turn the dial. There are also some other considerations for taking your shot to the next level: composition, lens selection, and a few more items that we will explore in this chapter. So strap on your seatbelt and hit the gas, because here we go!

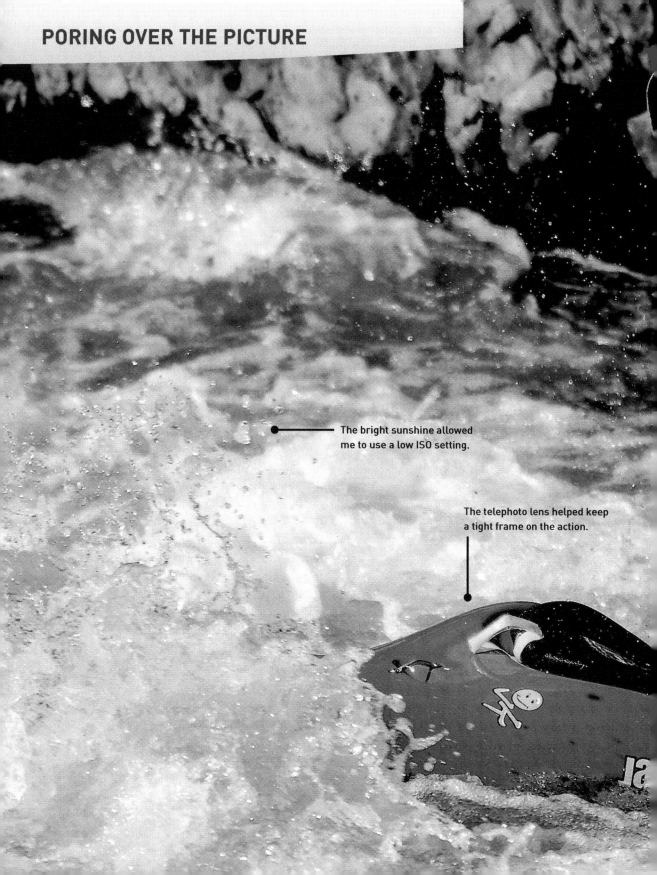

The bright sunshine allowed
me to use a low ISO setting.

The telephoto lens helped keep
a tight frame on the action.

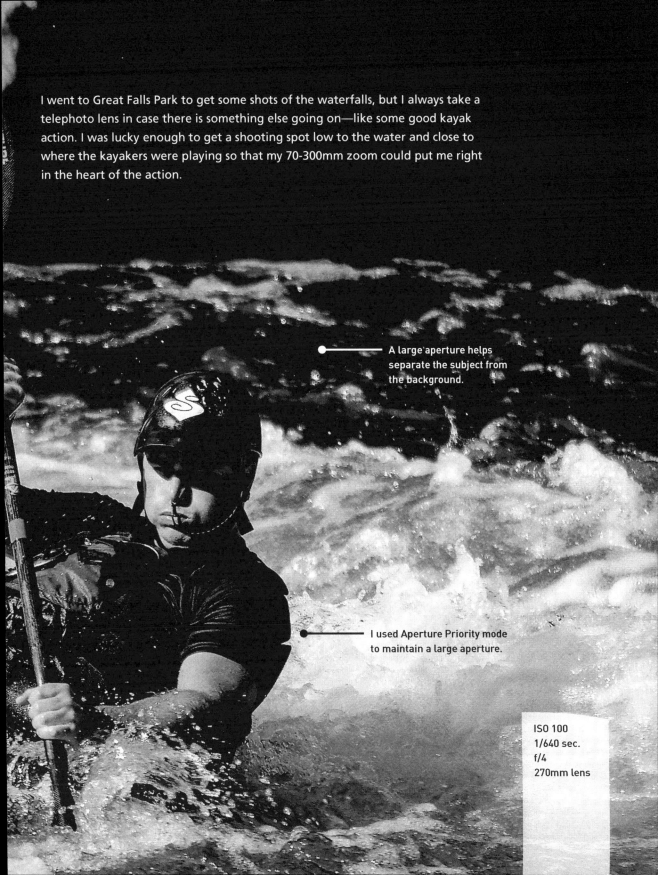

I went to Great Falls Park to get some shots of the waterfalls, but I always take a telephoto lens in case there is something else going on—like some good kayak action. I was lucky enough to get a shooting spot low to the water and close to where the kayakers were playing so that my 70-300mm zoom could put me right in the heart of the action.

A large aperture helps separate the subject from the background.

I used Aperture Priority mode to maintain a large aperture.

ISO 100
1/640 sec.
f/4
270mm lens

Things always look brighter under the big lights. The reality is that the human eye adjusts rapidly to lower light levels, which can make you feel like there should be plenty of light. That was the case when I began shooting this rodeo event. As it got later and later, I kept raising my ISO higher and higher. When I reached 800, I checked my menu to ensure that the noise reduction was turned on. I set my focus point for the middle and then just tried to anticipate the action so that I would be ready to catch photos such as this.

Shooting sports under the lights requires high ISO values.

I shot in the continuous drive mode using the Dynamic autofocus mode.

A large aperture helps key in on the main action.

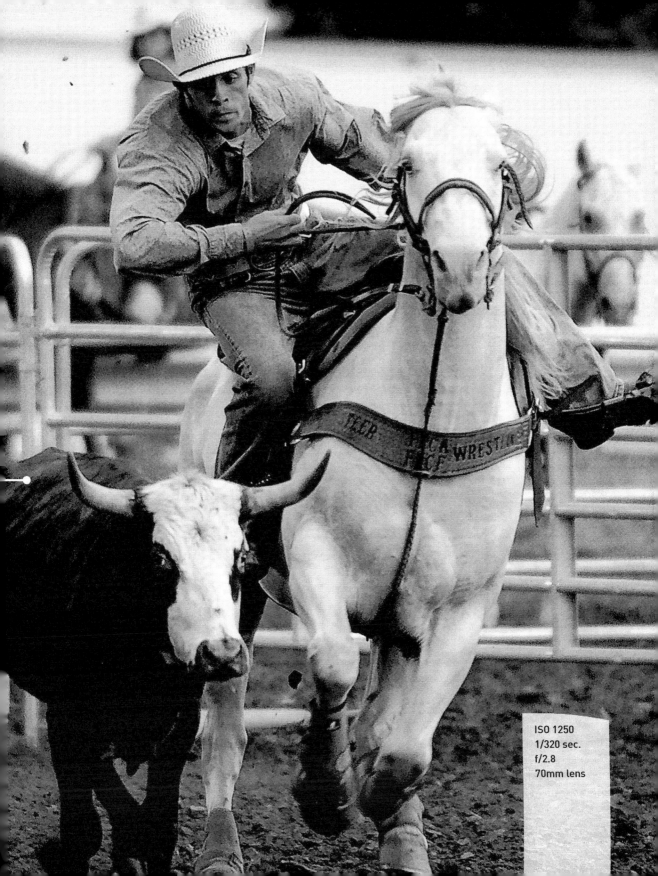

ISO 1250
1/320 sec.
f/2.8
70mm lens

STOP RIGHT THERE!

Shutter speed is the main tool in the photographer's arsenal for capturing great action shots. The ability to freeze a moment in time often makes the difference between a good shot and a great one. To take advantage of this concept, you should have a good grasp of the relationship between shutter speed and movement. When you press the shutter release button, your camera goes into action by opening the shutter curtain and then closing it after a predetermined length of time. The longer you leave your shutter open, the more your subject will move within the frame, so common sense dictates that the first thing to consider is just how fast your subject is moving.

Typically, you will be working in fractions of a second. Just how long those fractions are depends on several factors. Subject movement, while simple in concept, is actually based on three factors. The first is the direction of travel. Is the subject moving across your field of view (left to right) or traveling toward or away from you? The second consideration is the actual speed at which the subject is moving. There is a big difference between a moving sports car and a child on a bicycle. Finally, the distance from you to the subject has a direct bearing on how fast the action seems to be taking place. Let's take a brief look at each of these factors to see how they might affect your shooting.

DIRECTION OF TRAVEL

Typically, the first thing that people think about when taking an action shot is how fast the subject is moving, but in reality the first consideration should be the direction of travel. Where you are positioned in relation to the subject's direction of travel is critically important in selecting the proper shutter speed. When you open your shutter, the lens gathers light from your subject and records it on the camera sensor. If the subject is moving across your viewfinder, you need a faster shutter speed to keep that lateral movement from being recorded as a streak across your image. Subjects that are moving toward or away from your shooting location do not move across your viewfinder and appear to be more stationary. This allows you to use a slightly slower shutter speed (**Figure 5.1**). A subject that is moving in a diagonal direction—both across the frame and toward or away from you—requires a shutter speed in between the two.

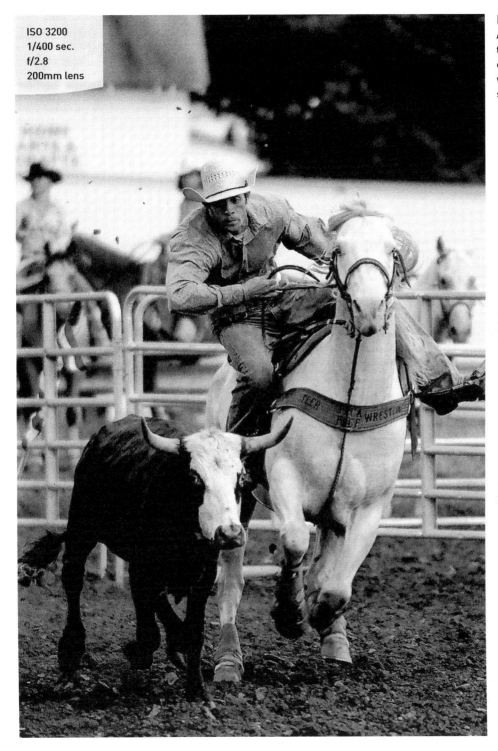

ISO 3200
1/400 sec.
f/2.8
200mm lens

FIGURE 5.1
Action coming
toward the camera
can be captured
with slower shutter
speeds.

SUBJECT SPEED

Once the angle of motion has been determined, you can then assess the speed at which the subject is traveling. The faster your subject moves, the faster your shutter speed needs to be in order to "freeze" that subject (**Figure 5.2**). A person walking across your frame might only require a shutter speed of 1/60 of a second, whereas a cyclist traveling in the same direction would call for 1/500 of a second. That same cyclist traveling toward you at the same rate of speed, rather than across the frame, might only require a shutter speed of 1/125 of a second. You can start to see how the relationship of speed and direction comes into play in your decision-making process.

FIGURE 5.2
A fast-moving
subject that is
crossing your path
will require a faster
shutter speed.

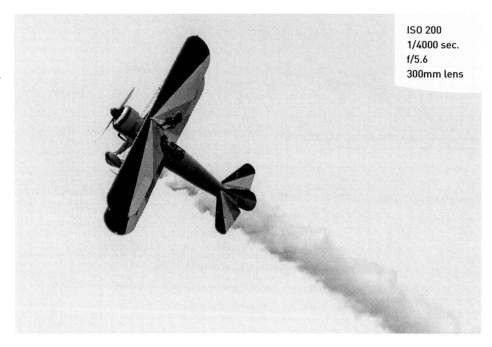

ISO 200
1/4000 sec.
f/5.6
300mm lens

SUBJECT-TO-CAMERA DISTANCE

So now we know both the direction and the speed of your subject. The final factor to address is the distance between you and the action. Picture yourself looking at a highway full of cars from up in a tall building a quarter of a mile from the road. As you stare down at the traffic moving along at 55 miles per hour, the cars and trucks seem to be slowly moving along the roadway. Now picture yourself standing in the median of that same road as the same traffic flies by at the same rate of speed.

Although the traffic is moving at the same speed, the shorter distance between you and the traffic makes the cars look like they are moving much faster. This is because your field of view is much narrower; therefore, the subjects are not going to present themselves within the frame for the same length of time. The concept of distance applies to the length of your lens as well (**Figure 5.3**). If you are using a wide-angle lens, you can probably get away with a slower shutter speed than if you were using a telephoto, which puts you in the heart of the action. It all has to do with your field of view. That telephoto gets you "closer" to the action—and the closer you are, the faster your subject will be moving across your viewfinder.

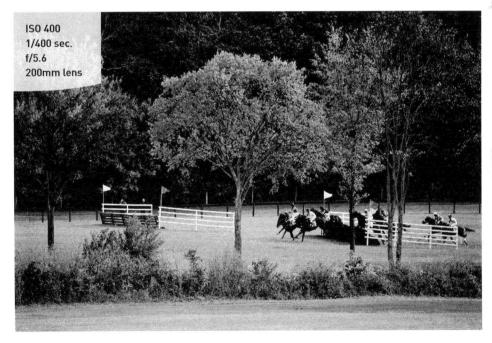

ISO 400
1/400 sec.
f/5.6
200mm lens

FIGURE 5.3
Because of the distance of the action from the camera, a slower shutter speed could be used to capture this action.

ZOOM IN TO BE SURE

When reviewing your shots on the LCD, don't be fooled by the display. The smaller your image is, the sharper it will look. To ensure that you are getting sharp, blur-free images, make sure that you zoom in on your LCD display.

To zoom in on your images, press the Playback button located at the top left on the rear of the camera and then press the Zoom In button (**Figure 5.4**). Continue pressing the Zoom In button to increase the zoom ratio. One trick that I use is to set the Multi-selector center button to Medium Magnification Zoom during playback mode. This allows me to quickly zoom in to a 50% view with a single press of the button. To set this up, you will need to assign the function in the Custom Setting menu.

FIGURE 5.4
Zooming in on your image helps you
confirm that the image is really sharp.

Zoom In

Zoom Out

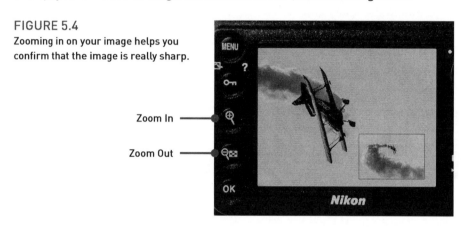

1. Press the Menu button, navigate to the Custom Setting menu, and select the Controls option. Press OK (**A**).

2. Highlight item f2 Multi-selector center button, and press OK (**B**).

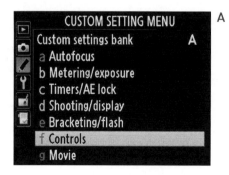

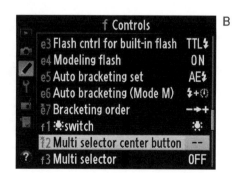

3. Highlight the Playback mode option, and press OK (**C**).

4. Select Zoom on/off, and press OK (**D**).

5. Choose your magnification level, and press OK (**E**).

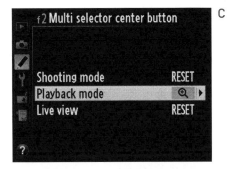

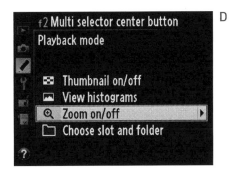

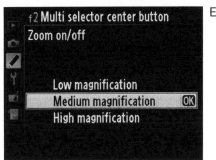

Now when you are reviewing images, you can press the Multi-selector button and quickly zoom in for a better look.

To zoom back out, simply press the Zoom Out button (the magnifying glass with the minus sign on it) or press the Playback button again.

USING SHUTTER PRIORITY (S) MODE TO STOP MOTION

In Chapter 4, you were introduced to the professional shooting modes. You'll remember that the mode that gives you ultimate control over shutter speed is Shutter Priority, or S, mode, where you are responsible for selecting the shutter speed while handing over the aperture selection to the camera. The ability to concentrate on just one exposure factor helps you quickly make changes on the fly while staying glued to your viewfinder and your subject.

There are a couple of things to consider when using Shutter Priority mode, both of which have to do with the amount of light that is available when shooting. Although you have control over which shutter speed you select in Shutter Priority mode, the range of shutter speeds that is available to you depends largely on how well your subject is lit.

Typically, when shooting fast-paced action, you will be working with very fast shutter speeds. This means that your lens will probably be set to its largest aperture. If the light is not sufficient for the shutter speed selected, you will need to do one of two things: select a lens that offers a larger working aperture, or raise the ISO of the camera. Working off the assumption that you have only one lens available, let's concentrate on balancing your exposure using the ISO.

Let's say that you are shooting a baseball game at night and want to get some great action shots. You set your camera to Shutter Priority mode and, after testing out some shutter speeds, determine that you need to shoot at 1/500 of a second to freeze the action on the field. When you place the viewfinder to your eye and press the shutter button halfway, you notice that the f-stop is blinking. This is your camera's way of telling you that the lens has now reached its maximum aperture and that you will be underexposed if you shoot your pictures at the currently selected shutter speed. You could slow your shutter speed down until the blinking goes away, but then you might get images with too much motion blur.

The alternative is to raise your ISO to a level that is high enough for a proper exposure. The key here is to always use the lowest ISO that you can get away with. That might mean ISO 200 in bright sunny conditions, or ISO 1600 and higher for an indoor or night situation (**Figure 5.5**). Just remember that the higher the ISO, the greater the amount of noise in your image. This is the reason that you see professional sports photographers using those mammoth lenses perched atop a monopod: they could use a smaller lens, but to get those very large apertures, they need a huge piece of glass on the front of the lens. The larger the glass on the front of the lens, the more light it gathers, and the larger the aperture for shooting. For the working pro, the large aperture translates into low ISO (thus, low noise), fast shutter speeds, and razor-sharp action.

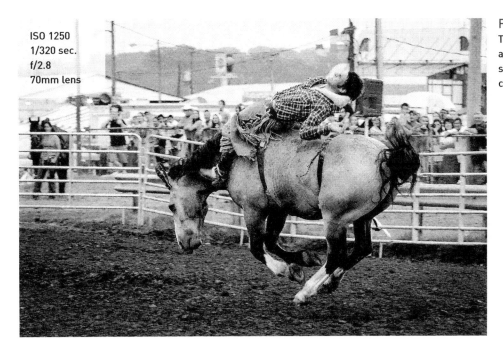

ISO 1250
1/320 sec.
f/2.8
70mm lens

FIGURE 5.5
The only way to stop action when the sun goes down is to crank up your ISO.

USING APERTURE PRIORITY (A) MODE TO ISOLATE YOUR SUBJECT

One of the benefits of working in Shutter Priority mode with fast shutter speeds is that, more often than not, you will be shooting with the largest aperture available on your lens. Shooting with a large aperture allows you to use faster shutter speeds, but it also narrows your depth of field.

To isolate your subject in order to focus your viewer's attention on it, a larger aperture is required. The larger aperture reduces the foreground and background sharpness: the larger the aperture, the more blurred they will be.

The reason that I bring this up here is that when you are shooting most sporting events, the idea is to isolate your main subject by having it in focus while the rest of the image has some amount of blur. This sharp focus draws your viewer right to the subject. Studies have shown that the eye is drawn to sharp areas before moving on to the blurry areas. Also, depending on what your subject matter is, there can be a tendency to get distracted by a busy background if everything in the photo is equally sharp. Without a narrow depth of field, it might be difficult for the viewer to establish exactly what the main subject is in your picture.

Let's look at how to use depth of field to bring focus to your subject. In the previous section, I told you that you should use Shutter Priority mode for getting those really fast shutter speeds to stop action. Generally speaking, Shutter Priority mode will be the mode you most often use for shooting sports and other action, but there will be times when you want to ensure that you are getting the narrowest depth of field possible in your image. The way to do this is by using Aperture Priority mode.

So how do you know when you should use Aperture Priority mode as opposed to Shutter Priority mode? It's not a simple answer, but your LCD screen can help you make this determination. The best scenario for using Aperture Priority mode is a brightly lit scene where maximum apertures will still give you plenty of shutter speed to stop the action.

Let's say that you are shooting a soccer game in the midday sun. If you have determined that you need something between 1/500 and 1/1250 of a second for stopping the action, you could just set your camera to a high shutter speed in Shutter Priority mode and start shooting. But you also want to be using an aperture of, say, f/4.5 to get that narrow depth of field. Here's the problem: if you set your camera to Shutter Priority mode and select 1/1000 of a second as a nice compromise, you might get that desired f-stop—but you might not. As the meter is trained on your moving subject, the light levels could rise or fall, which might actually change that desired f-stop to something higher like f/5.6 or even f/8. Now the depth of field is extended, and you will no longer get that nice isolation and separation that you wanted.

To rectify this, switch the camera to Aperture Priority mode and select f/4.5 as your aperture. Now, as you begin shooting, the camera holds that aperture and makes exposure adjustments with the shutter speed. As I said before, this works well when you have lots of light—enough light so that you can have a high enough shutter speed without introducing motion blur (**Figure 5.6**).

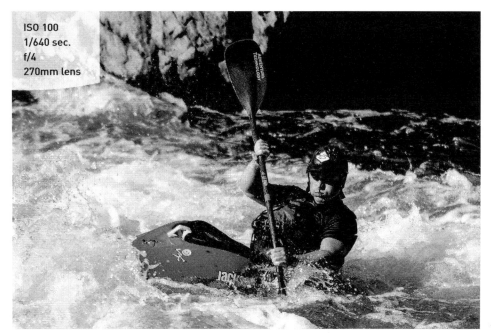

ISO 100
1/640 sec.
f/4
270mm lens

FIGURE 5.6
A sunny day means you can use Aperture Priority mode to lock in a large aperture while the camera sets a fast shutter speed.

KEEP THEM IN FOCUS WITH CONTINUOUS-SERVO FOCUS AND AF FOCUS POINT SELECTION

With the exposure issue handled for the moment, let's move on to an area that is equally important: focusing. If you have browsed your manual, you know that there are several focus modes to choose from in the D800. To get the greatest benefit from each of them, it is important to understand how they work and the situations where each mode will give you the best opportunity to grab a great shot. Because we are discussing subject movement, our first choice is going to be Continuous-servo AF mode (AF-C). AF-C mode uses the focus points in the camera to track a moving subject and then lock in the focus when the shutter button is completely depressed. As the subject moves, the camera uses something called predictive focus tracking to anticipate where the subject will be moving and then adjust focus accordingly.

SELECTING AND SHOOTING IN CONTINUOUS-SERVO AF FOCUS MODE

1. Press and hold the AF-mode button on the front of the camera.

2. Rotate the Main Command dial until the AF-C designation is visible in the viewfinder or the control panel.

3. Locate your subject in the viewfinder, then press and hold the shutter button halfway or press the AF-On button on the back of the camera to activate the focus mechanism.

4. The camera will maintain the subject's focus as long as it remains within one of the focus points in the viewfinder, or until you release the AF-On button or shutter button, or take a picture.

You should take note that holding down the shutter button for long periods of time will cause your battery to drain much faster because the camera will be constantly focusing on the subject.

When using the AF-C mode, you can change the AF-area mode to specify how the focus points are used. There are two modes to choose from.

Single-Point AF. This mode allows you to select a single focus point. The camera will ignore all other points and utilize only the point you specify. To select a point, set the camera in Single-Point AF mode by holding down the AF-mode button and rotating the Sub-command dial until you see the single-point designation. Next, use the Multi-selector to select the desired focus point, which will be highlighted in the viewfinder. You can lock in your point selection by rotating the lock lever to the L position.

Dynamic-area AF. This mode uses a focus point of your choosing as the primary focus but uses information from the surrounding points if your subject happens to move away from the point. You can select from three different areas: 9-, 21-, and 51-point. The area you use depends on how much subject movement there will be.

SETTING THE AF-AREA MODE TO DYNAMIC

1. To set the AF-area mode, press and hold the AF-mode button on the front of the camera.

2. Rotate the Sub-command dial until you see the desired setting in your viewfinder or control panel.

Select a focus point as described in the Single-Point AF section. Pressing the button in the center of the Multi-selector will reset your focus point to the center position.

Note that the AF-area mode is used to select the method with which the camera will focus the lens. This is different from the AF point, which is a cluster of small points that are visible in the viewfinder and are used to determine where you want the lens to focus (**Figure 5.7**).

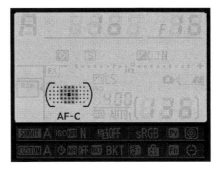

STOP AND GO WITH 3D-TRACKING AF

FIGURE 5.7
The Automatic Focus (AF) points are the 51 small boxes seen in the bottom-left area of the info screen.

If you are going to be changing between a moving target and one that is still, you should consider using the 3D-tracking AF mode. This mode mixes both the AF-C and Dynamic modes for shooting a subject that goes from stationary to moving without having to adjust your focus mode.

When you have a stationary subject, simply place your selected focus point on your subject and the camera will focus on it. If your subject begins to move out of focus, the camera will track the movement, keeping a sharp focus.

For example, suppose you are shooting a football game. The quarterback has brought the team to the line and is standing behind the center, waiting for the ball to be hiked. If you are using the 3D-tracking AF mode, you can place your focus point on the quarterback and start taking pictures of him as he stands at the line. As soon as the ball is hiked and the action starts, the camera will switch to tracking mode and follow his movement within the frame. This can be a little tricky at first, but once you master it, it will make your action shooting effortless.

To select 3D-tracking, simply follow the same steps listed for selecting Dynamic AF-area mode but instead select the 3D-tracking mode. It is important to know that the 3D-tracking AF mode uses color and contrast to locate and then follow the subject, so this mode might be less effective when everything is similar in tone or color.

MANUAL FOCUS FOR ANTICIPATED ACTION

While I utilize the automatic focus modes for the majority of my shooting, there are times when I like to fall back on manual focus. This is usually when I know when and where the action will occur and I want to capture the subject as it crosses a certain plane of focus. This is useful in sports like motocross or auto racing, where the subjects are on a defined track and I know exactly where I want to capture the action. I could try tracking the subject, but sometimes the view can be obscured by a curve. By pre-focusing the camera, all I have to do is wait for the subject to approach my point of focus and then start firing the camera.

Take a look at **Figure 5.8**. The horses in the steeplechase race were traveling from my right to left and were partly obscured by the hedge, so tracking them with 3D-tracking would have been difficult, if not impossible. To get my shot, I simply focused on the front of the hedge and waited for the horses to come into range. As they began their jump over the hedge, I started shooting and captured the horses and riders at the height of the action.

FIGURE 5.8
Pre-focus the camera to a point where you know the subject will be, and start shooting right before they get there.

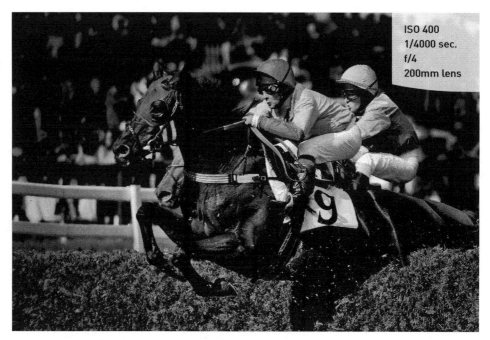

ISO 400
1/4000 sec.
f/4
200mm lens

When you want to use manual focus, just rotate the Focus-mode selector to the M position or set the focus switch on your lens to M (as discussed in Chapter 1). The camera will be able to assist you in focusing your camera using the focus points. Simply move the focus point over the area where you want the camera to focus, press the shutter button halfway to wake the rangefinder, and then turn the focus ring on your lens. When the camera is focused, you will see a circular in-focus indicator in the bottom of your viewfinder. The camera will hold this focus until you rotate the focus ring again or re-activate the AF system.

DRIVE MODES

The drive mode determines how fast your camera will take pictures. Single-shot is for taking one photograph at a time. With every full press of the shutter release button, the camera will take a single image. Continuous mode allows for a more rapid capture rate. Think of it like a machine gun. When you are using continuous mode, the camera will continue to take pictures as long as the shutter release button is held down.

KEEPING UP WITH THE CONTINUOUS SHOOTING MODE

Getting great focus is one thing, but capturing the best moment on the sensor can be difficult if you are shooting just one frame at a time. In the world of sports, and in life in general, things move pretty fast. If you blink, you might miss it. The same can be said for shooting in Single-frame mode. Fortunately, your D800 comes equipped with a continuous shooting—or "burst"—mode that lets you capture a series of images at up to five frames a second (**Figure 5.9**).

Using the continuous shooting mode causes the camera to keep taking images for as long as you hold down the shutter release button. In Single mode, you have to release the button and then press it again to take another picture.

FIGURE 5.9
Using the continu-
ous shooting mode
means that you are
sure to capture the
peak of the action.

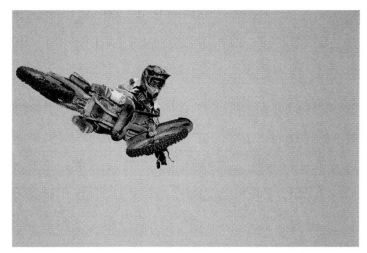

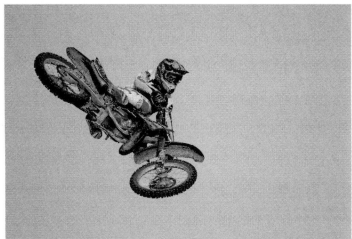

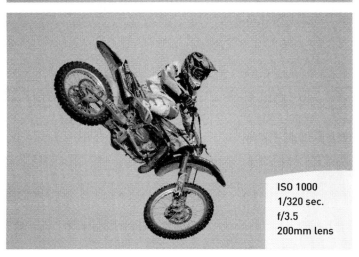

ISO 1000
1/320 sec.
f/3.5
200mm lens

SETTING UP AND SHOOTING IN THE CONTINUOUS SHOOTING MODE

The release mode selector switch is located on top of the camera. To select continuous mode, press the lock release button and rotate the release mode dial to either the CL or CH position.

The frame rate for the CL, or Continuous Low, mode can be adjusted to shoot anywhere from one to five frames a second (see the "Max Frame Rates" sidebar). The default for the CL mode is two frames a second. The CH, or Continuous High, mode will always fire at the maximum available frame rate.

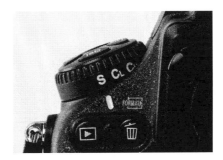

CHANGING THE CL MODE RATE

1. Press the Menu button, navigate to the d Shooting/display option in the Custom Setting menu, and press OK (**A**).

2. Select item d2 CL mode shooting speed, and press OK (**B**).

3. Set your new CL shooting speed, and press OK to lock in the change (**C**).

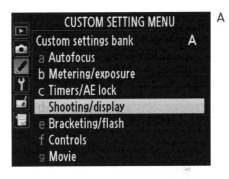

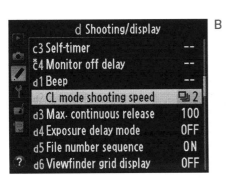

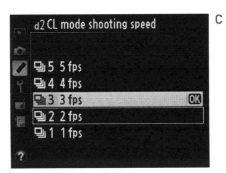

WATCHING THE BUFFER

Your camera has an internal memory, called a "buffer," where images are stored while they are being processed prior to being moved to your memory card. When the buffer fills up, the camera will stop shooting until space is made in the buffer for new images. The camera readout in the viewfinder tells you how many frames you have available in burst mode. Just look in the lower-right corner of the viewfinder to see the maximum number of images for burst shooting. As you shoot, the number will go down and then back up as the images are written to the memory card.

MAX FRAME RATES

While the D800 is by no means a speed demon when it comes to continuous frames, you can still squeeze some respectable frame rates out of it if you know how. When you are shooting in the full-frame FX mode (see page 79 in the user's manual), you are limited to a maximum of four frames a second. If you switch to a smaller frame size like 1.2x (30x20) and use the MB-D12 battery pack with an EN-EL18 battery, you can get up to six frames a second. See the chart on page 104 of the user's manual for more info.

A SENSE OF MOTION

Shooting action isn't always about freezing the action. There are times when you want to convey a sense of motion so that the viewer can get a feel for the movement and flow of an event. Two techniques you can use to achieve this effect are panning and motion blur.

PANNING

Panning has been used for decades to capture the speed of a moving object as it moves across the frame. It doesn't work well for subjects that are moving toward or away from you. Panning is achieved by following your subject across your frame, moving your camera along with the subject, and using a slower-than-normal shutter speed so that the background (and sometimes even a bit of the subject) has a sideways blur but the main portion of your subject is sharp and blur-free. The key to a great panning shot is selecting the right shutter speed: too fast and you won't get the desired blurring of the background; too slow and the subject will have too much blur and will not be recognizable. Practice the technique until you can achieve a smooth motion with your camera that follows along with your subject. The other thing to remember when panning is to follow through even after the shutter has closed. This will keep the motion smooth and give you better images.

In **Figure 5.10**, I used the panning technique to follow this jet as it took off in front of me. I set the camera to the continuous shooting mode, and I used Shutter Priority mode to select a shutter speed of 1/125 of a second while the focus mode was on Dynamic. Even though my aperture was f/18, I knew that the panning motion would blur my background.

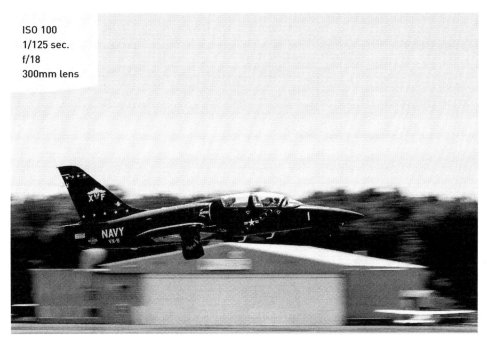

ISO 100
1/125 sec.
f/18
300mm lens

FIGURE 5.10
Following the subject as it moves across the field of view allows for a slower shutter speed and adds a sense of motion by blurring the background.

MOTION BLUR

Another way to let the viewer in on the feel of the action is to simply include some blur in the image. This isn't accidental blur from choosing the wrong shutter speed. This blur is more exaggerated, and it tells a story. In **Figure 5.11**, I was interested in capturing the movement of the merry-go-round. A fast shutter speed would have surely frozen the action, but it would not have told the story of the movement of the ride and the operator who was standing in the middle. Instead of moving with the action, I let the movement of the merry-go-round create the blur as I held the camera stationary.

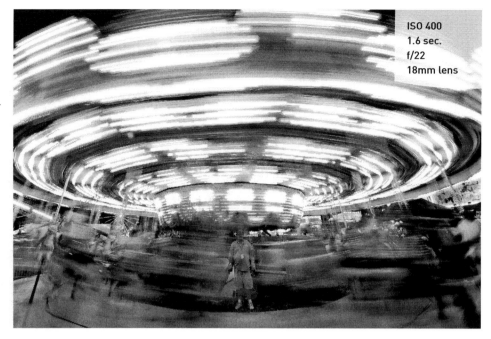

FIGURE 5.11
The movement of the ride coupled with the slow shutter speed conveys the spinning action of the merry-go-round as the operator mans his post in the middle.

ISO 400
1.6 sec.
f/22
18mm lens

Just as in panning, there is no preordained shutter speed to use for this effect. It is simply a matter of trial and error until you have a look that conveys the action. I try to get some area of the subject that is frozen. The key to this technique is the correct shutter speed combined with keeping the camera still during the exposure. You are trying to capture the motion of the subject, not the photographer or the camera, so use a good shooting stance or even a tripod.

TIPS FOR SHOOTING ACTION

GIVE THEM SOMEWHERE TO GO

Whether you are shooting something as simple as your child's soccer match or as complex as the aerial acrobatics of a motorcycle jumper, where you place the subject in the frame is equally as important as how well you expose the image. A poorly composed shot can completely ruin a great moment by not holding the viewer's attention.

The one mistake I see many times in action photography is that the photographer doesn't use the frame properly. If you are dealing with a subject that is moving horizontally across your field of view, give the subject somewhere to go by placing them to the side of the frame, with their motion leading toward the middle of the frame (**Figure 5.12**). This offsetting of the subject will introduce a sense of direction and anticipation for the viewer. Unless you are going to completely fill the image with the action, try to avoid placing your subject in the middle of the frame.

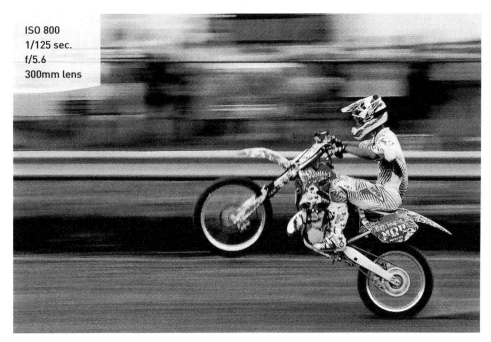

ISO 800
1/125 sec.
f/5.6
300mm lens

FIGURE 5.12
Try to leave space in front of your subject to lead the action in a direction.

GET IN FRONT OF THE ACTION

Here's another one. When shooting action, show the action coming toward you (**Figure 5.13**). Don't shoot the action going away from you. People want to see faces. Faces convey the action, the drive, the sense of urgency, and the emotion of the moment. So if you are shooting action involving people, always position yourself so that the action is either coming at you or at least perpendicular to your position.

FIGURE 5.13
Shooting from
the front with a
telephoto gives a
feeling that the
action is coming
right at you.

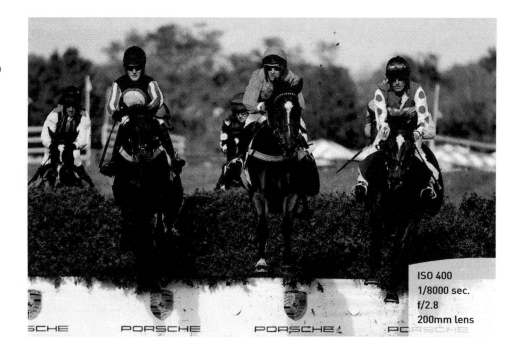

ISO 400
1/8000 sec.
f/2.8
200mm lens

PUT YOUR CAMERA IN A DIFFERENT PLACE

Changing your vantage point is a great way of finding new angles. Shooting from a low position with a wide-angle lens might let you incorporate some foreground to give depth to the image. Shooting from farther away with a telephoto lens will compress the elements in a scene and allow you to crop in tighter on the action. Don't be afraid to experiment and try new things.

The image in **Figure 5.14** is one of my favorite action shots, and it all happened because I tried something different.

As I was waiting for the race to begin, the horses started running out of their holding area and passing within a few yards of me. I had a wide-angle lens on the camera, and instead of bringing it up to eye level, I held it down at my side and started shooting frames in continuous mode. The AF focus mode was picking up the horse and getting great focus, and I knew that my shutter speed was set very high from the last race. The wide-angle lens captured the horse in the foreground, the trees in the middle ground, and the great-looking sky overhead. The horse was positioned to the right of the frame, running toward the empty space on the left. It was also placed in the lower third of the frame, giving an excellent "rule of thirds" balance. (See Chapter 7, "Landscape Photography," for more on the rule of thirds.) And this image is the result—just because I said, "What the heck?" and tried something a little outside the box.

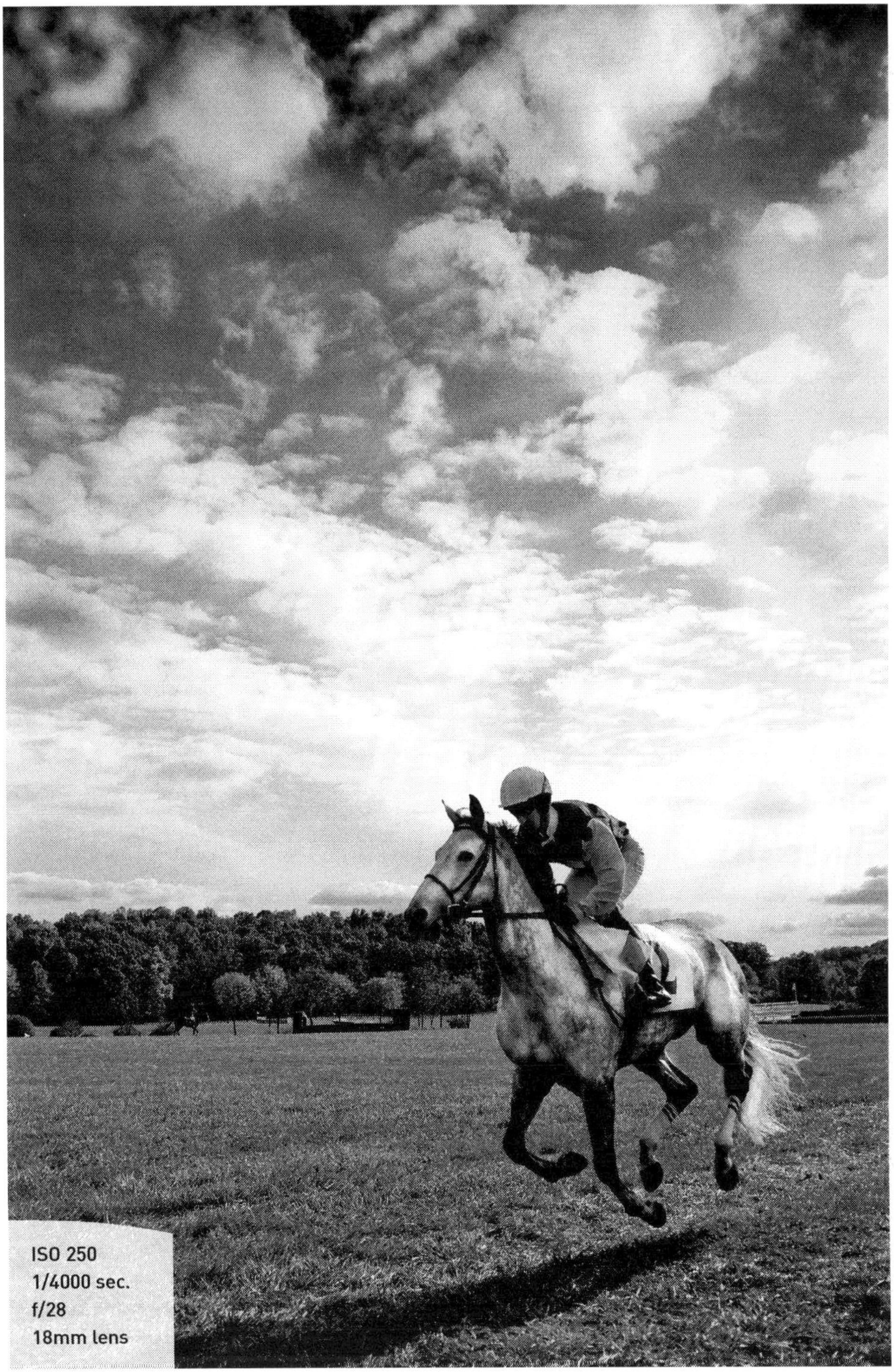

FIGURE 5.14
Putting your cam-
era in a different
place can yield
pleasing results.

ISO 250
1/4000 sec.
f/28
18mm lens

Chapter 5 Assignments

The mechanics of motion

For this first assignment, you need to find some action. Explore the relationship between the speed of an object and its direction of travel. Use the same shutter speed to record your subject moving toward you and across your view. Try using the same shutter speed for both to compare the difference made by the direction of travel.

Wide vs. telephoto

Just as with the first assignment, photograph a subject moving in different directions, but this time, use a wide-angle lens and then a telephoto. Check out how the telephoto setting on the zoom lens will require faster shutter speeds than the lens at its wide-angle setting.

Getting a feel for focusing modes

We discussed two different ways to autofocus for action: Dynamic and 3D-tracking. Starting with Dynamic mode, find a moving subject and use the mode to get familiar with the way the mode works.

Now repeat the process using the 3D-tracking AF mode. The point of the exercise is to become familiar enough with the two modes to decide which one to use for the situation you are photographing.

Anticipating the spot using manual focus

For this assignment, you will need to find a subject that you know will cross a specific line that you can pre-focus on. A street with moderate traffic works well for this. Focus on a spot on the street that the cars will travel across (don't forget to set your lens for manual focus). To do this right, you need to set the drive mode on the camera to continuous mode. Now, when a car approaches the spot, start shooting. Try shooting in three- or four-frame bursts.

Following the action

Panning is a great way to show motion. To begin, find a subject that will move across your path at a steady speed and practice following it in your viewfinder from side to side. Now, with the camera in Shutter Priority mode, set your shutter speed to 1/30 of a second and the focus mode to Dynamic. Now pan along with the subject and shoot as it moves across your view. Experiment with different shutter speeds and focal lengths. Panning is one of those skills that takes some time to get a feel for, so try it with different types of subjects moving at different speeds.

Feeling the movement

Instead of panning with the motion, use a stationary camera position and adjust the shutter speed until you get a blurred effect that gives the sense of motion but still allows you to identify the subject. There is a big difference between a slightly blurred photo that looks like you just picked the wrong shutter speed and one that looks intentional for the purpose of showing motion. Just like panning, it will take some experimentation to find just the right shutter speed to achieve the desired effect.

Share your results with the book's Flickr group!

Join the group here: www.flickr.com/groups/d800fromsnapshotstogreatshots

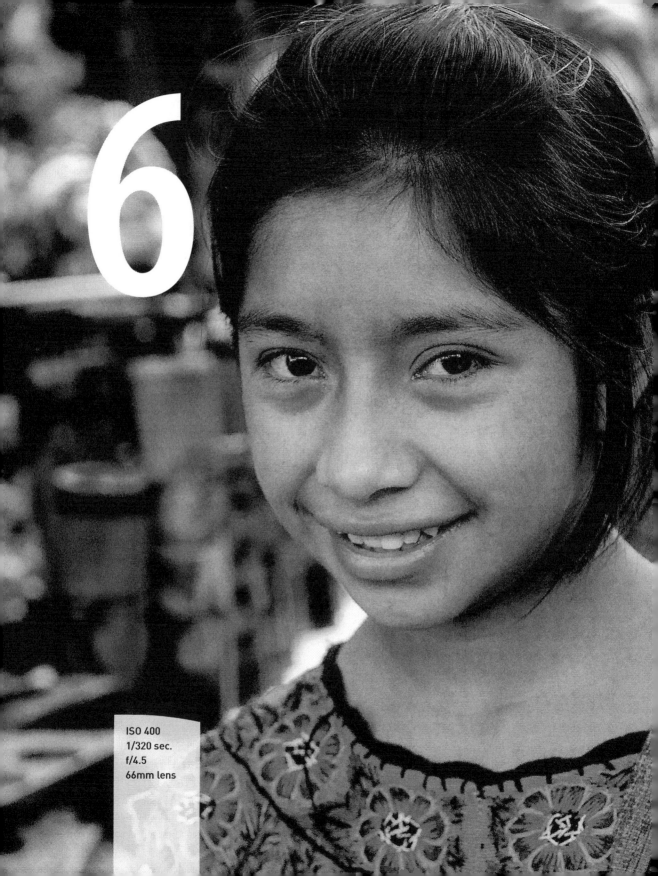

6

ISO 400
1/320 sec.
f/4.5
66mm lens

Say Cheese!

SETTINGS AND FEATURES TO MAKE GREAT PORTRAITS

Taking pictures of people is one of the great joys of photography. You will experience a great sense of accomplishment when you capture the spirit and personality of someone in a photograph. At the same time, you have a great responsibility because the person in front of the camera is depending on you to make them look good. You can't always change how someone looks, but you can control the way you photograph that individual. In this chapter, we will explore some camera features and techniques that can help you create great portraits.

While climbing through the Bayon temple in Cambodia, I happened upon this young monk sitting quietly in a corner. His colorful robes were such a great contrast to the old stone walls of the temple. The area he was sitting in happened to be in the shade, which helped to soften the shadows and allowed me to capture more detail in the darker shadow areas.

The image was composed to show a larger portion of the surroundings.

A small aperture of f/11 ensured that the subject and background would be in focus.

The monk was positioned in the lower-right third of the frame to add to the composition.

The vivid color of the monk's robe adds contrast to the photo and draws the viewer's eyes to the main subject.

ISO 200
1/60 sec.
f/11
35mm lens

PORING OVER THE PICTURE

When shooting portraits in outdoor locations, I always look for a variety of backdrop possibilities so that I have options depending on the lighting conditions. This photo shoot took place in a small central park in my city, where I had lots of great soft, natural light that was perfect for portraits of this girl.

The subject was framed off-center to improve the composition.

Using a telephoto lens let me crop tightly without having to get in the model's face.

A large aperture helped blur the background.

ISO 400
1/100 sec.
f/5.6
120mm lens

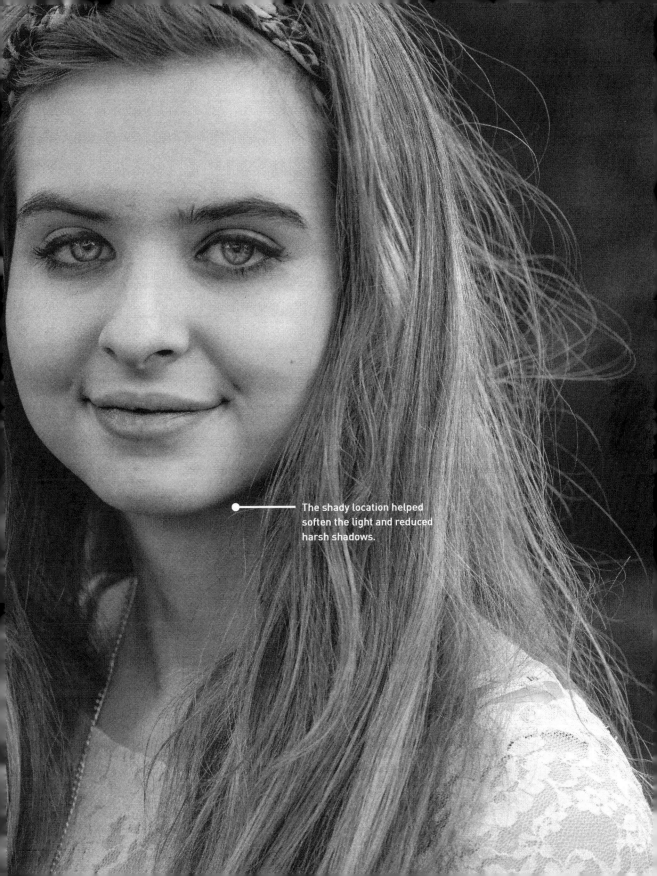

The shady location helped soften the light and reduced harsh shadows.

USING APERTURE PRIORITY MODE

If you took a poll of portrait photographers to see which shooting mode was most often used for portraits, the answer would certainly be Aperture Priority (A) mode. Selecting the right aperture is important for placing the most critically sharp area of the photo on your subject, while simultaneously blurring all of the distracting background clutter (**Figure 6.1**). Not only will a large aperture give the narrowest depth of field, it will also allow you to shoot in lower light levels at lower ISO settings.

This isn't to say that you have to use the largest aperture on your lens. A good place to begin is f/5.6. This will give you enough depth of field to keep the entire face in focus, while providing enough blur to eliminate distractions in the background. This isn't a hard-and-fast setting; it's just a good, all-around number to start with. Your aperture might change depending on the focal length of the lens you are using and on the amount of blur that you want for your foreground and background elements.

FIGURE 6.1
Using a wide aperture, especially with a longer lens, blurs distracting background details.

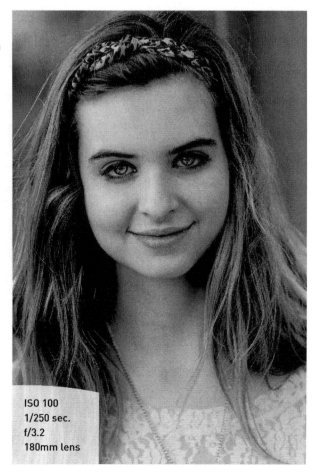

ISO 100
1/250 sec.
f/3.2
180mm lens

GO WIDE FOR ENVIRONMENTAL PORTRAITS

There will be times when your subject's environment is of great significance to the story you want to tell. This might mean using a smaller aperture to get more detail in the background or foreground. Once again, by using Aperture Priority mode, you can set your aperture to a higher f-stop, such as f/8 or f/11, and include the important details of the scene that surrounds your subject.

Using a wider-than-normal lens can also assist in getting more depth of field as well as showing the surrounding area. A wide-angle lens requires less stopping down of the aperture (making the aperture smaller) to achieve an acceptable depth of field. This is because wide-angle lenses cover a greater area, so the depth of field appears to cover a greater percentage of the scene.

A wider lens might also be necessary to relay more information about the scenery (**Figure 6.2**). Select a lens length that is wide enough to tell the story but not so wide that you distort the subject. There's little in the world of portraiture quite as unflattering as giving someone a big, distorted nose (unless you are going for that sort of look). When shooting a portrait with a wide-angle lens, keep the subject away from the edge of the frame. This will reduce the distortion, especially in very wide focal lengths. As the lens length increases, distortion will be reduced. I generally don't like to go wider than about 24mm for portraits.

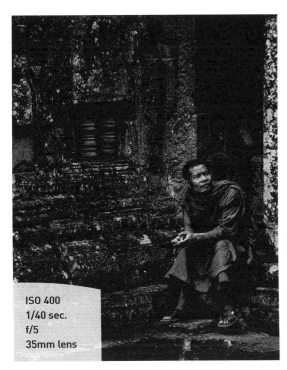

ISO 400
1/40 sec.
f/5
35mm lens

FIGURE 6.2
A wide-angle lens allows you to capture more of the environment in the scene without having to increase the distance between you and the subject.

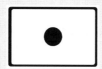
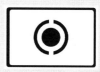
METERING MODES FOR PORTRAITS

For most portrait situations, the Matrix metering mode is ideal. (For more on how metering works, see the "Metering Basics" sidebar.) This mode measures light values from all portions of the viewfinder and then establishes a proper exposure for the scene. The only problem that you might encounter when using this metering mode is when you have very light or dark backgrounds in your portrait shots.

In these instances, the meter might be fooled into using the wrong exposure information because it will be trying to lighten or darken the entire scene based on the prominence of dark or light areas (**Figure 6.6**). You can deal with this in one of two ways. You can use exposure compensation, which we cover in Chapter 7, "Landscape Photography," to dial in adjustments for over- and underexposure. Or you can change the metering mode to Center-weighted metering. The Center-weighted metering mode uses only the center area of the viewfinder (about 9 percent) to get its exposure information. This is the best way to achieve proper exposure for most portraits; metering off skin tones, averaged with hair and clothing, will often give a more accurate exposure (**Figure 6.7**). This metering mode is also great to use when the subject is strongly backlit.

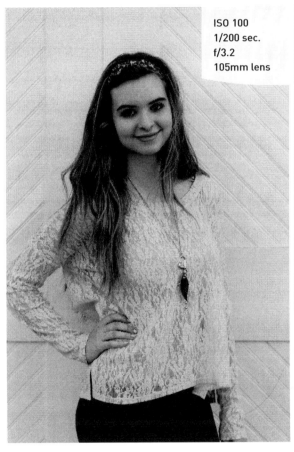

ISO 100
1/200 sec.
f/3.2
105mm lens

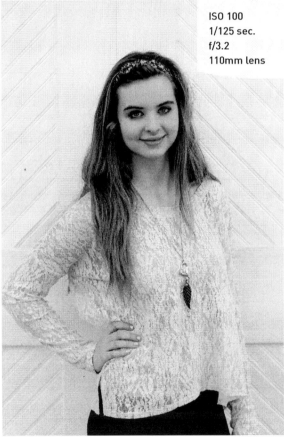

ISO 100
1/125 sec.
f/3.2
110mm lens

FIGURE 6.6
The light background color and clothing fooled the meter into choosing a slightly underexposed setting for the photo.

FIGURE 6.7
When I switched to the Center-weighted metering mode, my camera was able to ignore much of the background and add a little more time to the exposure.

Changing your metering mode is as simple as rotating the Metering selector knob on the back of the camera to the Center-weighted icon. You can change the actual area used in calculating the exposure in the Custom Setting menu.

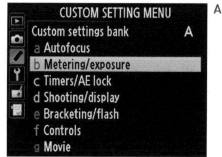

1. Press the Menu button, navigate to the Custom Setting menu, highlight b Metering/exposure, and press OK (A).

2. Highlight b5 Center-weighted area, and press OK (B).

3. The default setting is 12 mm. If you want a larger or smaller area, just highlight it, and press OK to lock it in (C).

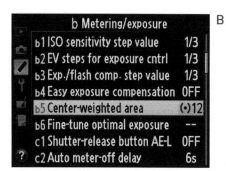

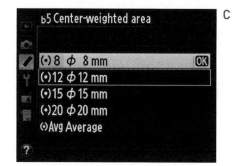

USING THE AE-L (AUTO EXPOSURE LOCK) FEATURE

There will often be times when your subject is not in the center of the frame but you still want to use the Center-weighted metering mode. So how can you get an accurate reading if the subject isn't in the center? Try using the AE-L (Auto Exposure Lock) feature to hold the exposure setting while you recompose.

AE Lock lets you use the exposure setting from any portion of the scene that you think is appropriate, and then lock that setting in regardless of how the scene looks when you recompose. An example of this would be when you're shooting a photograph of someone and a large amount of blue sky appears in the picture. Normally, the meter might be fooled by all that bright sky and try to reduce the exposure.

Using AE Lock, you can establish the correct metering by zooming in on the subject (or even pointing the camera toward the ground), taking the meter reading, locking it in with the AE-L feature, and then recomposing and taking your photo with the locked-in exposure.

SHOOTING WITH THE AE LOCK FEATURE

1. Find the AE Lock button on the back of the camera and place your thumb on it.

2. While looking through the viewfinder, place the focus point on your subject and press the shutter release button halfway to get a meter reading, and focus the camera.

3. Press and hold the AE Lock button to lock in the meter reading. You should see the AE-L indicator in the viewfinder.

4. While pressing in the AE-L button, recompose your shot and take the photo.

5. To take more than one photo without having to take another meter reading, just hold down the AE Lock button until you are done using the meter setting.

FOCUSING: THE EYES HAVE IT

It has been said that the eyes are the windows to the soul, and nothing could be truer when you are taking a photograph of someone (**Figure 6.8**). You could have the perfect composition and exposure, but if the eyes aren't sharp, the entire image suffers. While there are many different focusing modes to choose from on your D800, for portrait work you can't beat AF-S (Single-Servo AF) mode using a single focusing point. AF-S focusing will establish a single focus for the lens and then hold it until you take the photograph; the other focusing modes continue focusing until the photograph is taken. The single-point selection lets you place the focusing point right on your subject's eye and set that spot as the critical focus spot. Using AF-S mode lets you get that focus and recompose all in one motion.

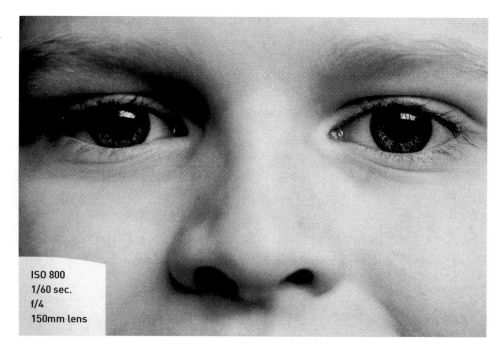

FIGURE 6.8
When photograph-
ing people, you
should almost
always place the
emphasis on the
eyes.

ISO 800
1/60 sec.
f/4
150mm lens

SETTING UP FOR AF-S FOCUS MODE

1. Press and hold the AF-mode button.
2. Rotate the Main Command dial until you see AF-S in the control panel.

SETTING YOUR FOCUS TO A SINGLE POINT

1. Press the AF-mode button again and rotate the Sub-command dial until you see the single-point indicator in the control panel.
2. While looking through the viewfinder, use the Multi-selector to select which cursor you want to use as your focus point.

Now, to shoot using this focus point, place that point on your subject's eye and press the shutter button halfway to lock in the focus. While still holding the shutter button down halfway, recompose if necessary and then press the button the rest of the way to take your shot.

I typically use the center point for focus selection. I find it easier to place that point directly on the location where my critical focus should be established and then recompose the shot. Even though the single point can be selected from any of the focus points, it typically takes longer to figure out where that point should be in relation to my subject. By using the center point, I can quickly establish focus and get on with my shooting.

CLASSIC BLACK AND WHITE PORTRAITS

There is something timeless about a black and white portrait. It eliminates the distraction of color and puts all the emphasis on the subject. To get great black and whites without having to resort to any image-processing software, set your picture control to Monochrome (**Figure 6.9**). You should know that the picture controls are automatically applied when shooting with the JPEG file format. If you are shooting in RAW, the picture that shows up on your rear LCD display will look black and white, but it will appear as a color image when you open it in your software. You can use image-editing software to apply the Monochrome, or any other, picture control to your RAW image.

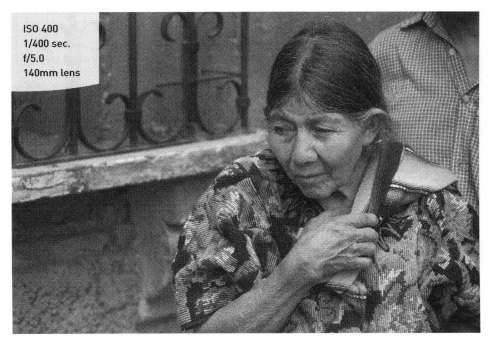

ISO 400
1/400 sec.
f/5.0
140mm lens

FIGURE 6.9
Getting high-quality black and white portraits can be as simple as setting the picture control to Monochrome.

The real key to using the Monochrome picture control is to customize it for your portrait subject. The control can be changed to alter the sharpness and contrast. For any subject you would like to look somewhat soft, set the Sharpness setting to 0 or 1. For anyone who you want to look really detailed, try a setting of 6 or 7. I typically like to leave Contrast at a setting of around –1 or –2. This gives me a nice range of tones throughout the image.

The other adjustment that you should try is to change the picture control's Filter effect from None to one of the four available settings (Yellow, Orange, Red, and Green). Using the filters will have the effect of either lightening or darkening the skin tones. The Red and Yellow filters usually lighten skin, while the Green filter can make skin appear a bit darker. Experiment to see which one works best for your subject.

SETTING YOUR PICTURE CONTROL TO MONOCHROME

Press the Lock button on the back of the camera to bring up the Set Picture Control screen, highlight Monochrome, and press OK (**A**).

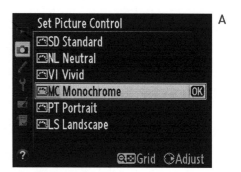

CUSTOMIZING YOUR MONOCHROME PICTURE CONTROL

1. Follow the previous step to get to the Picture Control menu and highlight Monochrome, but instead of pressing the OK button, press the Multi-Selector to the right to enter the customization menu (**B**).

2. Once you have modified the settings, press the OK button to save your changes. When you return to the Picture Control menu, you will now see a small star next to the MC. This is your clue that you have altered the default settings for that particular control (**C**).

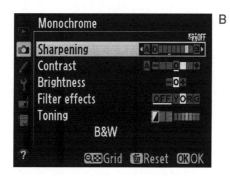

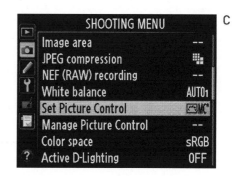

THE PORTRAIT PICTURE CONTROL FOR BETTER SKIN TONES

As long as we are talking about picture controls for portraits, there is another control on your D800 that has been tuned specifically for this type of shooting. Oddly enough, it's called Portrait. To set this control on your camera, simply follow the same directions as earlier, except this time, select the Portrait control (PT) instead of Monochrome. There are also individual options for the Portrait control that, like the Monochrome control, include sharpness and contrast. You can also change the saturation (how intense the colors will be) and hue, which lets you change the skin tones from more reddish to more yellowish. I prefer brighter colors, so I like to boost the Saturation setting to +2 and leave everything else at the defaults. You won't be able to use the same adjustments for everyone, especially when it comes to color tone, so do some experimenting to see what works best.

USE FILL FLASH FOR REDUCING SHADOWS

A common problem when taking pictures of people outside, especially during the midday hours, is that the overhead sun can create dark shadows under the eyes and chin. You could have your subject turn his or her face to the sun, but that is usually considered cruel and unusual punishment. So how can you have your subject's back to the sun and still get a decent exposure of the face? Try turning on your flash to fill in the shadows (**Figure 6.10**). This also works well when you are photographing someone with a ball cap on. The bill of the hat tends to create heavy shadows over the eyes, and the fill flash will lighten up those areas while providing a really nice catchlight in the eyes.

The key to using the flash as a fill is to not use it on full power. If you do, the camera will try to balance the flash with the daylight, and you will get a very flat and featureless face.

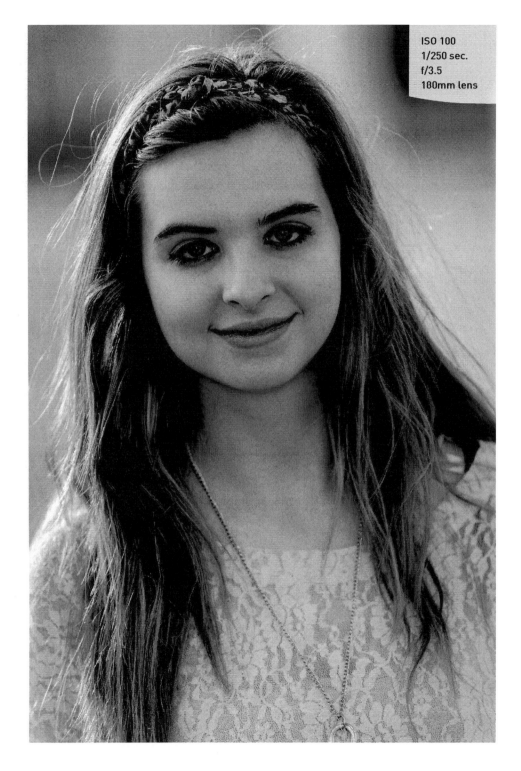

FIGURE 6.10
I used a little fill flash to lighten the subject, who was standing in a shaded area with strong light behind her.

ISO 100
1/250 sec.
f/3.5
180mm lens

CATCHLIGHT

A *catchlight* is that little sparkle that adds life to the eyes. When you are photographing a person with a light source in front of them, you will usually get a reflection of that light in the eye, be it your flash, the sun, or something else brightly reflecting in the eye. The light is reflected off the surface of the eyes as bright highlights and serves to bring attention to the eyes.

SETTING UP AND SHOOTING WITH FILL FLASH

1. Press the pop-up flash button (**A**) to raise your pop-up flash into the ready position.

2. Press and hold the flash compensation button on the front of the camera (**B**), and then rotate the Sub-command dial to reduce the flash exposure by –0.3. Look in the control panel to see the compensation readout.

3. Take a photograph and check your playback LCD to see if it looks good. If it doesn't, try reducing the flash's power in 1/3-stop increments.

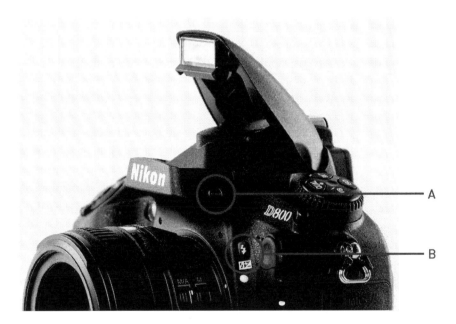

One problem that can quickly surface when using the on-camera flash is red-eye. Not to worry, though—we will talk about that in Chapter 8, "Mood Lighting."

PORTRAITS ON THE MOVE

Not all portraits are shot with the subject sitting in a chair, posed and ready for the picture. Sometimes you might want to get an action shot that says something about the person, similar to an environmental portrait. Children, especially, just like to move. Why fight it? Set up an action portrait instead.

For the photo in **Figure 6.11**, I used the Portrait picture control and set my camera to Shutter Priority mode. I knew that there would be a good deal of movement involved, and I wanted to make sure that I had a fairly high shutter speed to freeze the action, so I set it to 1/320 of a second. I set the focus mode to AF-C and the drive mode to Continuous, and I just let it rip. There were quite a few throwaway shots, but I was able to capture one that conveyed the energy and action.

FIGURE 6.11
A high ISO allowed me to use a fast shutter speed to stop the action, along with a small aperture to increase depth of field.

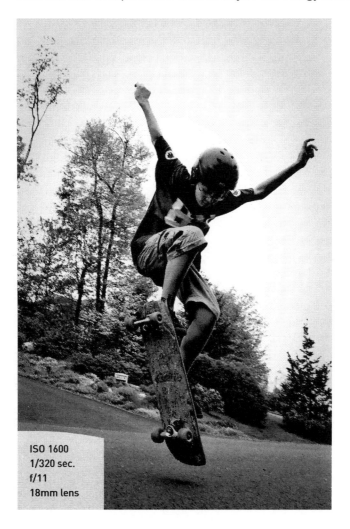

ISO 1600
1/320 sec.
f/11
18mm lens

TIPS FOR SHOOTING BETTER PORTRAITS

Before we get to the assignments for this chapter, I thought it might be a good idea to leave you with a few extra pointers on shooting portraits that don't necessarily have anything specific to do with your camera. There are entire books that cover things like portrait lighting, posing, and so on. But here are a few pointers that will make your people pics look a lot better.

AVOID THE CENTER OF THE FRAME

This falls under the category of composition. Place your subject to the side of the frame (**Figure 6.12**)—it just looks more interesting than plunking them smack dab in the middle (**Figure 6.13**).

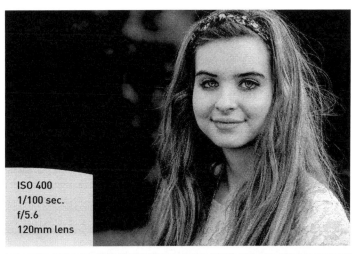

ISO 400
1/100 sec.
f/5.6
120mm lens

FIGURE 6.12
Try cropping in a bit, and place the subject's face off-center to improve the shot.

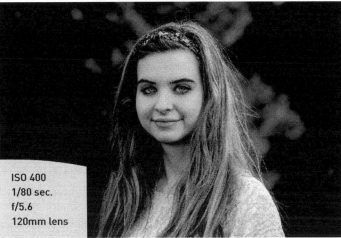

ISO 400
1/80 sec.
f/5.6
120mm lens

FIGURE 6.13
Having the subject in the middle of the frame with so much empty space on the sides can make for a less-than-interesting portrait.

CHOOSE THE RIGHT LENS

Choosing the correct lens can make a huge impact on your portraits. A wide-angle lens can distort the features of your subject, which can lead to an unflattering portrait (**Figure 6.14**). Select a longer focal length if you will be close to your subject (**Figure 6.15**).

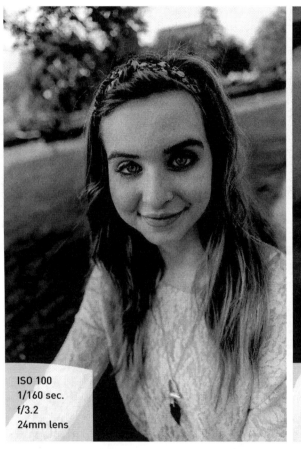

ISO 100
1/160 sec.
f/3.2
24mm lens

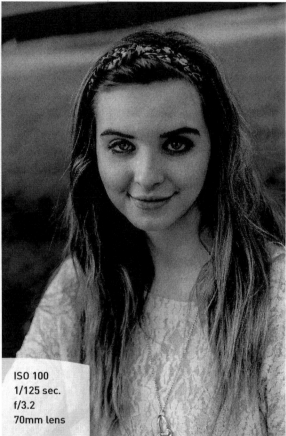

ISO 100
1/125 sec.
f/3.2
70mm lens

FIGURE 6.14
At this close distance, the 24mm lens is distorting the subject's face.

FIGURE 6.15
By zooming out to 70mm, I am able to remove the distortion for a much better photo.

DON'T CUT THEM OFF AT THE KNEES

There is an old rule about photographing people: never crop the picture at a joint. This means no cropping at the ankles or the knees. If you need to crop at the legs, the proper place to crop is mid-shin or mid-thigh (**Figure 6.16**).

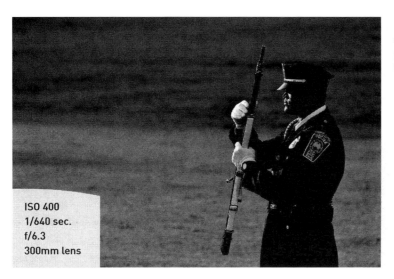

FIGURE 6.16
A good crop for people is at mid-thigh or mid-shin.

ISO 400
1/640 sec.
f/6.3
300mm lens

USE THE FRAME

Have you ever noticed that most people are taller than they are wide? Turn your camera vertically for a more pleasing composition (**Figure 6.17**).

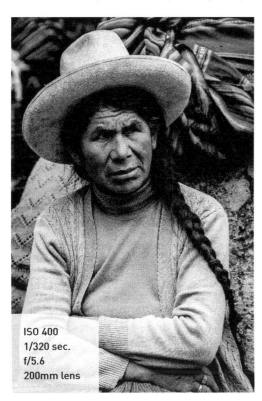

FIGURE 6.17
Get in the habit of turning your camera to a vertical position when shooting portraits. This is also referred to as portrait orientation.

ISO 400
1/320 sec.
f/5.6
200mm lens

SUNBLOCK FOR PORTRAITS

The midday sun can be harsh and can do unflattering things to people's faces. If you can, find a shady spot out of the direct sunlight. You will get softer shadows, smoother skin tones, and better detail. This holds true for overcast skies as well (**Figure 6.18**). Just be sure to adjust your white balance accordingly.

GIVE THEM A HEALTHY GLOW

Nearly everyone looks better with a warm, healthy glow. Some of the best light of the day happens just a little before sundown, so shoot at that time if you can (**Figure 6.19**).

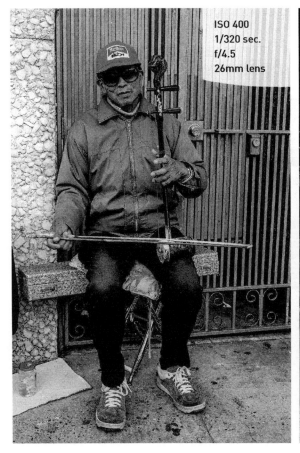

ISO 400
1/320 sec.
f/4.5
26mm lens

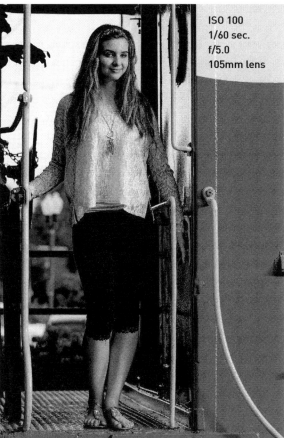

ISO 100
1/60 sec.
f/5.0
105mm lens

FIGURE 6.18
The lack of harsh shadows in this photograph of a street musician is directly due to his shady location.

FIGURE 6.19
You just can't beat the glow of the late afternoon sun for adding warmth to your portraits.

KEEP AN EYE ON YOUR BACKGROUND

Sometimes it's easy to get so caught up in taking a great shot that you forget about the smaller details. Try to keep an eye on what is going on behind your subject so they don't end up with things popping out of their heads (**Figures 6.20** and **6.21**).

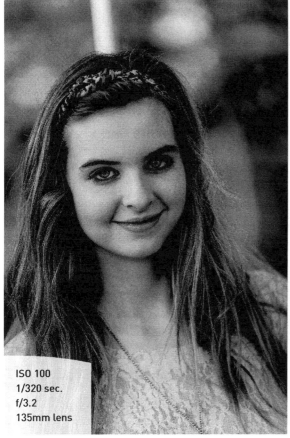

ISO 100
1/320 sec.
f/3.2
135mm lens

FIGURE 6.20
The yellow handrail in the background is coming right out of the subject's head.

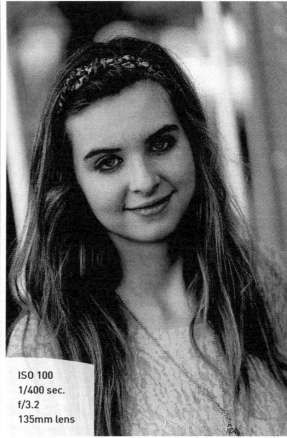

ISO 100
1/400 sec.
f/3.2
135mm lens

FIGURE 6.21
By moving the camera position a little to the left, I was able to move the handrail to the side, where it is less distracting.

FRAME THE SCENE

Using elements in the scene to create a frame around your subject is a great way to draw the viewer in. You don't have to use a window frame to do this. Just look for elements in the foreground that could be used to force the viewer's eye toward your subject (**Figure 6.22**).

FIGURE 6.22
The colorful red and yellow elements of the caboose make a great frame for the subject.

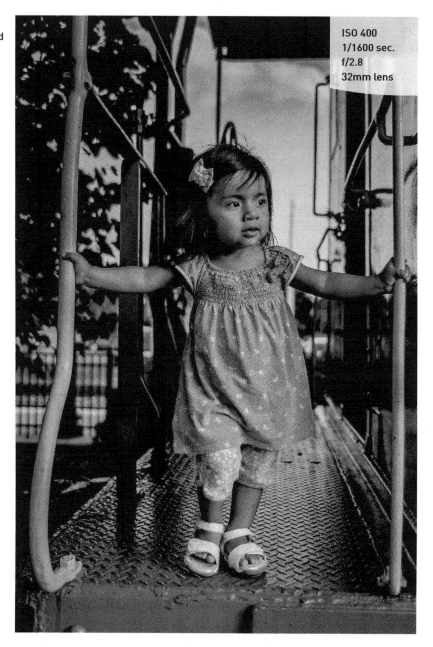

ISO 400
1/1600 sec.
f/2.8
32mm lens

GET DOWN ON THEIR LEVEL

If you want better pictures of children, don't shoot from an adult's eye level. Getting the camera down to the child's level will make your images look more personal (**Figure 6.23**).

ELIMINATE SPACE BETWEEN YOUR SUBJECTS

One of the problems you can encounter when taking portraits of more than one person is that of personal space. What feels like a close distance to the subjects can look impersonal to the viewer. Have your subjects move close together, eliminating any open space between them (**Figure 6.24**).

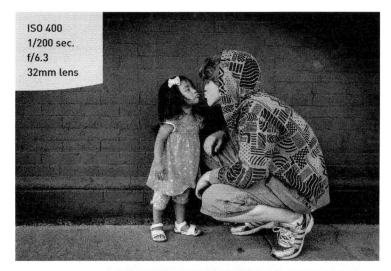

ISO 400
1/200 sec.
f/6.3
32mm lens

FIGURE 6.23
Sometimes taking photographs of children means getting low to the ground, but the end result is a much better image.

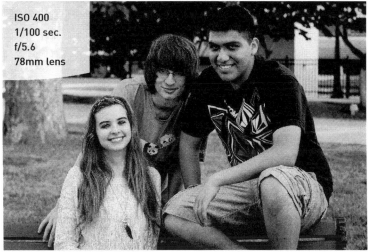

ISO 400
1/100 sec.
f/5.6
78mm lens

FIGURE 6.24
Getting your subjects to move in close together can sometimes be a challenge, but the results are worth the effort.

DON'T BE AFRAID TO GET CLOSE

When you are taking someone's picture, don't be afraid of getting close and filling the frame (**Figure 6.25**). This doesn't mean you have to shoot from a foot away; try zooming in to capture the details.

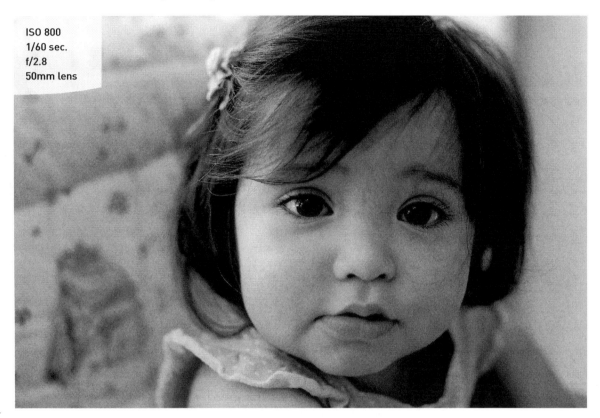

ISO 800
1/60 sec.
f/2.8
50mm lens

FIGURE 6.25
Filling the frame with the subject's face can lead to a much more intimate portrait.

Chapter 6 Assignments

Depth of field in portraits

Let's start with something simple. Grab your favorite person and start experimenting with using different aperture settings. Shoot wide open (the widest your lens goes, such as f/3.5 or f/5.6) and then really stopped down (like f/22). Look at the difference in the depth of field and how it plays an important role in placing the attention on your subject. (Make sure you don't have your subject standing against the background. Give some distance so that there is a good blurring effect of the background at the wide f-stop setting.)

Discovering the qualities of natural light

Pick a nice sunny day and try shooting some portraits in the midday sun. If your subject is willing, have them turn so the sun is in their face. If they are still speaking to you after blinding them, have them turn their back to the sun. Try this with and without the fill flash so you can see the difference. Finally, move them into a completely shaded spot and take a few more.

Picking the right metering method

Find a very dark or light background and place your subject in front of it. Now take a couple of shots, giving a lot of space around your subject for the background to show. Now switch metering modes and use the AE Lock feature to get a more accurate reading of your subject. Notice the differences in exposure between the metering methods.

Picture controls for portraits

Have some fun playing with the different picture controls. Try the Portrait control as compared to the Standard. Then try out Monochrome and play with the different color filter options to see how they affect skin tones.

Share your results with the book's Flickr group!

Join the group here: www.flickr.com/groups/d800fromsnapshotstogreatshots

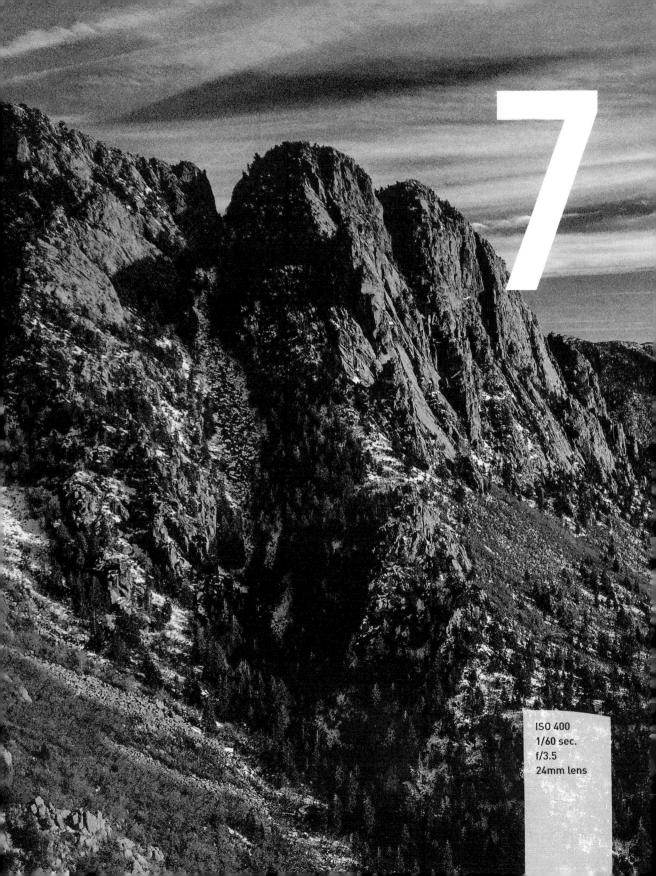

7

ISO 400
1/60 sec.
f/3.5
24mm lens

Landscape Photography

TIPS, TOOLS, AND TECHNIQUES TO GET THE MOST OUT OF YOUR LANDSCAPE PHOTOGRAPHY

There has always been something about shooting landscapes that has brought a sense of joy to my photography. It might have something to do with being outdoors and working at the mercy of Mother Nature. Maybe it's the way it challenges me to visualize the landscape and try to capture it with my camera. It truly is a celebration of light, composition, and the world we live in.

In this chapter, we will explore some of the features of the D800 that not only improve the look of your landscape photography, but also make it easier to take great shots. We will also explore some typical scenarios and discuss methods to bring out the best in your landscape photography.

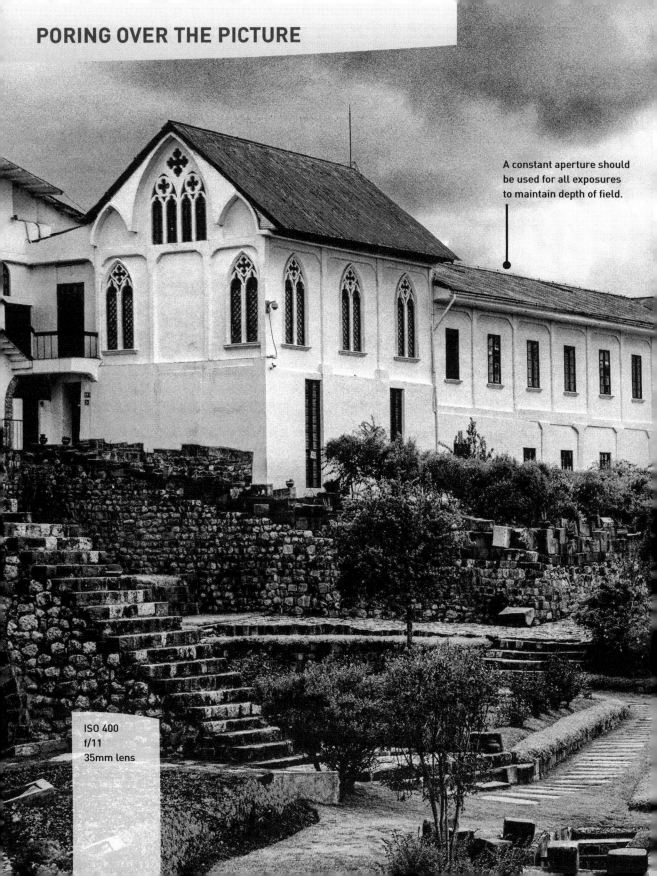

PORING OVER THE PICTURE

A constant aperture should be used for all exposures to maintain depth of field.

ISO 400
f/11
35mm lens

HDR photography has rapidly become one of the most popular and controversial types of photography in recent years. Some purists believe that combining multiple exposures is like cheating. Others believe it is a viable art form that is just using another piece of technology to help photographers realize their vision. Personally, I think that if you have the right subject, HDR can make for a pretty cool photograph, which is why I chose it for this particular location—lots of clouds, a bright white building, and dark foliage. HDR helped me capture all of it.

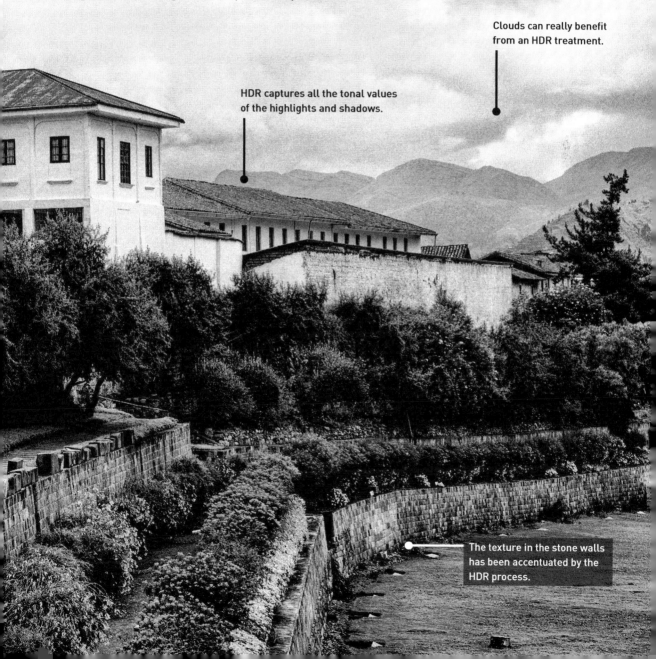

Clouds can really benefit from an HDR treatment.

HDR captures all the tonal values of the highlights and shadows.

The texture in the stone walls has been accentuated by the HDR process.

PORING OVER THE PICTURE

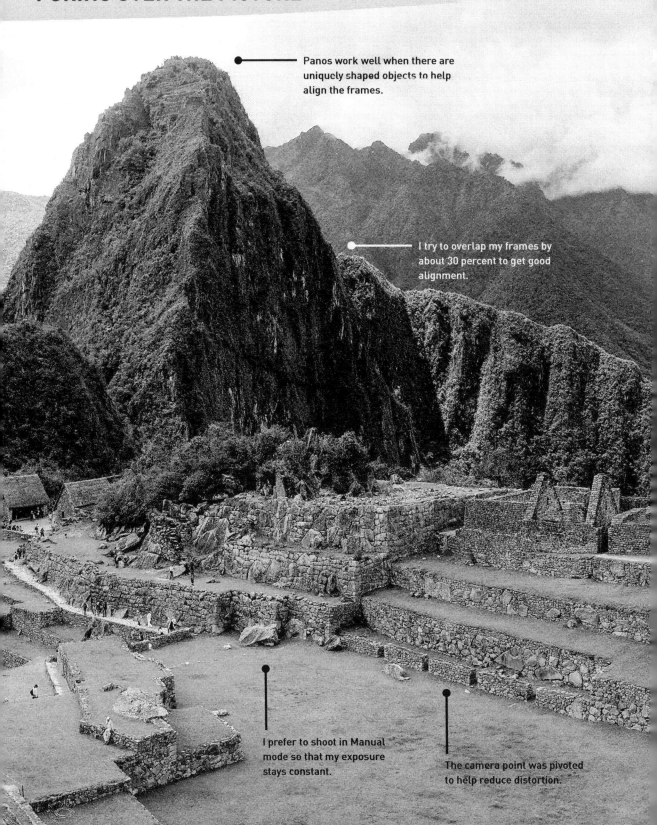

Panos work well when there are uniquely shaped objects to help align the frames.

I try to overlap my frames by about 30 percent to get good alignment.

I prefer to shoot in Manual mode so that my exposure stays constant.

The camera point was pivoted to help reduce distortion.

Sometimes you will find a scene that you can't cover in just one frame. You could try to use a wide-angle lens, but you might end up with too much sky or foreground and small scenery with little detail. That's where the panorama comes into play. By capturing multiple exposures and then combining them in an imaging program such as Adobe Photoshop or Photoshop Elements, you can create panoramic images that really show off an amazing vista.

ISO 800
1/100 sec.
f/13
26mm lens

SHARP AND IN FOCUS: USING TRIPODS

Throughout the previous chapters we have concentrated on using the camera to create great images. We will continue that trend through this chapter, but there is one additional piece of equipment that is crucial in the world of landscape shooting: the tripod. There are a couple of reasons why tripods are so critical to your landscape work, the first being the time of day that you will be working. For reasons that will be explained later, the best light for most landscape work happens at sunrise and just before sunset. While this is the best time to shoot, it's also kind of dark. That means you'll be working with slow shutter speeds. Slow shutter speeds mean camera shake. Camera shake equals bad photos.

The second reason is also related to the amount of light that you're gathering with your camera. When taking landscape photos, you will usually want to be working with very small apertures, as they give you lots of depth of field. This also means that, once again, you will be working with slower-than-normal shutter speeds.

Slow shutter = camera shake = bad photos.

Do you see the pattern here? The one tool in your arsenal to truly defeat the camera shake issue and ensure tack-sharp photos is a good tripod (**Figure 7.1**).

FIGURE 7.1
A sturdy tripod is the key to sharp landscape photos. (Photo: Scott Kelby)

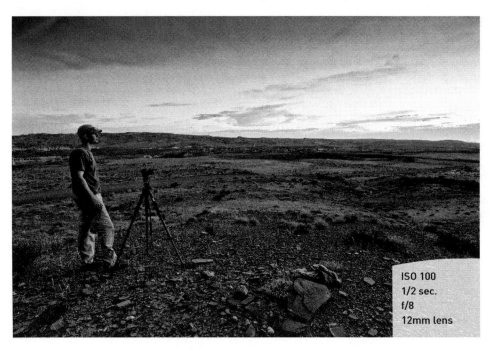

ISO 100
1/2 sec.
f/8
12mm lens

So what should you look for in a tripod? Well, first make sure it is sturdy enough to support your camera and any lens that you might want to use. Next, check the height of the tripod. Bending over all day to look through the viewfinder of a camera on a short tripod can wreak havoc on your back. Finally, think about getting a tripod that utilizes a quick-release head. This usually employs a plate that screws into the bottom of the camera and then quickly snaps into place on the tripod. This will be especially handy if you are going to move between shooting by hand and using the tripod. You'll find more information about tripods in the bonus chapter "Pimp My Ride."

TRIPOD STABILITY

Most tripods have a center column that allows the user to extend the height of the camera above the point where the tripod legs join together. This might seem like a great idea, but the reality is that the farther you raise that column, the less stable your tripod becomes. Think of a tall building that sways near the top. To get the most solid base for your camera, always try to use it with the center column at its lowest point so that your camera is right at the apex of the tripod legs.

VR LENSES AND TRIPODS DON'T MIX

If you are using Vibration Reduction (VR) lenses on your camera, you need to remember to turn this feature off when you use a tripod (**Figure 7.2**). This is because the Vibration Reduction, while trying to minimize camera movement, can actually create movement when the camera is already stable. To turn off the VR feature, just slide the VR selector switch on the side of the lens to the Off position.

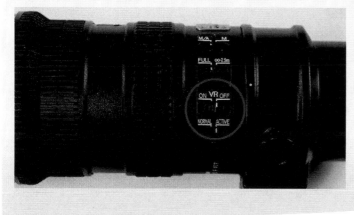

FIGURE 7.2
Turn off the Vibration Reduction feature when using a tripod.

SELECTING THE PROPER ISO

When shooting most landscape scenes, the ISO is the one factor that should only be increased as a last resort. While it is easy to select a higher ISO to get a smaller aperture, the noise that it can introduce into your images can be quite harmful. The noise is not only visible as large grainy artifacts; it can also be multicolored, which further degrades the image quality and color balance.

Take a look at **Figures 7.3** and **7.4**, which show a photograph taken with an ISO of 1600. The purpose was to shorten the shutter speed and still use a small aperture setting of f/22. The problem is that the noise level is so high that, in addition to being distracting, it is obscuring fine details in the canyon wall.

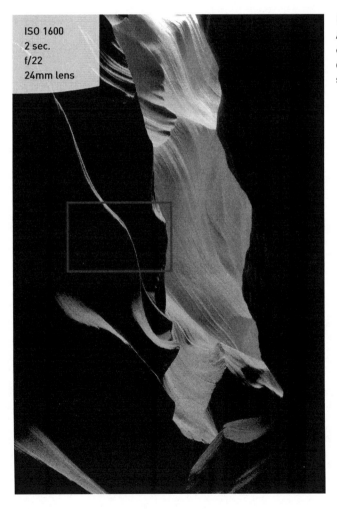

ISO 1600
2 sec.
f/22
24mm lens

FIGURE 7.3
A high ISO setting created a lot of digital noise in the shadows.

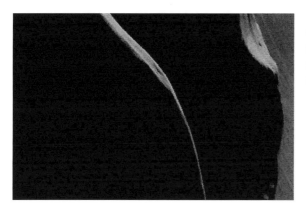

FIGURE 7.4
When the image
is enlarged, the
noise is even
more apparent.

Now check out another image that was taken in the same canyon light but with
a much lower ISO setting (**Figures 7.5** and **7.6**). As you can see, the noise levels are
much lower, which means that my blacks look black, and the fine details are beauti-
fully captured.

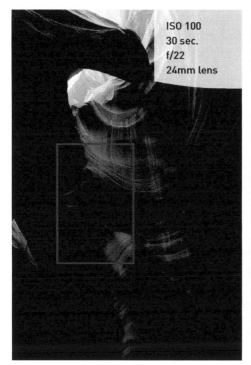

ISO 100
30 sec.
f/22
24mm lens

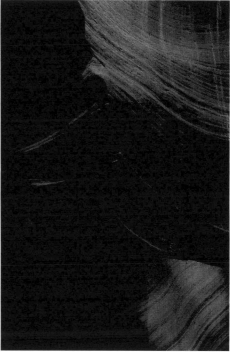

FIGURE 7.5
By lowering the ISO to 100, I was able to
avoid the noise and capture a clean image.

FIGURE 7.6
Zooming in shows that the noise levels
for this image are almost nonexistent.

When shooting landscapes, set your ISO to the lowest possible setting at all times. Between the use of Vibration Reduction lenses (if you are shooting handheld) and a good tripod, there should be few circumstances where you would need to shoot landscapes with anything above an ISO of 400.

As you start shooting with shutter speeds that exceed 1 second, the level of image noise can increase. Your camera has a feature called Long Exposure Noise Reduction that you can turn on to combat noise from long exposures and high ISOs.

SETTING UP LONG EXPOSURE NR

1. Press the Menu button, then use the Multi-selector to get to the Shooting menu.
2. Using the Multi-selector, locate the Long exposure NR menu item, and then press OK (**A**). Change this option to On, and press the OK button (**B**).

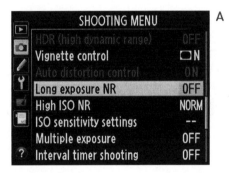
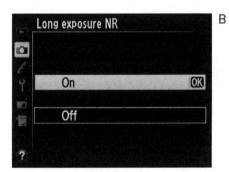

That's all there is to it. Now when you shoot, your camera will be aware of the settings and work toward minimizing unwanted noise in your images.

SELECTING A WHITE BALANCE

This probably seems like a no-brainer. If it's sunny, select Daylight. If it's overcast, choose the Shade or Cloudy setting. Those choices wouldn't be wrong for those circumstances, but why limit yourself? Sometimes you can actually change the mood of the photo by selecting a white balance that doesn't quite fit the light for the scene that you are shooting.

Figure 7.7 is an example of a correct white balance. It was late afternoon and the sun was starting to move low in the sky, giving everything that warm afternoon glow. The white balance for this image was set to Daylight.

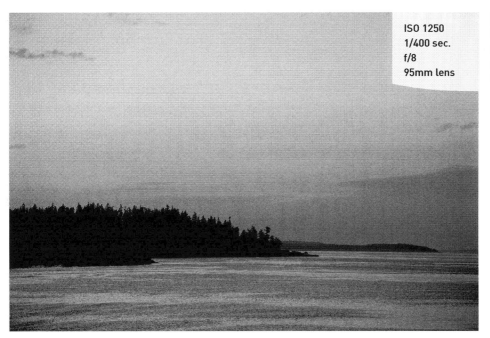

ISO 1250
1/400 sec.
f/8
95mm lens

FIGURE 7.7
Using the "proper" white balance yields predictable results.

But what if I want to make the scene look like it was shot in the early morning hours? Simple. I just change the white balance to Fluorescent, which is a much cooler setting (**Figure 7.8**).

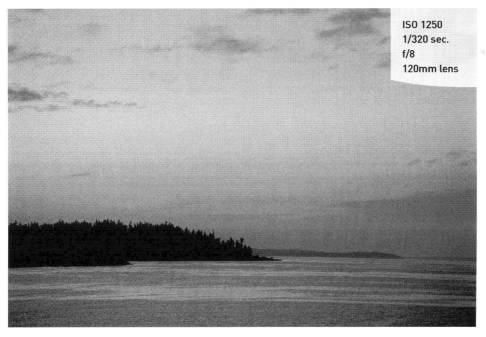

ISO 1250
1/320 sec.
f/8
120mm lens

FIGURE 7.8
Changing the white balance to Fluorescent gives the impression that the picture was taken at a different time of day than it really was.

So how do you know what a good white balance selection is? You could just take a guess, but an easier way is to take a shot, review it on the LCD, and keep the one you like. I actually prefer to preview the effect using the Live View function. Live View will display the scene you are getting ready to shoot and will do so using the current white balance settings. If you hold the WB button and turn the Main Command dial while Live View is turned on, the changes in white balance will be displayed in the preview monitor. To activate Live View, press the LV button on the back of the camera. When you are done, press the LV button again to turn it off.

USING THE LANDSCAPE PICTURE CONTROL

When shooting landscapes, I always look for great color and contrast. This is one of the reasons that so many landscape shots are taken in the early morning or during sunset. The light is much more vibrant and colorful at these times of day and adds a sense of drama to an image. There are also much longer and deeper shadows because of the angle of the light. These shadows are what give depth to your image.

Manual Callout

Check out pages 163–173 in your camera manual for more information on setting picture controls.

You can help boost vibrancy and contrast, especially in the less-than-golden hours of the day, by using the Landscape picture control (**Figure 7.9**). Just as in the Landscape mode found in the automatic scene modes, you can set up your landscape shooting so that you capture images with increased sharpness and a slight boost in blues and greens. This control will add some pop to your landscapes without the need for additional processing in any software.

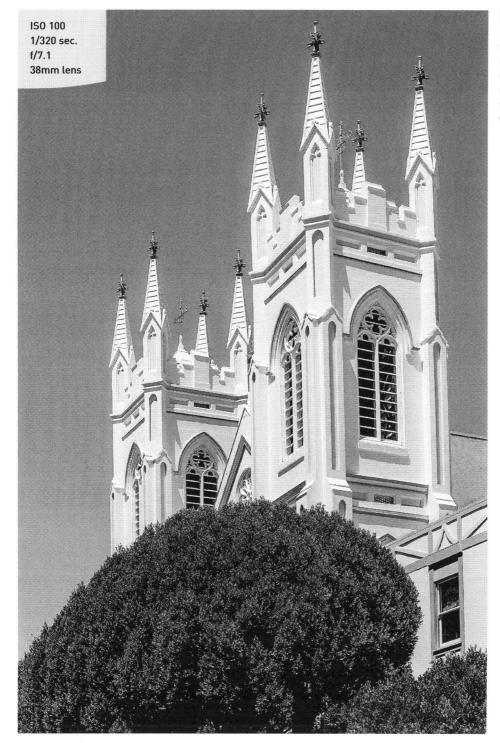

ISO 100
1/320 sec.
f/7.1
38mm lens

FIGURE 7.9
Using the Land-
scape picture
control can add
sharpness and
more vivid color
to skies and
vegetation.

SETTING UP THE LANDSCAPE PICTURE CONTROL

1. You can set the Landscape picture control by using the menu system, but there is an easier method. To quickly access the controls, press the Lock button on the back of the camera (**A**).

2. Look at the rear LCD monitor, use the Multi-selector to choose Landscape, and press OK when done (**B**).

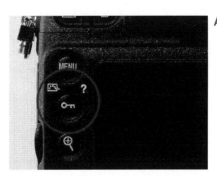

A

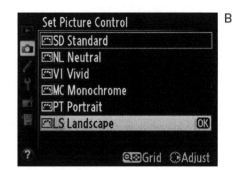

B

The camera will now apply the Landscape picture control to all of your photos. This style will be locked in to the camera even after turning it off and back on again, so make sure to change it back to Standard when you are done with your landscape shoot.

PICTURE CONTROLS FOR RAW FILES

When you set up the picture control, the camera will apply the changes to your file as it is saved and show you the result on your LCD monitor. If you are shooting with the RAW format and set a picture control, the result will show up on your LCD monitor, but all of the picture control adjustments will go away when you open the image for processing. That's because a RAW file has no camera processing applied. There are programs—like Adobe Camera Raw—that will let you add the picture control look back to your RAW file, so check your software manual for more info.

TAMING BRIGHT SKIES WITH EXPOSURE COMPENSATION

Balancing exposure in scenes that have a wide contrast in tonal ranges can be extremely challenging. The one thing you should try to avoid is overexposing your skies to the point of blowing out your highlights (unless, of course, that is the look you are going for). It's one thing to have white clouds, but it's a completely different and bad thing to have no detail at all in those clouds. This usually happens when the camera is trying to gain exposure in the darker areas of the image (**Figure 7.10**). The one way to tell if you have blown out your highlights is to turn on the Highlight Alert, or "blinkies," feature on your camera (see the "How I Shoot" section in Chapter 4). When you take a shot where the highlights are exposed beyond the point of having any detail, that area will blink in your LCD display if you have set up the Highlights display option. It is up to you to determine if that particular area is important enough to regain detail by altering your exposure. If the answer is yes, then the easiest way to go about it is to use some exposure compensation.

With this feature, you can force your camera to choose an exposure that ranges, in 1/3-stop increments, from five stops over to five stops under the metered exposure (**Figure 7.11**).

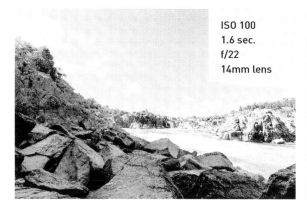

ISO 100
1.6 sec.
f/22
14mm lens

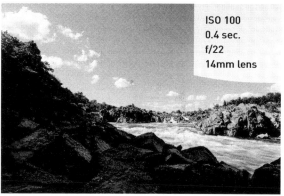

ISO 100
0.4 sec.
f/22
14mm lens

FIGURE 7.10
The rocks in the foreground are properly exposed, but the sky and river have no detail in the highlights.

FIGURE 7.11
A compensation of two stops of underexposure brought back the detail in the highlights.

HIGH-KEY AND LOW-KEY IMAGES

When you hear someone refer to a subject as being *high key*, it usually means that the entire image is composed of a very bright subject with very few shadow areas—think snow or beach. It makes sense, then, that a *low-key* subject has very few highlight areas and a predominance of shadow areas. Think of a cityscape at night as an example of a low-key photo.

USING EXPOSURE COMPENSATION TO REGAIN DETAIL IN HIGHLIGHTS

1. Activate the camera meter by lightly pressing the shutter release button.

2. Using your index finger, press and hold the Exposure Compensation button to change the over-/underexposure setting by rotating the Main Command dial.

3. Rotate the Main Command dial to the right one click, and take another picture (each click of the Main Command dial is a 1/3-stop exposure change).

4. If the blinkies are gone, you are good to go. If not, keep subtracting from your exposure by 1/3 of a stop until you have a good exposure in the highlights.

I generally keep my camera set to −1/3 stop for most of my landscape work unless I am working with a location that is very dark or low key.

Note that any exposure compensation will remain in place even after turning the camera off and then on again. Don't forget to reset it once you have successfully captured your image. Also, exposure compensation works across all of the shooting modes. If you change between modes (e.g., from Program to Aperture Priority), the camera will hold the compensation you set in the previous mode.

SHOOTING BEAUTIFUL BLACK AND WHITE LANDSCAPES

There's nothing as timeless as a beautiful black and white landscape photo. For many, it is the purest form of photography. The genre conjures up thoughts of Ansel Adams out in Yosemite Valley, capturing stunning monoliths with his 8x10 view camera. Well, just because you are shooting with a digital camera doesn't mean you can't create your own stunning photos using the power of the Monochrome picture control. (See the "Classic Black and White Portraits" section of Chapter 6 for instructions on setting up this feature.) Not only can you shoot in black and white, you can also customize the camera to apply built-in filters to lighten or darken different elements within your scene, as well as add contrast and definition.

The four filter colors are red, yellow, green, and orange. The most typically used filters in black and white photography are red and yellow. This is because the color of these filters will darken opposite colors and lighten similar colors. So if you want to darken a blue sky, you would use a yellow filter, because blue is the opposite of yellow. To darken green foliage, you would use a red filter. Check out the series of shots in **Figure 7.12** with different filters applied.

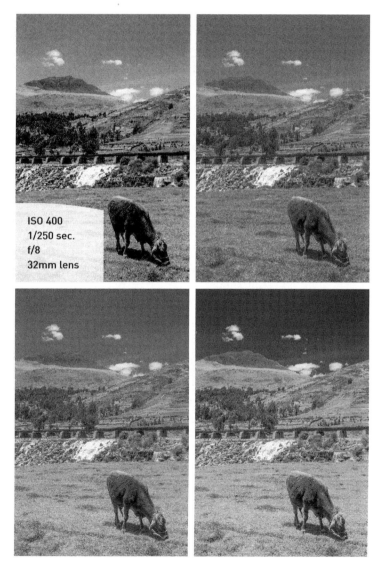

ISO 400
1/250 sec.
f/8
32mm lens

FIGURE 7.12
Adding color filter settings to the Monochrome picture control allows you to lighten or darken elements in your scene. The top right image has no filter applied to it. The bottom left has a green filter, and the bottom right has a yellow filter.

You can see that there is no real difference in contrast between the color image and the black and white image with no filter. The green filter has the effect of darkening the skies slightly and giving a significantly lighter look to the vegetation. Using the yellow filter makes the vegetation a little lighter but dramatically darkens the sky. There is no right or wrong to choosing a filter for your black and white shots—it's pretty much whatever you prefer. In this instance, I think I prefer the image with the green filter.

Other options in the Monochrome picture control enable you to adjust the sharpness and contrast and even add some color toning (like sepia) to the final image. This information is also in the "Classic Black and White Portraits" section of Chapter 6. I like to have Sharpness set to 5 and Contrast set to +1 for my landscape images. This gives an overall look to the black and white image that is reminiscent of the classic black and white films. Experiment with the various settings to find the combination that is most pleasing to you. Just remember that the Monochrome picture control is automatically applied and saved to a JPEG file but will be lost when you open your RAW files.

THE GOLDEN LIGHT

If you ask any professional landscape photographer what their favorite time of day to shoot is, chances are they will tell you it's the hours surrounding daybreak and sunset (**Figures 7.13** and **7.14**). The reason for this is that the light is coming from a very low angle to the landscape, which creates shadows and gives depth and character. There is also a quality to the light that seems cleaner and is more colorful than the light you get when shooting at midday. One thing that can dramatically improve any morning or evening shot is the presence of clouds. The sun will fill the underside of the clouds with a palette of colors and add drama to your image.

WARM AND COOL COLOR TEMPERATURES

These two terms are used to describe the overall color cast of an image. Reds and yellows are said to be *warm*, which is usually the look that you get from the late afternoon sun. Blue is usually the predominant color when talking about a *cool* cast.

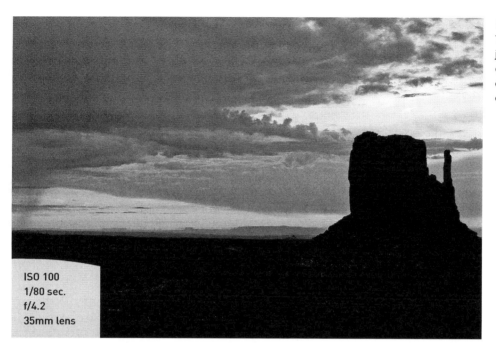

FIGURE 7.13
The few minutes
just prior to sunrise
can add great
colors to a partly
cloudy sky.

ISO 100
1/80 sec.
f/4.2
35mm lens

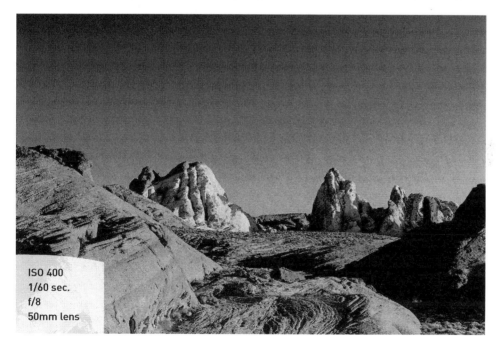

FIGURE 7.14
Late afternoon sun
is usually warmer
and adds drama
and warmth.

ISO 400
1/60 sec.
f/8
50mm lens

WHERE TO FOCUS

Large landscape scenes are great fun to photograph, but they can present a problem: where exactly do you focus when you want everything to be sharp? Since our goal is to create a great landscape photo, we will need to concentrate on how to best create an image that is tack sharp, with a depth of field that renders great focus throughout the scene.

I have already stressed the importance of a good tripod when shooting landscapes. The tripod lets you concentrate on the aperture portion of the exposure without worrying about how long your shutter will be open. This is because the tripod provides the stability to handle any shutter speed you might need when shooting at small apertures. I find that for most of my landscape work I set my camera to Aperture Priority mode and the ISO to 100 (for a clean, noise-free image).

However, shooting with the smallest aperture on your lens doesn't necessarily mean that you will get the proper sharpness throughout your image. The real key is knowing where in the scene to focus your lens to maximize the depth of field for your chosen aperture. To do this, you must utilize something called the "hyper focal distance" of your lens.

Hyper focal distance, also referred to as HFD, is the point of focus that will give you the greatest acceptable sharpness from a point near your camera all the way out to infinity. If you combine good HFD practice with a small aperture, you will get images that are sharp to infinity.

There are a couple of ways to do this, and the one that is probably the easiest is, as you might guess, the one that is most widely used by working pros. When you have your shot all set up and composed, focus on an object that is about one-third of the distance into your frame (**Figure 7.15**). It is usually pretty close to the proper distance and will render favorable results. When you have the focus set, take a photograph and then zoom in on the preview on your LCD to check the sharpness of your image.

One thing to remember is that as your lens gets wider in focal length, your HFD will be closer to the camera position. This is because the wider the lens, the greater depth of field you can achieve. This is yet another reason why a good wide-angle lens is indispensable to the landscape shooter.

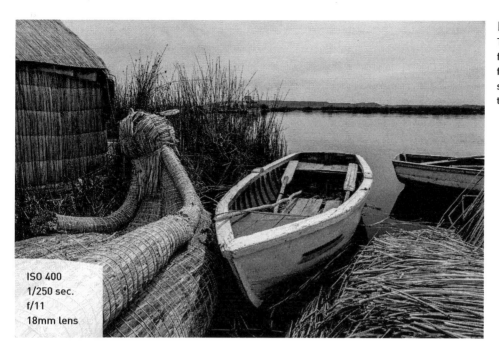

FIGURE 7.15
To get maximum
focus from near to
far, the focus was
set on the back of
the center boat.

ISO 400
1/250 sec.
f/11
18mm lens

TACK SHARP

Here's one of those terms that photographers like to throw around. *Tack sharp* refers not only to the focus of an image but also to the overall sharpness of the image. This usually means that there is excellent depth of field in terms of sharp focus for all elements in the image. It also means that there is no sign of camera shake, which can give soft edges to subjects that should look nice and crisp. To get your images tack sharp, use a small depth of field, don't forget your tripod, use the self-timer to activate the shutter if no cable release is handy, and practice achieving good hyper focal distance (HFD) when picking your point of focus.

EASIER FOCUSING

There's no denying that the automatic focus features on the D800 are great, but sometimes it just pays to turn them off and focus manually. This is especially true if you are shooting on a tripod: once you have your shot composed in the viewfinder and you are ready to focus, chances are that the area you want to focus on is not going to be in the area of one of the focus points. Often this is the case when you have a foreground element that is fairly low in the frame. You could use a single focus point set low in your viewfinder and then pan the camera down until it rests on your subject. But then you would have to press the shutter button halfway to focus the camera and then try to recompose and lock down the tripod. It's no easy task.

But you can have the best of both worlds by having the camera focus for you, then switching to manual focus to comfortably recompose your shot (**Figure 7.16**).

FIGURE 7.16
Using the hyper focal distance (HFD) one-third rule, I focused on the small lagoon area, then switched the lens to manual focus before recomposing for the final shot.

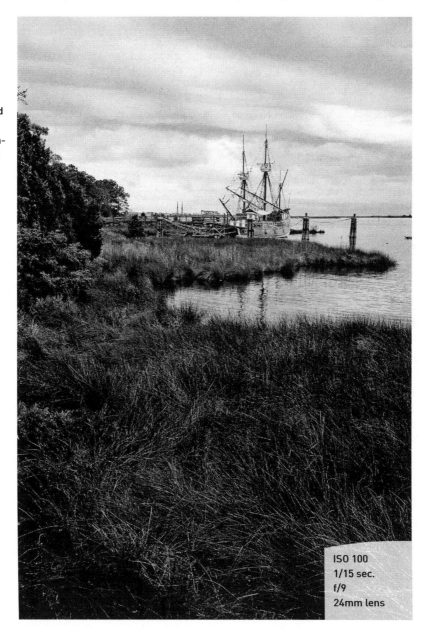

ISO 100
1/15 sec.
f/9
24mm lens

1. Set up your shot and find the area that you want to focus on.

2. Pan your tripod head so that your active focus point is on that spot.

3. Press the shutter button halfway to focus the camera.

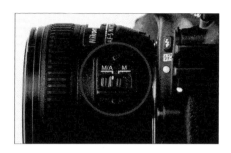

4. Switch the camera to manual focus by sliding the switch on the lens barrel from M/A to M.

5. Recompose the composition on the tripod, and then take the shot.

The camera will fire without trying to refocus the lens. This works especially well for wide-angle lenses, which can be difficult to focus in Manual mode.

MAKING WATER FLUID

There's little that is quite as satisfying for the landscape shooter as capturing a silky waterfall shot. Creating the smooth-flowing effect is as simple as adjusting your shutter speed to allow the water to be in motion while the shutter is open. The key is to have your camera on a stable platform (such as a tripod) so that you can use a shutter speed that's long enough to work (**Figure 7.17**). To achieve a great effect, use a shutter speed that is 1/15 of a second or longer.

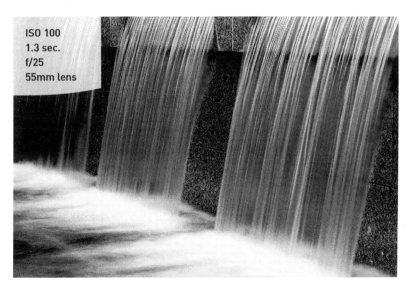

ISO 100
1.3 sec.
f/25
55mm lens

FIGURE 7.17
To get really long exposures of water features, you need to bring along a good tripod.

SETTING UP FOR A WATERFALL SHOT

1. Attach the camera to your tripod, then compose and focus your shot.

2. Make sure the ISO is set to 100.

3. Using Aperture Priority mode, set your aperture to the smallest opening (such as f/22 or f/36).

4. Press the shutter button halfway so the camera takes a meter reading.

5. Check to see if the shutter speed is 1/15 of a second or slower.

6. Take a photo and then check the image on the LCD.

You can also use Shutter Priority mode for this effect by dialing in the desired shutter speed and having the camera set the aperture for you. I prefer to use Aperture Priority to ensure that I have the greatest depth of field possible.

If the water is blinking on the LCD, indicating a loss of detail in the highlights, then use the exposure compensation feature (as discussed earlier in this chapter) to bring details back into the waterfall. You will need to have the Highlight Alert feature turned on to check for overexposure (see "How I Shoot" in Chapter 4).

There is a possibility that you will not be able to have a shutter speed that is long enough to capture a smooth, silky effect, especially if you are shooting in bright daylight conditions. To overcome this obstacle, you need a filter for your lens— either a polarizing filter or a neutral density filter. The polarizing filter redirects wavelengths of light to create more vibrant colors, reduce reflections, and darken blue skies. It also lengthens exposure times by about two stops due to the darkness of the filter (this amount can vary depending on the brand of filter used). It is a handy filter for landscape work. The neutral density filter is typically just a dark piece of glass that serves to darken the scene by one, two, or three stops (**Figure 7.18**). This allows you to use slower shutter speeds during bright conditions. Think of it as sunglasses for your camera lens. You will find more discussion on filters in the bonus chapter "Pimp My Ride."

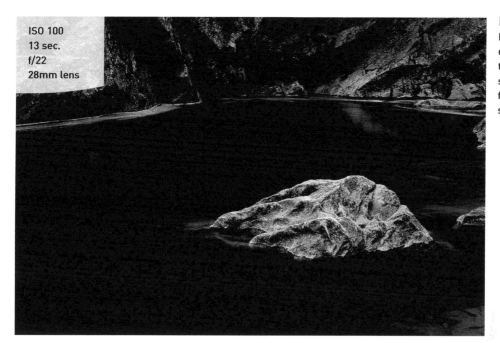

ISO 100
13 sec.
f/22
28mm lens

FIGURE 7.18
I used a neutral
density filter to add
two stops of expo-
sure, thus allowing
for a longer expo-
sure time.

DIRECTING THE VIEWER:
A WORD ABOUT COMPOSITION

As a photographer, it's your job to lead the viewer through your image. You accom-
plish this by utilizing the principles of composition, which is the arrangement of
elements in the scene that draw the viewer's eyes through your image and hold their
attention. As the director of this viewing, you need to understand how people see
and then use that information to focus their attention on the most important elements in your image.

There is a general order at which we look at elements in a photograph. The first is
brightness. The eye wants to travel to the brightest object within a scene. So if you
have a bright sky, it's probably the first place the eye will travel to. The second order
of attention is sharpness. Sharp, detailed elements will get more attention than soft,
blurry areas. Finally, the eye will move to vivid colors while leaving the dull, flat colors for last. It is important to know these essentials in order to grab—and keep—the
viewer's attention and then direct them through the frame.

In **Figure 7.19**, the eye is drawn to the bright white cloud in the middle of the frame. From there, it is pulled toward the sharpness and color of the large boulder that is anchoring the lower-left portion of the image. The eye moves around the curved section of stone at the bottom of the frame, where it is then lifted back up to the sky and clouds, right back to the beginning. The elements within the image all help to keep the eye moving but never leave the frame.

FIGURE 7.19
The composition of the elements pulls the viewer's eyes around the image, leading from one element to the next in a circular pattern.

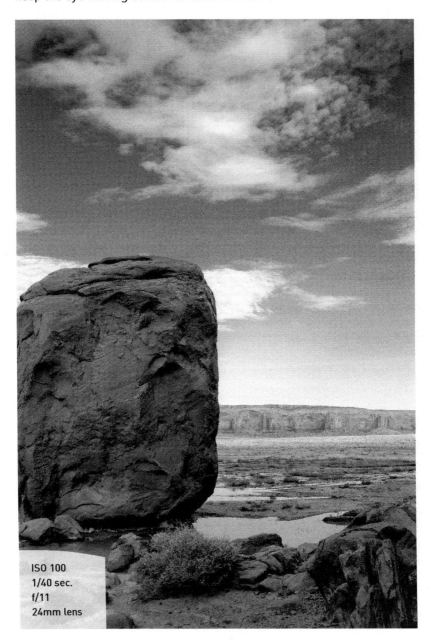

ISO 100
1/40 sec.
f/11
24mm lens

RULE OF THIRDS

There are, in fact, quite a few philosophies concerning composition. The easiest one to begin with is known as the "rule of thirds." Using this principle, you simply divide your viewfinder into thirds by imagining two horizontal and two vertical lines that divide the frame equally.

The key to using this method of composition is to have your main subject located at or near one of the intersecting points (**Figure 7.20**).

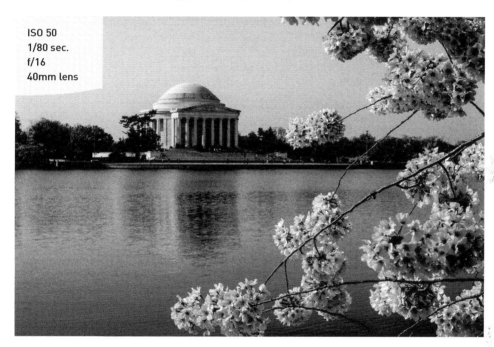

ISO 50
1/80 sec.
f/16
40mm lens

FIGURE 7.20
Placing the Jefferson Memorial in the upper-left portion of the image creates a much more interesting composition than having it dead center in the frame. Additionally, the horizon line is running across the top third of the frame.

By placing your subject near these intersecting lines, you are giving the viewer space to move within the frame. The one thing you don't want to do is place your subject smack dab in the middle of the frame. This is sometimes referred to as "bull's eye" composition, and it requires the right subject matter for it to work. It's not always wrong, but it will usually be less appealing and may not hold the viewer's attention.

Speaking of the middle of the frame: the other general rule of thirds deals with horizon lines. Generally speaking, you should position the horizon one-third of the way up or down in the frame. Splitting the frame in half by placing your horizon in the middle of the picture is akin to placing the subject in the middle of the frame; it doesn't lend a sense of importance to either the sky or the ground.

The D800 has a visual tool for assisting you in composing your photo in the viewfinder in the form of a grid overlay. The grid can be turned on using the camera menu system so that three horizontal and three vertical grid lines appear in the viewfinder. This won't necessarily help with aligning things in thirds, but it will help you keep your horizons straight and give you some visual alignment cues.

USING A GRID OVERLAY IN THE VIEWFINDER

1. Press the Menu button, then use the Multi-selector to navigate to the Custom Setting menu and select d Shooting/display. Press OK (**A**).

2. Highlight d6 Viewfinder grid display, press OK, set the feature to On, and press OK once again to lock in your changes (**B**).

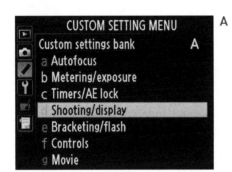
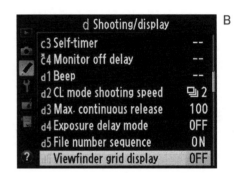

Now when you look through the viewfinder you will see a new grid overlay. Don't ask me how they do that, but it is a very cool feature. When using the Live View mode for shooting, you can turn on the grid feature by pressing the Info button until the grid appears in the LCD monitor.

CREATING DEPTH

Because a photograph is a flat, two-dimensional space, you need to create a sense of depth by using the elements in the scene to create a three-dimensional feel. This is accomplished by including different and distinct spaces for the eye to travel: a foreground, middle ground, and background. By using these three spaces, you draw the viewer in and render depth to your image.

The scene shown in **Figure 7.21**, a small grove of old trees in Washington, DC, illustrates this well. The tree on the left strongly defines the foreground area. The tree on the right defines the middle ground, and the thicker area of trees in the background provides a contrasting canopy that adds dimension to the image.

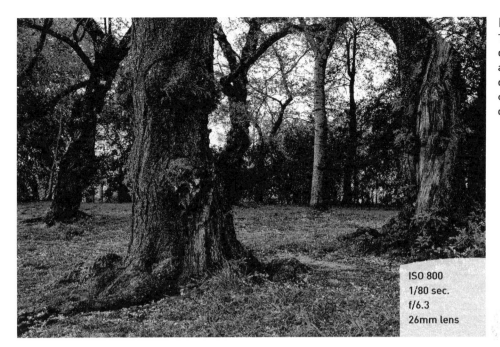

FIGURE 7.21
The distinctly
different trees
at different
distances help to
create a three-
dimensional feel.

ISO 800
1/80 sec.
f/6.3
26mm lens

ADVANCED TECHNIQUES TO EXPLORE

This section comes with a warning attached. All of the techniques and topics up to this point have been centered on your camera. The following two sections, covering panoramas and high dynamic range (HDR) images, require you to use image-processing software to complete the photograph. They are, however, important enough that you should know how to correctly shoot for success should you choose to explore these two popular techniques.

SHOOTING PANORAMAS

If you have ever visited the Grand Canyon, you know just how large and wide open it truly is—so much so that it would be difficult to capture its splendor in just one frame. The same can be said for a mountain range or a cityscape or any extremely wide vista. There are two methods that you can use to capture the feeling of this type of scene.

THE "FAKE" PANORAMA

The first method is to shoot with your lens set to its widest focal length and then crop out the top and bottom portion of the frame in your imaging software. Panoramic images are generally two or three times wider than a normal image.

CREATING A FAKE PANORAMA

1. To create the look of the panorama, find your widest lens focal length. In my case, it would be the 14mm setting on the 14–24mm lens.

2. Using the guidelines discussed earlier in the chapter, compose and focus your scene, and select the smallest aperture possible.

3. Shoot your image using whichever technique and shooting mode you desire. That's all there is to it from a photography standpoint.

4. Open the image in your favorite image-processing software and crop the extraneous foreground and sky from the image, leaving you with a wide panorama of the scene.

Figure 7.22 shows an example using a photo taken in Death Valley National Park.

As you can see, the image was shot with a wide perspective, using a 14mm lens. While it is not a bad photo, the clouds get distracting near the top of the frame. This isn't a problem, though, because it was shot for the express purpose of creating a "fake" panorama. Now look at the same image, cropped for panoramic view (**Figure 7.23**). As you can see, it makes a huge difference in the image and gives much higher visual impact by reducing the clouds and drawing your eyes across the length of the horizon.

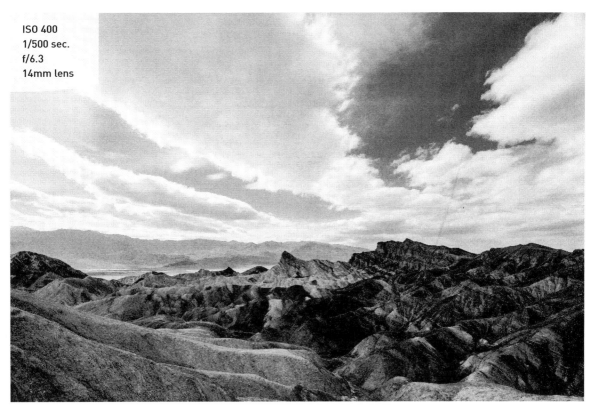

ISO 400
1/500 sec.
f/6.3
14mm lens

FIGURE 7.22

This is a nice image, but it lacks visual impact and I don't like the look of the clouds at the top of the frame.

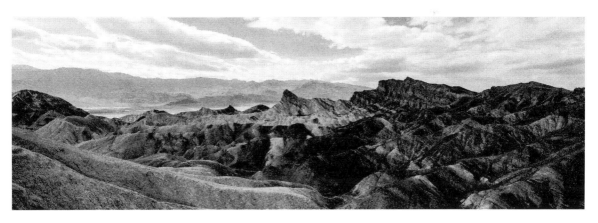

FIGURE 7.23

Cropping gives the feeling of a sweeping vista and makes the shot visually appealing.

FIGURE 7.24
Here you see
the makings of a
panorama, with six
shots overlapping
by about 30 percent
from frame to
frame.

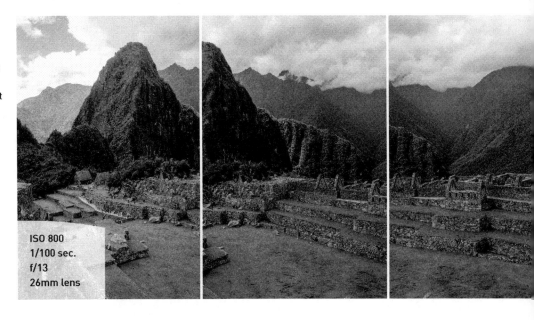

ISO 800
1/100 sec.
f/13
26mm lens

THE MULTIPLE-IMAGE PANORAMA

The reason the previous method is sometimes referred to as a "fake" panorama is because it is made with a standard-size frame and then cropped down to a narrow perspective. To shoot a true panorama, you need to use either a special panorama camera that shoots a very wide frame, or the following method, which requires the combining of multiple frames.

The multiple-image pano has gained in popularity in the past few years; this is principally due to advances in image-processing software. Many software options are available now that will take multiple images, align them, and then "stitch" them into a single panoramic image. The real key to shooting a multiple-image pano is to overlap your shots by about 30 percent from one frame to the next (**Figures 7.24** and **7.25**). It is possible to hand-hold the camera while capturing your images, but the best method for capturing great panoramic images is to use a tripod.

Now that you have your series of overlapping images, you can import them into your image-processing software to stitch them together and create a single panoramic image.

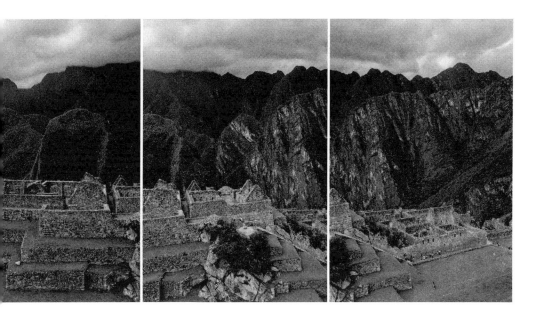

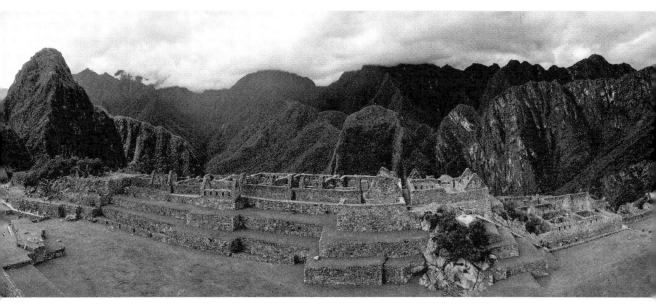

FIGURE 7.25
I used Adobe Photoshop to combine all of the exposures into one large panoramic image.

SHOOTING PROPERLY FOR A MULTIPLE-IMAGE PANORAMA

1. Mount your camera on your tripod and make sure it is level.

2. Choose a focal length for your lens that is somewhere between 35mm and 50mm.

3. In Aperture Priority mode, use a very small aperture for the greatest depth of field. Take a meter reading of a bright part of the scene, and make note of it.

4. Now change your camera to Manual mode (M), and dial in the aperture and shutter speed that you obtained in the previous step.

5. Set your lens to manual focus, and then focus your lens for the area of interest using the HFD method of finding a point one-third of the way into the scene. (If you use the autofocus, you risk getting different points of focus from image to image, which will make the image stitching more difficult for the software.)

6. While carefully panning your camera, shoot your images to cover the entire area of the scene from one end to the other, leaving a 30-percent overlap from one frame to the next.

7. For the final step, use your favorite imaging software to combine all of the photographs into a single panoramic image.

SORTING YOUR SHOTS FOR THE MULTI-IMAGE PANORAMA

If you shoot more than one series of shots for your panoramas, it can sometimes be difficult to know when one series of images ends and the other begins. Here is a quick tip for separating your images.

Set up your camera using the steps listed here. Now, before you take your first good exposure in the series, hold up one finger in front of the camera and take a shot. Now move your hand away and begin taking your overlapping images. When you have taken your last shot, hold two fingers in front of the camera and take another shot.

Now, when you go to review your images, use the series of shots that falls between the frames with one and two fingers in them. Then just repeat the process for your next panorama series.

SHOOTING HIGH DYNAMIC RANGE (HDR) IMAGES

One of the more recent trends in digital photography is the use of high dynamic range (HDR) to capture the full range of tonal values in your final image. Typically, when you photograph a scene that has a wide range of tones from shadows to highlights, you have to make a decision regarding which tonal values you are going to empha-size, and then adjust your exposure accordingly. This is because your camera has a limited dynamic range, at least as compared to the human eye. HDR photography allows you to capture multiple exposures for the highlights, shadows, and midtones and then combine them into a single image using software (**Figures 7.26** through **7.29**).

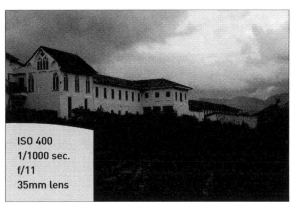

FIGURE 7.26
Underexposing two stops will render more detail in the highlight areas of the clouds.

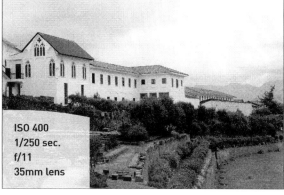

FIGURE 7.27
This is the normal exposure as dictated by the camera meter.

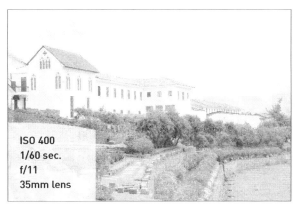

FIGURE 7.28
Overexposing by two stops ensures that the darker areas are exposed for detail in the shadows.

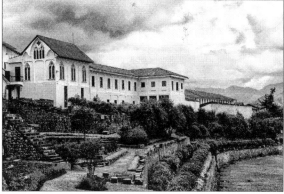

FIGURE 7.29
This is the final HDR image that was rendered from the three other exposures you see here.

A number of software applications allow you to combine the images and then perform a process called "tone mapping," whereby the complete range of exposures is represented in a single image. I will not be covering the software applications, but I will explore the process of shooting a scene to help you render properly captured images for the HDR process. Note that using a tripod is absolutely necessary for this technique, since you need to have perfect alignment of each image when they are combined.

SETTING UP FOR SHOOTING AN HDR IMAGE

1. Set your ISO to 100, if you can, to ensure clean, noise-free images.

2. Set your program mode to Aperture Priority. During the shooting process, you will be taking five shots of the same scene, creating an overexposed image, an underexposed image, and a normal exposure. Since the camera is going to be adjusting the exposure, you want it to make changes to the shutter speed, not the aperture, so that your depth of field is consistent.

3. Set your camera file format to RAW. This is extremely important because the RAW format contains a much larger range of exposure values than a JPEG file, and the HDR software needs this information.

4. Focus the camera using the manual focus method discussed earlier in the chapter, compose your shot, and secure the tripod.

5. Press the BKT button and rotate the Main Command dial two clicks to the right until you see 5F in the control panel (you should see two marks to the left and right of the center mark).

6. The bracketing can be set up for smaller than one-stop increments, but you should have yours set to 1.0 (indicated in the top right of the control panel as you hold the BKT button). If it is smaller, use the Sub-command dial to change it to 1.0.

7. Set your shooting mode to Continuous High (CH) so that the exposures can be taken in rapid succession. This is helpful if there are elements in the scene that might move, like clouds.

8. Finally, focus your image and then use a release cable such as the Nikon MC-30 to take five frames (check out Chapter 11, "Advanced Techniques," for a way to take your photos without the use of a cable).

A software program—such as Photoshop, Photomatix Pro, HDR Expose 2, or Nik HDR Efex Pro—can be used to process your exposure-bracketed images into a single HDR file. You can find more information on HDR photography and creating HDR images in the Tutorials section at www.photowalkpro.com.

BRACKETING YOUR EXPOSURES

In HDR, *bracketing* is the process of capturing a series of exposures at different stop intervals. You can bracket your exposures even if you aren't going to be using HDR. Sometimes this is helpful when you have a tricky lighting situation and want to ensure that you have just the right exposure to capture the look you're after. In HDR, you bracket to the plus and minus side of a "normal" exposure, but you can also bracket all of your exposures to the over or under side of normal. It all depends on what you are after. If you aren't sure whether you are getting enough shadow detail, you can bracket a little toward the overexposed side. The same is true for highlights. You can bracket in increments as small as a third of a stop. This means that you can capture several images with very subtle exposure variances and then decide later which one is best. If you want to bracket just to one side of a normal exposure, set your exposure compensation to +1 or –1, whichever way you need, and then use the bracketing feature to automatically bracket your exposures.

Chapter 7 Assignments

We've covered a lot of ground in this chapter, so it's definitely time to put this knowledge to work in order to get familiar with these new camera settings and techniques.

Comparing depth of field: Wide-angle vs. telephoto

Speaking of depth of field, you should also practice using the hyper focal distance of your lens to maximize the depth of field. You can do this by picking a focal length to work with on your lens.

If you have a zoom lens, try using the longest length. Compose your image and find an object to focus on. Set your aperture to f/22 and take a photo.

Now do the same thing with the zoom lens at its widest focal length. Use the same aperture and focus point.

Review the images and compare the depth of field when using a wide-angle lens as opposed to a telephoto lens. Try this again with a large aperture as well.

Applying hyper focal distance to your landscapes

Pick a scene that once again has objects that are near the camera position and something that is clearly defined in the background. Try using a wide to medium-wide focal length for this (18–35mm). Use a small aperture and focus on the object in the foreground; then recompose and take a shot.

Without moving the camera position, use the object in the background as your point of focus and take another shot.

Finally, find a point that is one-third of the way into the frame from near to far and use that as the focus point.

Compare all of the images to see which method delivered the greatest range of depth of field from near to infinity.

Placing your horizons

Find a location with a defined horizon and, using the rule-of-thirds grid overlay, shoot the horizon along the top third of the frame, in the middle of the frame, and along the bottom third of the frame.

Share your results with the book's Flickr group!

Join the group here: www.flickr.com/groups/d800fromsnapshotstogreatshots

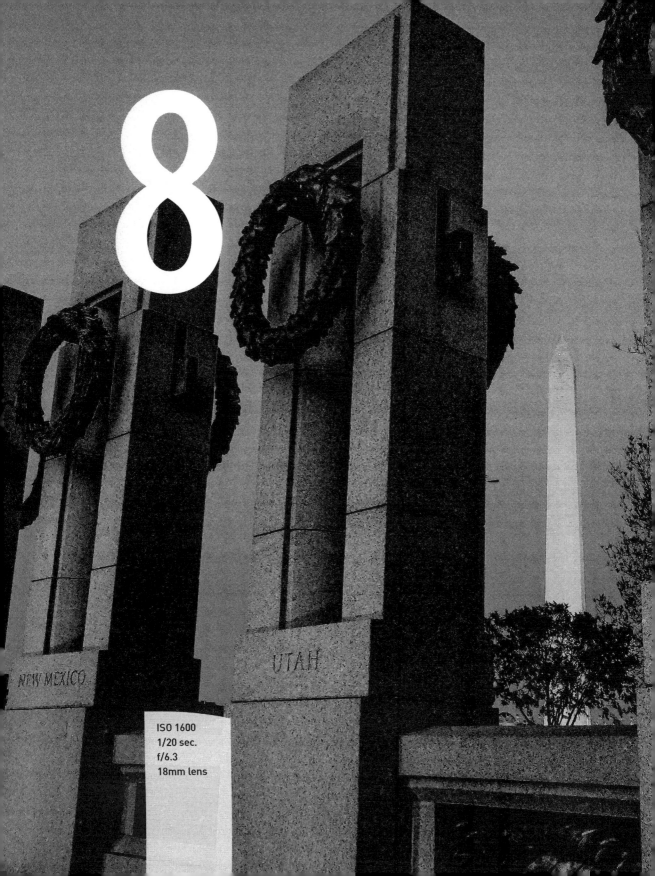

8

NEW MEXICO

UTAH

ISO 1600
1/20 sec.
f/6.3
18mm lens

Mood Lighting

SHOOTING WHEN THE LIGHTS GET LOW

There is no reason to put your camera away when the sun goes down. Your D800 has some great features that let you work with available light as well as the built-in flash. In this chapter, we will explore ways to push your camera's technology to the limit in order to capture great photos in difficult lighting situations. We will also explore the use of flash and how best to utilize your built-in flash features to improve your photography. But let's first look at working with low-level available light.

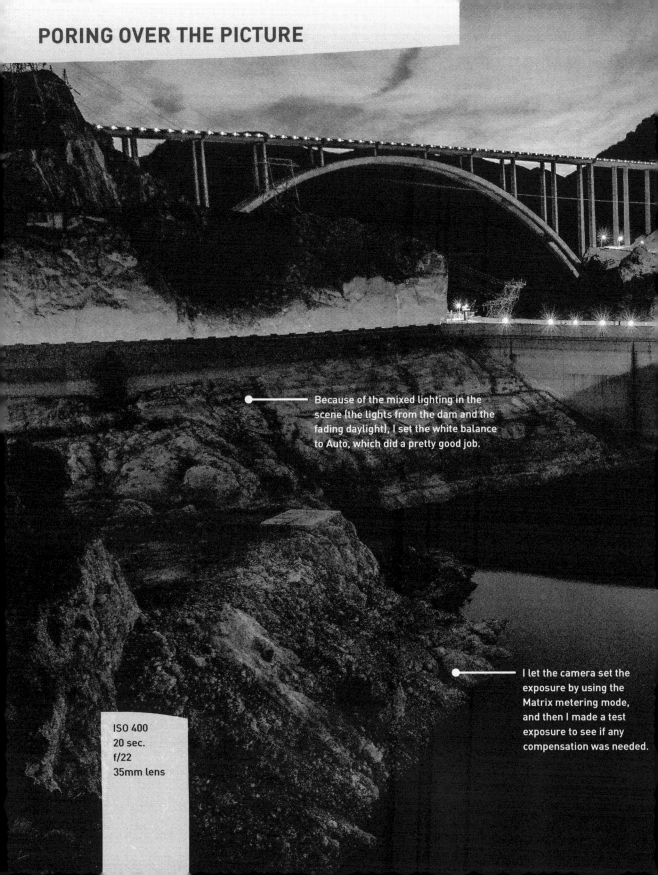

PORING OVER THE PICTURE

Because of the mixed lighting in the scene (the lights from the dam and the fading daylight), I set the white balance to Auto, which did a pretty good job.

I let the camera set the exposure by using the Matrix metering mode, and then I made a test exposure to see if any compensation was needed.

ISO 400
20 sec.
f/22
35mm lens

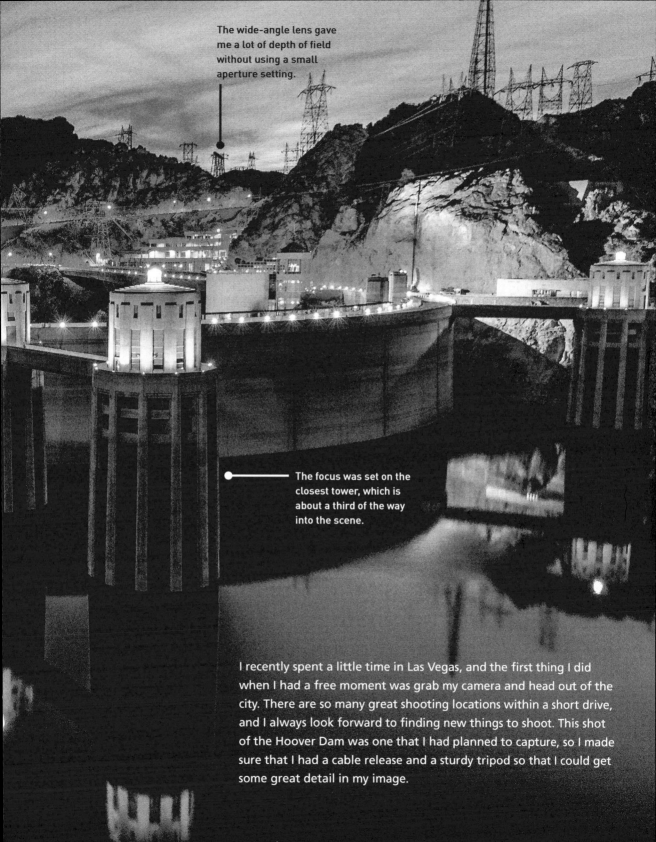

The wide-angle lens gave me a lot of depth of field without using a small aperture setting.

The focus was set on the closest tower, which is about a third of the way into the scene.

I recently spent a little time in Las Vegas, and the first thing I did when I had a free moment was grab my camera and head out of the city. There are so many great shooting locations within a short drive, and I always look forward to finding new things to shoot. This shot of the Hoover Dam was one that I had planned to capture, so I made sure that I had a cable release and a sturdy tripod so that I could get some great detail in my image.

PORING OVER THE PICTURE

While walking the back streets of Kuala Lumpur in Malaysia, I came across a small Hindu temple where these small figures were lined up on a wall. They seemed to be just waiting for me to take their picture, and all I had to do was figure out the best way to capture the moment. I went with a long lens and a small aperture to minimize the overall detail and focus on one representative figure.

I used a large aperture to blur the figures in the foreground and background.

The Daylight white balance setting gives the image an overall warm feeling.

I turned on the Vibration Reduction feature to get the sharpest image possible.

ISO 1600
1/20 sec.
f/5.3
200mm lens

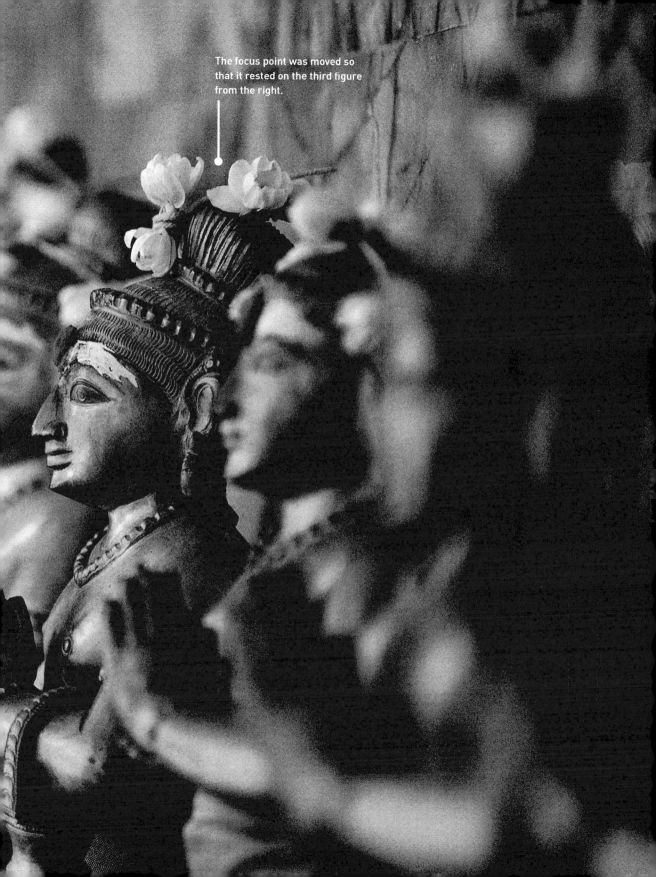

The focus point was moved so that it rested on the third figure from the right.

RAISING THE ISO: THE SIMPLE SOLUTION

Let's begin with the obvious way to keep shooting when the lights get low: raising the ISO (**Figure 8.1**). By now you know how to change the ISO by using the ISO button and the Main Command dial. In typical shooting situations, you should keep the ISO in the 100–800 range. This will keep your pictures nice and clean by keeping the digital noise to a minimum. But as the available light gets low, you might find yourself working in the higher ranges of the ISO scale, which could lead to more noise in your image.

You could use the flash, but that has a limited range (15–20 feet) that might not work for you. Also, you could be in a situation where flash is prohibited, or at least frowned upon, like at a wedding or in a museum.

And what about a tripod in combination with a long shutter speed? That is also an option, and we'll cover it a little further into the chapter. The problem with using a tripod and a slow shutter speed in low-light photography, though, is that it performs best when subjects aren't moving. Besides, try to set up a tripod in a museum and see how quickly you grab the attention of the security guards.

FIGURE 8.1
To get this shot of the praying idols without using a tripod, I had to turn up the ISO setting.

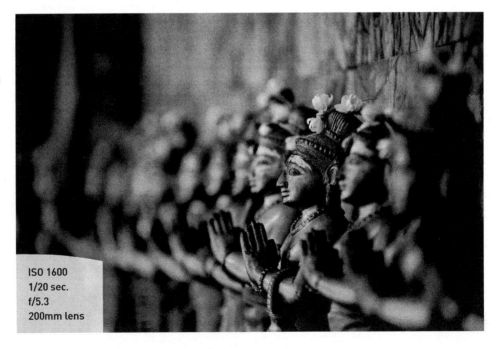

ISO 1600
1/20 sec.
f/5.3
200mm lens

So if the only choice to get the shot is to raise the ISO to 800 or higher, make sure that you turn on the High ISO Noise Reduction feature. This menu function is set to Off by default, but as you start using higher ISO values you should consider turning it on.

TURNING ON THE HIGH ISO NOISE REDUCTION

1. Press the Menu button and then highlight the High ISO NR option in the Shooting menu, and press OK (**A**).

2. Set your desired level of noise reduction: low for ISO settings around 800 and higher as you raise the ISO setting (**B**).

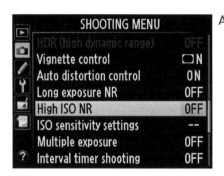

A

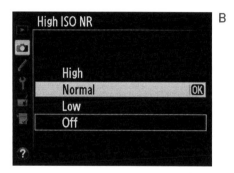

B

To see the effect of noise reduction, you need to zoom in and take a closer look (**Figures 8.2** and **8.3**).

Turning on the High ISO Noise Reduction feature slightly increases the processing time for your images, so if you are shooting in the continuous drive mode, you might see a little reduction in the speed of your frames per second.

NOISE REDUCTION SAVES SPACE

When shooting at very high ISO settings, running Noise Reduction can save you space on your memory card. If you are saving your photos as JPEGs, the camera will compress the information in the image to take up less space. When you have excessive noise, you can literally add megabytes to the file size. This is because the camera has to deal with more information: it views the noise in the image as photo information and, therefore, tries not to lose that information during the compression process. That means more noise equals bigger files. So not only will turning on the Noise Reduction feature improve the look of your image, it will also save you some space so you can take a few more shots.

FIGURE 8.2
Here is an enlarge-
ment of a flower
shot without any
noise reduction.

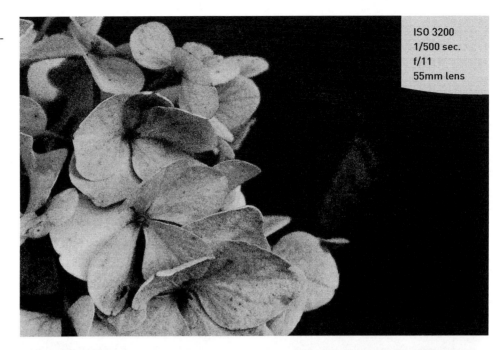

ISO 3200
1/500 sec.
f/11
55mm lens

FIGURE 8.3
Here is the same
flower photo-
graphed with
High ISO Noise
Reduction turned
set to normal.
While it doesn't get
rid of all the noise,
it certainly reduces
the effect and
improves the look
of your image.

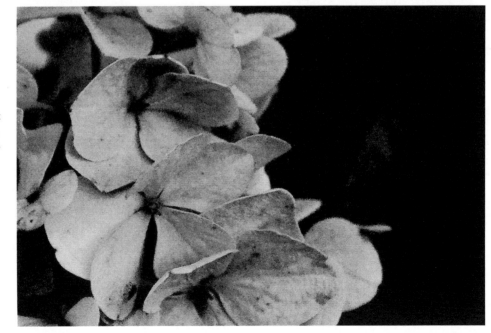

USING VERY HIGH ISOS

Is ISO 6400 just not enough for you? Well, in that case, you will need to set your camera to the expanded ISO setting. These settings open up another two stops of ISO, raising the new limit to 25600. The new settings will not appear in your ISO scale as numbers, but as Hi 1 for ISO 12800 and Hi 2 for 25600.

To access these higher ISO settings, simply press the ISO button and rotate the Main Command dial past 6400 to the H settings. You can raise the ISO in 1/3-stop increments from Hi 0.3 to Hi 1. The jump to Hi 2 is a single stop, with no 1/3-stop increments in between.

A word of warning about the expanded ISO settings: although it is great to have these high ISO settings available during low-light shooting, they should always be your last resort. Even with noise reduction turned on, the amount of visible noise will be extremely high. Although they should be avoided, you might find yourself at a nighttime sporting event under the lights, which would require an ISO of 6400 to improve your shutter speeds and capture the action (**Figure 8.4**).

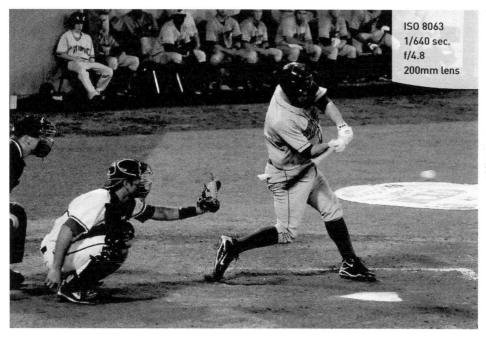

ISO 8063
1/640 sec.
f/4.8
200mm lens

FIGURE 8.4
The only way to get a fast enough shutter speed during this night-time baseball game was to raise the ISO to H0.3 (8063).

STABILIZING THE SITUATION

If you purchased your camera with the Vibration Reduction (VR) lens, you already own a great tool to squeeze two stops of exposure out of your camera when shooting without a tripod (**Figure 8.5**). Typically, the average person can hand-hold their camera down to about 1/60 of a second before blurriness results due to hand shake. As the length of the lens is increased (or zoomed), the ability to handhold at slow shutter speeds (1/60 and slower) and still get sharp images is further reduced.

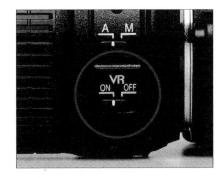

FIGURE 8.5
Turning on the VR switch will help you shoot in low-light conditions.

The Nikon VR lenses contain small gyro sensors and servo-actuated optical elements, which correct for camera shake and stabilize the image. The VR function is so good that it is possible to improve your handheld photography by two or three stops, meaning that if you are pretty solid at a shutter speed of 1/60 of a second, the VR feature lets you shoot at 1/15, and possibly even 1/8, of a second (**Figures 8.6** and **8.7**). When shooting in low-light situations, make sure you set the VR switch on the side of your lens to the On position.

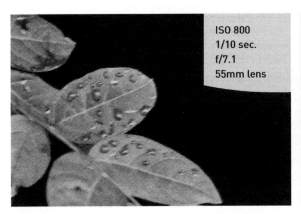

ISO 800
1/10 sec.
f/7.1
55mm lens

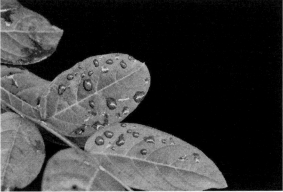

FIGURE 8.6
This image was shot hand-held with the VR turned off.

FIGURE 8.7
Here is the same subject shot with the same camera settings, but this time I turned the VR on.

Whether you are shooting with a tripod or even resting your camera on a wall, you can increase the sharpness of your pictures by taking your hands out of the equation. Whenever you use your finger to depress the shutter release button, you are increasing the chance that there will be a little bit of shake in your image. To eliminate this possibility, try setting your camera up to use the self-timer. To turn on the self-timer, just press the self-timer button on the side of the camera, directly beneath the flash button. There are four self-timer modes: 2, 5, 10, and 20 seconds. I generally use the 2-second mode to cut down on time between exposures. If you want to use one of the other modes, you will need to change this in the Setup menu under the Self-Timer Delay setting.

FOCUSING IN LOW LIGHT

The D800 has a great focusing system, but occasionally the light levels might be too low for the camera to achieve an accurate focus. There are a few things that you can do to overcome this obstacle.

First, you should know that the camera utilizes contrast in the viewfinder to establish a point of focus. This is why your camera will not be able to focus when you point it at a white wall or a cloudless sky. It simply can't find any contrast in the scene to work with. Knowing this, you might be able to use a single focus point in AF-S mode to find an area of contrast that is at the same distance as your subject. You can then hold that focus by holding down the shutter button halfway (or by pressing the AF-ON button) and recomposing your image.

Then there are those times when there just isn't anything there for you to focus on. A perfect example of this would be a fireworks display. If you point your lens to the night sky in any automatic focus (AF) mode, it will just keep searching for—and not finding—a focus point. On these occasions, you can simply turn off the autofocus feature and manually focus the lens (**Figure 8.8**). Look for the A/M switch on the side of the lens and slide it to the M position. Don't forget to put it back in A mode at the end of your shoot.

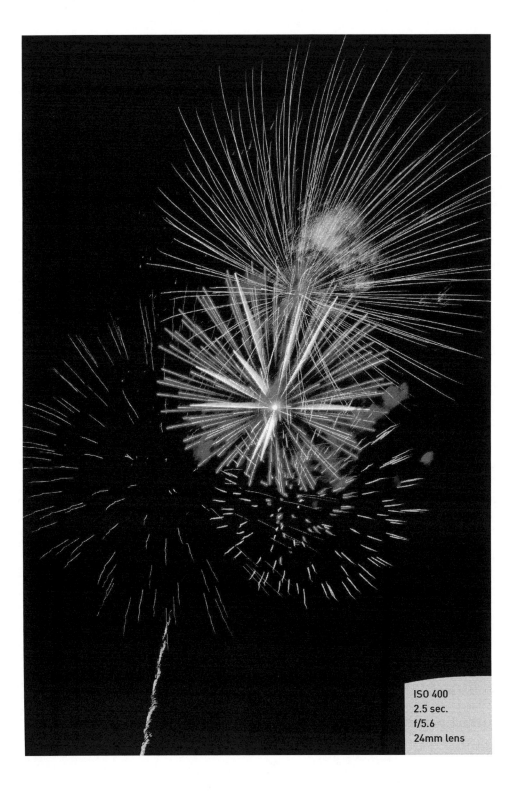

FIGURE 8.8
Focusing on the
night sky is best
done in Manual
focus mode.

ISO 400
2.5 sec.
f/5.6
24mm lens

AF ASSIST

Another way to ensure good focus is to use the D800's AF Assist feature. AF Assist uses a small, bright beam of light from the front of the camera to shine some light on the scene, which assists the autofocus system in locating more detail. This feature is automatically activated when using the flash (except in Landscape, Sports, and Flash Off modes for the following reasons: in Landscape mode, the subject is usually too far away; in Sports mode, the subject is probably moving; and in Flash Off mode, you've disabled the flash entirely). Also, AF Assist will be disabled when shooting in the AF-C or Manual focus mode, as well as when the feature is turned off in the camera menu. AF Assist should be enabled by default, but you can check the menu just to make sure.

TURNING ON THE AF ASSIST FEATURE

1. Press the Menu button, access the Custom Setting menu, locate the a Autofocus section, and press OK (A).

2. Navigate to the item a8 Built-in AF-Assist illuminator, and press the OK button (B).

3. Set the option to On, and press the OK button to complete the setup (C).

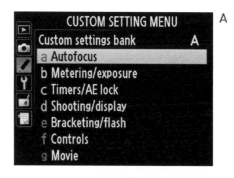

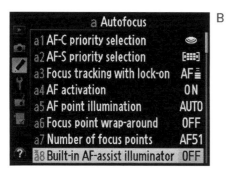

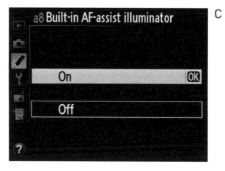

SHOOTING LONG EXPOSURES

We have covered some of the techniques for shooting in low light, so let's go through the process of capturing a night or low-light scene for maximum image quality (**Figure 8.9**). The first thing to consider is that in order to shoot in low light with a low ISO, you will need to use shutter speeds that are longer than you could possibly hand-hold (longer than 1/15 of a second). This will require the use of a tripod or stable surface for you to place your camera on. For maximum quality, the ISO should be low —somewhere below 400. The Long Exposure Noise Reduction feature should be turned on to minimize the effects of exposing for longer durations. (To set this up, see Chapter 7.)

FIGURE 8.9
A long exposure and a tripod were necessary to catch the lights of the Hoover Dam at twilight.

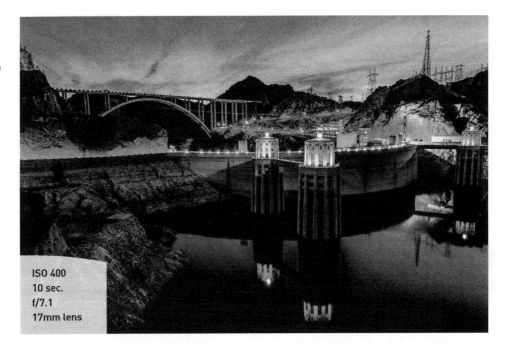

ISO 400
10 sec.
f/7.1
17mm lens

Once you have the noise reduction turned on, set your camera to Aperture Priority (A) mode. That way, you can concentrate on the aperture that you believe is most appropriate and let the camera determine the best shutter speed. If it is too dark for the autofocus to function properly, try manually focusing. Finally, consider using a remote cable (see the bonus chapter) to activate the shutter. If you don't have one, check out the sidebar "Self-Time Your Way to Sharper Images." Once you shoot the image, you may notice some lag time before it is displayed on the rear LCD. This is due to the noise reduction process, which can take anywhere from a fraction of a second up to 30 seconds, depending on the length of the exposure. Typically, the noise reduction process will take the same amount of time as the exposure itself.

The basic idea behind the term *flash synchronization (flash sync* for short) is that when you take a photograph using the flash, the camera needs to ensure that the shutter is fully open at the time that the flash goes off. This is not an issue if you are using a long shutter speed such as 1/15 of a second but does become more critical for fast shutter speeds. To ensure that the flash and shutter are synchronized so that the flash is going off while the shutter is open, the D800 implements a top sync speed of 1/250 of a second. This means that when you are using the flash, you will not be able to have your shutter speed be any faster than 1/250. If you did use a faster shutter speed, the shutter would actually start closing before the flash fired, which would cause a black area to appear in the frame where the light from the flash was blocked by the shutter.

USING THE BUILT-IN FLASH

There are going to be times when you have to turn to your camera's built-in flash to get the shot. The pop-up flash on the D800 is not extremely powerful, but with the camera's advanced metering system it does a pretty good job of lighting up the night…or just filling in the shadows.

If you are working with one of the automatic scene modes, the flash should automatically activate when needed. If, however, you are working in one of the professional modes you will have to turn the flash on for yourself. To do this, just press the pop-up flash button located on the front of the camera (**Figure 8.10**). Once the flash is up, it is ready to go (**Figure 8.11**). It's that simple.

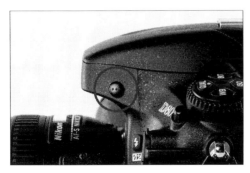

FIGURE 8.10
A quick press of the pop-up flash button will release the built-in flash up to its ready position.

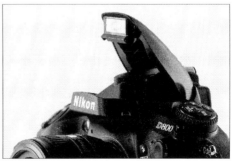

FIGURE 8.11
The pop-up flash in its ready position.

FLASH RANGE

Because the pop-up flash is fairly small, it does not have enough power to illuminate a large space (**Figure 8.12**). The effective distance varies depending on the ISO setting. At ISO 200, the range is about 14 feet. This range can be extended to as far as 28 feet when the camera is set to an ISO of 1600. For the best image quality, your ISO setting should not go above 800. Anything higher will begin to introduce excessive noise into your photos. Check out page 187 of your manual for a chart that shows the effective flash range for differing ISO and aperture settings.

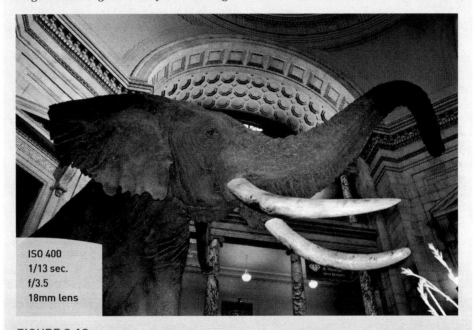

ISO 400
1/13 sec.
f/3.5
18mm lens

FIGURE 8.12
The pop-up flash filled in shadows on the elephant while the long exposure time allowed the ambient light to illuminate the rest of the scene.

SHUTTER SPEEDS

The standard flash synchronization speed for your camera is between 1/60 and 1/250 of a second. When you are working with the built-in flash in Program mode, the camera will typically adjust the shutter speed between these settings depending on the amount of ambient light.

The real key to using the flash to get great pictures is to control the shutter speed. The goal is to balance the light from the flash with the existing light so that everything in the picture has an even illumination. Let's take a look at the shutter speeds for the other modes.

Manual (M): You can adjust the shutter speed to as fast as 1/250 of a second all the way down to 30 seconds. The lens aperture is adjusted independently, so you will need to do a little experimentation to see what works best.

Shutter Priority (S): You can adjust the shutter speed to as fast as 1/250 of a second all the way down to 30 seconds. The lens aperture will adjust accordingly, but at long exposures the lens will typically be set to its smallest aperture.

Aperture Priority (A): This mode will allow you to adjust the aperture but will adjust the shutter speed between 1/250 and 1/60 of a second in the standard flash mode.

FLASH SHUTTER SPEED

You can adjust the flash shutter speed in the menu so that a slower shutter speed can be used when you are in Program mode or Aperture Priority mode. You can select a speed from 1/60 of a second to 30 seconds. This setting also affects the red-eye, slow-sync, and rear-curtain sync settings. Check out page 300 in your manual for more information.

METERING MODES

The built-in flash uses a technology called TTL (Through The Lens) metering to determine the appropriate amount of flash power to output for a good exposure. When you depress the shutter button, the camera quickly adjusts focus while gathering information from the entire scene to measure the amount of ambient light. As you press the shutter button down completely, the flash uses that exposure information and fires a predetermined amount of light at your subject during the exposure.

The default setting for the flash meter mode is TTL. The meter can also be set to Manual mode. In Manual flash mode, you can determine how much power you want coming out of the flash, ranging from full power all the way down to 1/128 power. Each setting from full power on down will cut the power by half. This is the equivalent of reducing flash exposure by one stop with each power reduction.

SETTING THE FLASH TO THE MANUAL POWER SETTING

1. Press the Menu button, navigate to the Custom Setting menu, highlight the setting called e Bracketing/flash, and press OK (**A**).

2. Highlight the item labeled e3 Flash cntrl for built-in flash, and press OK (**B**).

3. Highlight the Manual option, and press OK (**C**).

4. Select the amount of flash power you want to use, and press OK (**D**).

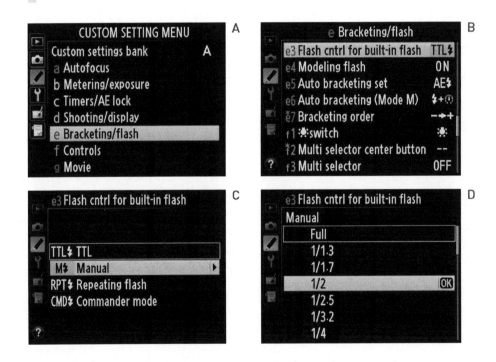

Don't forget to set the flash back to TTL when you are done, because the camera will hold this setting until you change it.

COMPENSATING FOR THE FLASH EXPOSURE

The TTL system will usually do an excellent job of balancing the flash and ambient light for your exposure, but it does have the limitation of not knowing what effect you want in your image. You may want more or less flash in a particular shot. You can achieve this by using the Flash Exposure Compensation feature.

Just as with exposure compensation, flash compensation allows you to dial in a change in the flash output in increments of 1/3 of a stop. You will probably use this most often to tone down the effects of your flash, especially when you are using the flash as a subtle fill light (**Figures 8.13** and **8.14**). The range of compensation goes from +1 stop down to –3 stops.

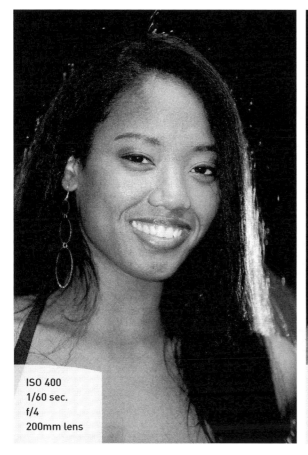

ISO 400
1/60 sec.
f/4
200mm lens

FIGURE 8.13

This shot was taken with the pop-up flash set to normal power. As you can see, it was trying too hard to illuminate my subject.

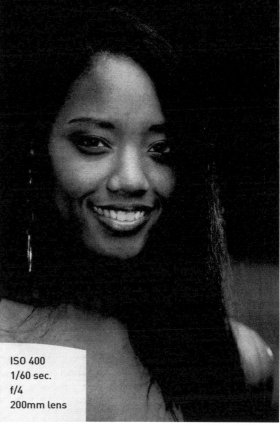

ISO 400
1/60 sec.
f/4
200mm lens

FIGURE 8.14

This image was made with the same camera settings. The difference is that the flash compensation was set to –1.3 stops.

USING THE FLASH EXPOSURE COMPENSATION FEATURE TO CHANGE THE FLASH OUTPUT

1. With the flash in the upright and ready position, press and hold the flash compensation button.

2. While holding down the button, rotate the Sub-command dial to set the amount of compensation you desire. Turning to the right increases the flash power 1/3 of a stop with each click of the dial. Turning left decreases the flash power.

3. Press the shutter button halfway to return to shooting mode, and then take the picture.

4. Review your image to see if more or less flash compensation is required, and repeat these steps as necessary.

You can view the amount of flash compensation in the control panel or in the viewfinder. You can also see the amount of compensation by activating the info screen prior to changing the compensation (**Figure 8.15**).

The Flash Exposure Compensation feature does not reset itself when the camera is turned off, so whatever compensation you have set will remain in effect until you change it. Your only clue to knowing that the flash output is changed will be the presence of the Flash Exposure Compensation symbol in the viewfinder. It will disappear when a zero compensation is set.

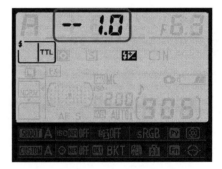

FIGURE 8.15
Using the info screen is an easy way to see how much compensation you have set.

REDUCING RED-EYE

We've all seen the result of using on-camera flashes when photographing people: the dreaded red-eye! This demonic effect is the result of the light from the flash entering the pupil and then reflecting back as an eerie red glow. The closer the flash is to the lens, the greater the chance that you will get red-eye. This is especially true when it is dark and the subject's pupils are fully dilated. There are two ways to combat this problem. The first is to get the flash away from the lens. That's not really an option, though, if you are using the pop-up flash. Therefore, you will need to turn to the Red-Eye Reduction feature.

This is a simple feature that shines a light from the camera at the subject, causing their pupils to shrink, thus eliminating or reducing the effects of red-eye (**Figure 8.16**).

The feature is set to Off by default and needs to be turned on by using the information screen or by using the flash compensation button.

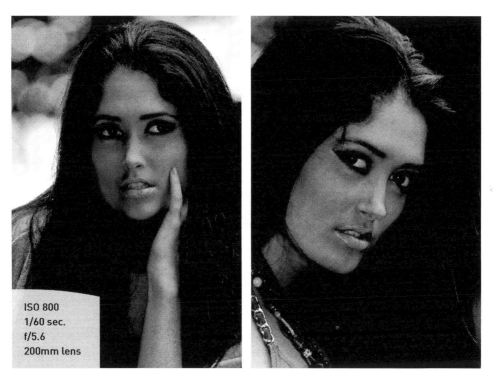

ISO 800
1/60 sec.
f/5.6
200mm lens

FIGURE 8.16
The picture on the left did not utilize red-eye reduction, thus the glowing red eyes. Notice that the pupils on the image on the right, without red-eye, are smaller as a result of using the red-eye reduction lamp.

TURN ON THE LIGHTS!

When you're shooting indoors, another way to reduce red-eye—or just shorten the length of time that the reduction lamp needs to be shining into your subject's eyes—is to turn on a lot of lights. The brighter the ambient light levels, the smaller the subject's pupils will be. This will reduce the time necessary for the red-eye reduction lamp to shine. It will also allow you to take more candid pictures because your subjects won't be required to stare at the red-eye lamp while waiting for their pupils to reduce.

TURNING ON THE RED-EYE REDUCTION FEATURE

1. Press and hold the flash compensation button on the front of the camera.

2. Rotate the Main Command dial until you see the red-eye reduction symbol in the control panel or info screen.

3. With red-eye reduction activated, compose your photo and then press the shutter release button to take the picture.

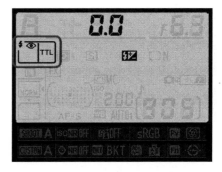

When red-eye reduction is activated, the camera will not fire the instant that you press the shutter release button. Instead, the red-eye reduction lamp will illuminate for a second or two and then fire the flash for the exposure. This is important to remember, as people have a tendency to move around, so you will need to instruct them to hold still for a moment while the lamp works its magic.

Truth be told, I rarely shoot with red-eye reduction turned on because of the time it takes before being able to take a picture. If I am after candid shots and have to use the flash, I will take my chances on red-eye and try to fix the problem in my image-processing software or even in the camera's retouching menu.

REAR CURTAIN SYNC

There are five flash synchronization modes in the D800. There's Front Curtain Sync, Red-Eye Reduction, Red-Eye Reduction with Slow Sync, Slow Sync, and Rear Curtain Sync. You may be asking, "What in the world does synchronization do, and what's with these 'curtains'?" Good questions.

When your camera fires, there are two curtains that open and close to make up the shutter. The first, or front, curtain moves out of the way, exposing the camera sensor to the light. At the end of the exposure, the second, or rear, curtain moves in front of the sensor, ending that picture cycle. In flash photography, timing is extremely important because the flash fires in milliseconds and the shutter is usually opening in tenths or hundredths of a second. To make sure these two functions happen in order, the camera usually fires the flash just as the first curtain moves out of the way (see the "Flash Sync" sidebar, earlier in this chapter).

In Slow Sync mode, the camera knows to balance the flash with a longer shutter speed. In Rear Curtain Sync mode, the flash will not fire until just before the second shutter curtain ends the exposure. So why have this mode at all? Well, there might be times when you want to have a longer exposure to balance out the light from the background to go with the subject needing the flash. Rear Curtain Sync adds some creativity by capturing the movement of light with a longer exposure while freezing the subject with the flash. Imagine taking a photograph of a friend standing in Times Square at night with all the traffic moving about and the bright lights of the streets overhead. If the flash fires at the beginning of the exposure, and then the objects around the subject move, those objects will often blur or even obscure the subject a bit. If the camera is set to Rear Curtain Sync mode, though, all of the movement is recorded using the existing light first, and then the subject is "frozen" by the flash at the end by the exposure.

There is no right or wrong to it. It's just a decision on what type of effect it is that you would like to create. Many times, Rear Curtain Sync is used for artistic purposes or to record movement in the scene without it overlapping the flash-exposed subject (**Figure 8.17**). To make sure that the main subject is always getting the final pop of the flash, I leave my camera set to Rear Curtain Sync most of the time.

Figure 8.18 shows an example of a fairly long exposure to record the light trails from the passing traffic, with a burst of flash at the end that gives a ghostly appearance to the subject.

If you intend to use a long exposure with front curtain synchronization, you need to have your subject remain fairly still so that any movement that occurs after the flash goes off will be minimized in the image.

FIGURE 8.17
The effect of using Rear Curtain Sync is most evident during long flash exposures.

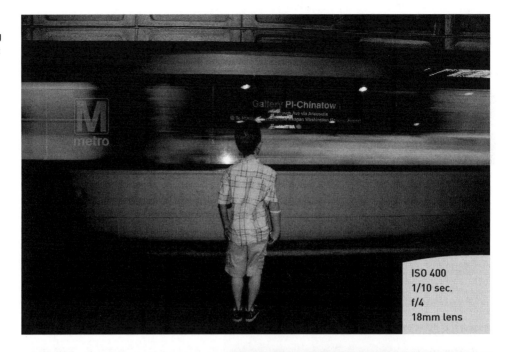

ISO 400
1/10 sec.
f/4
18mm lens

FIGURE 8.18
This effect was created using Rear Curtain Sync—the flash fired at the end of a single exposure.

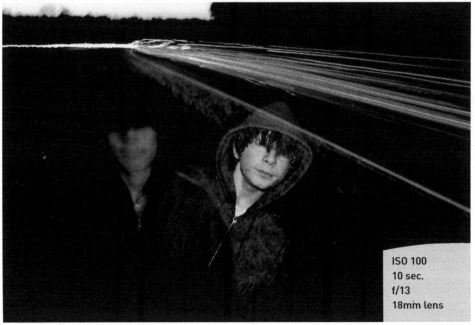

ISO 100
10 sec.
f/13
18mm lens

CHANGING THE FLASH SYNC MODE

1. Press and hold the flash compensation button.

2. Rotate the Main Command dial to change the mode.

3. To use the Slow Sync mode, change the shooting mode to Program or Aperture Priority.

4. You can view the flash sync mode changes by looking at the control panel or info screen (**Figure 8.19**).

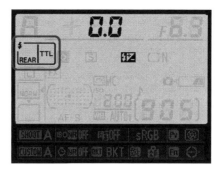

FIGURE 8.19

Look at the info screen to view your changes to the flash sync mode.

FLASH AND GLASS

If you find yourself in a situation where you want to use your flash to shoot through a window or display case, try placing your lens right against the glass so that the reflection of the flash won't be visible in your image (**Figures 8.20** and **8.21**). This is extremely useful in museums and aquariums.

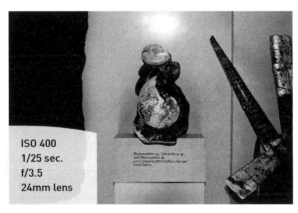

ISO 400
1/25 sec.
f/3.5
24mm lens

FIGURE 8.20

The bright spot at the top of the frame is a result of the flash reflecting off the display case.

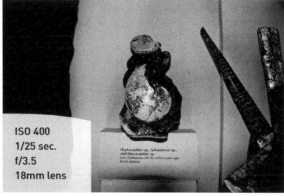

ISO 400
1/25 sec.
f/3.5
18mm lens

FIGURE 8.21

To eliminate the reflection, place the lens against the glass or as close to it as possible. This might also require zooming the lens out a little.

A FEW WORDS ABOUT EXTERNAL FLASH

We have discussed several ways to get control over the built-in pop-up flash on the D800. The reality is that, as flashes go, it will only render fairly average results. For people photography, it is probably one of the most unflattering light sources that you could ever use. This isn't because the flash isn't good—it's actually very sophisticated for its size. The problem is that light should come from any direction besides the camera to best flatter a human subject.

Manual Callout

For more information on the use of external Speedlight flashes on your D800, check out pages 380–384 of your manual.

When the light emanates from directly above the lens, it gives the effect of a photo-copier. Imagine putting your face down on a scanner: the result would be a flatly lit, featureless photo.

To really make your flash photography come alive with possibilities, you should con-sider buying an external flash such as the Nikon SB-700 AF Speedlight. The SB-700 has a swiveling flash head and more power, and it communicates with the camera and the TTL system to deliver balanced flash exposures. To see how to control an external Speedlight using your camera's pop-up flash, be sure to check out the bonus chapter.

Chapter 8 Assignments

Now that we have looked at the possibilities of shooting after dark, it's time to put it all to the test. These assignments cover the full range of shooting possibilities, both with flash and with-out. Let's get started.

How steady are your hands?

It's important to know just what your limits are in terms of hand-holding your camera and still getting sharp pictures. This will change depending on the focal length of the lens you are working with. Wider-angle lenses are more forgiving than telephoto lenses, so check this out for your longest and shortest lenses. Using a zoom lens, set your lens to its longest focal length and then, with the camera set to ISO 100 and the mode set to Shutter Priority, turn off the VR and start taking pictures with lower and lower shutter speeds. Review each image on the LCD at a zoomed-in magnification to take note of when you start seeing visible camera shake in your images. It will probably be about 1 over the focal length (1/125 of a second for a 125mm lens length).

Now do the same for the wide-angle setting on the lens. My limit is about 1/30 of a second. These shutter speeds are with the Vibration Reduction feature turned off. If you have a VR lens, try it with and without the VR feature enabled to see just how slow you can set your shutter while getting sharp results.

Pushing your ISO to the extreme

Find a place to shoot where the ambient light level is low. This could be at night or indoors in a darkened room. Using the mode of your choice, start increasing the ISO from 100 until you get to 25600 (Hi 2). Make sure you evaluate the level of noise in your image, especially in the shadow areas. Only you can decide how much noise is acceptable in your pictures. I can tell you from personal experience that I never like to stray above the ISO 800 mark.

Getting rid of the noise

Turn on the High ISO Noise Reduction feature and repeat the previous assignment. Find your acceptable limits with the noise reduction turned on. Also pay attention to how much detail is lost in your shadows with this function enabled.

Long exposures in the dark

If you don't have a tripod, find a stable place to set your camera outside and try some long exposures. Set your camera to Aperture Priority mode and then use the self-timer to activate the camera (this will keep you from shaking the camera while pressing the shutter button).

Shoot in an area that has some level of ambient light, be it a streetlight, traffic lights, or even a full moon. The idea is to get some late-night, low-light exposures.

Testing the limits of the pop-up flash

Wait for the lights to get low, and then press that pop-up flash button to start using the built-in flash. Try using the different shooting modes to see how they affect your exposures. Use the Flash Exposure Compensation feature to take a series of pictures while adjusting from –3 stops all the way to +1 stops so that you become familiar with how much latitude you will get from this feature.

Getting the red out

Find a friend with some patience and a tolerance for bright lights. Have them sit in a darkened room or outside at night and then take their picture with the flash. Now turn on the Red-Eye Reduction feature to see if you get better results. Don't forget to have them sit still while the red-eye lamp does its thing.

Getting creative with Rear Curtain Sync

Now it's time for a little creative fun. Set your camera up for Rear Curtain Sync and start shooting. Moving targets are best. Experiment with Shutter and Aperture Priority modes to lower the shutter speeds and exaggerate the effect. Try using a low ISO so the camera is forced to use longer shutter speeds. Be creative and have some fun!

Share your results with the book's Flickr group!

Join the group here: www.flickr.com/groups/d800fromsnapshotstogreatshots

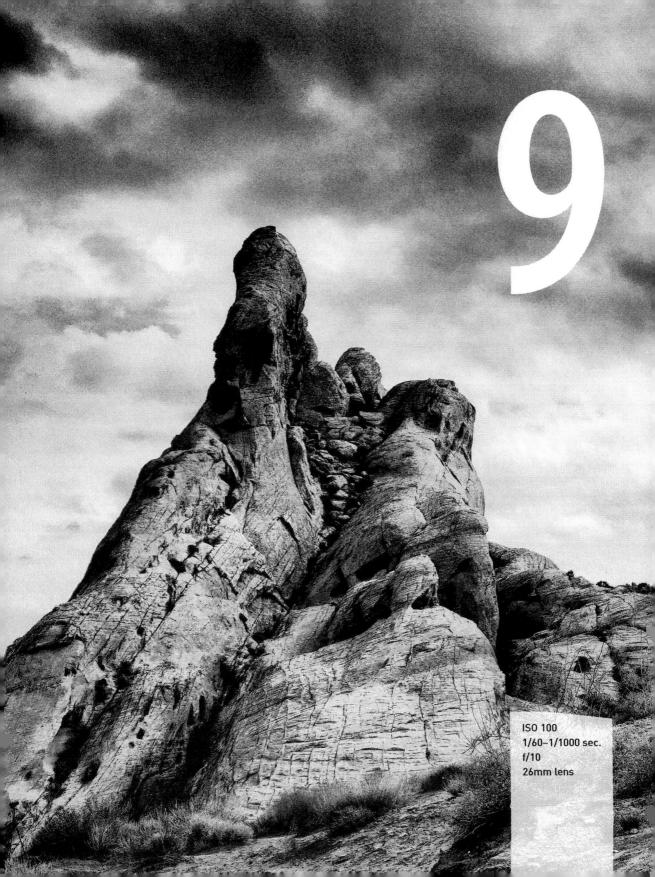

9

ISO 100
1/60–1/1000 sec.
f/10
26mm lens

Expanding the Exposure

CAMERA FEATURES AND TECHNIQUES TO INCREASE THE TONAL RANGE OF YOUR IMAGES

As good as the D800 is at finding the right exposure for a given scene, it can be very difficult to capture a wide range of tonal values in a single snap. Taking photographs will quickly remind you of just how sophisticated the human eye is and how hard it is to re-create what you see. The eye is capable of seeing a much larger range of tonal values—from dark shadows to bright highlights—and quickly adjusting between them. Unfortunately, the camera can only capture a single click and has to do the best it can at capturing all the values. So what's a photographer to do when the scene is contrasty and hard to capture? Read on and see.

PORING OVER THE PICTURE

Photography in the midday sun can be a pretty challenging prospect. The sun is usually high in the sky, and the light is bright and creates a lot of contrast between highlights and shadows. Of course, sometimes you don't have the luxury of coming back to a location when the light is perfect, and you have to make do with the light you have. That was the case when I shot this plane at a local air show. The show wasn't open during the early morning or late afternoon, when the light is more favorable, so I turned to the HDR feature in the D800 to help capture the subject.

The horizon line was placed in the lower third of the frame.

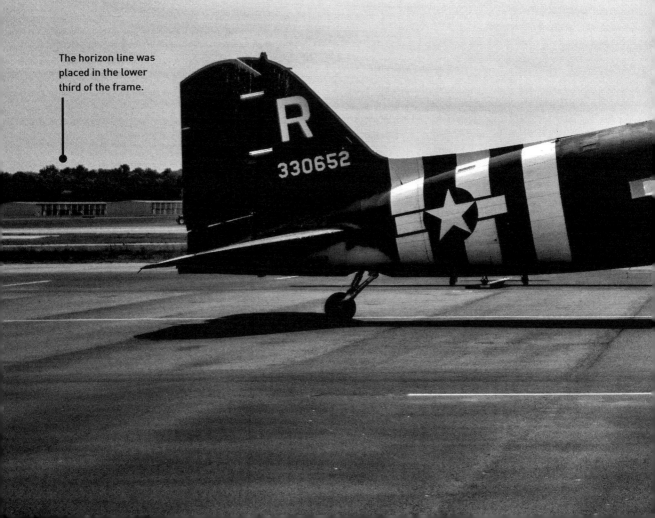

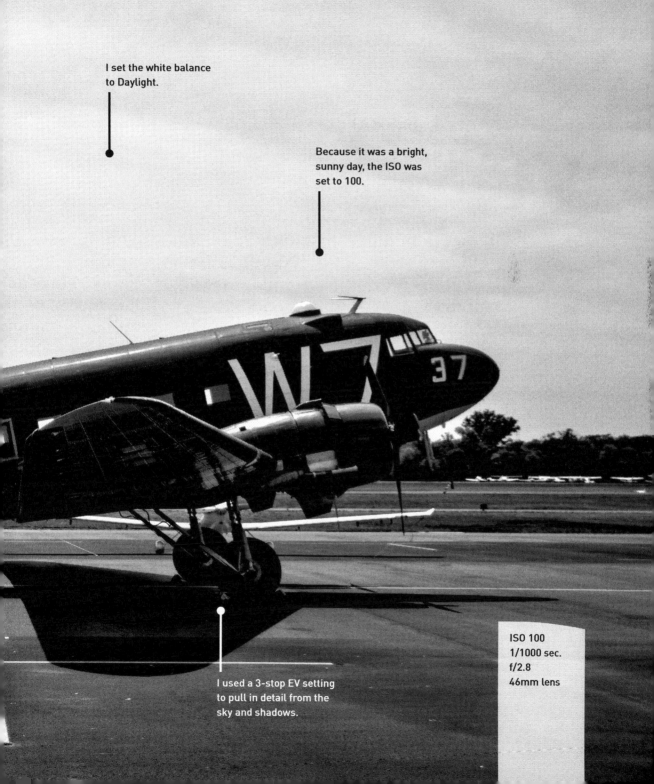

I set the white balance to Daylight.

Because it was a bright, sunny day, the ISO was set to 100.

I used a 3-stop EV setting to pull in detail from the sky and shadows.

ISO 100
1/1000 sec.
f/2.8
46mm lens

PORING OVER THE PICTURE

Although it's preferable to shoot in the best of lighting conditions, sometimes it's just not practical, and you need to take your photos when the opportunity arises. Such was the case with this image that was taken late in the afternoon but before the good light around sunset. I was still able to capture a nice shot, though, by using the technology in my camera to help expand the dynamic range and capture more of the shadow and highlight details.

Detail in the clouds was maintained using the Active D-Lighting (ADL) feature.

The high ADL setting captured good detail in the shadows.

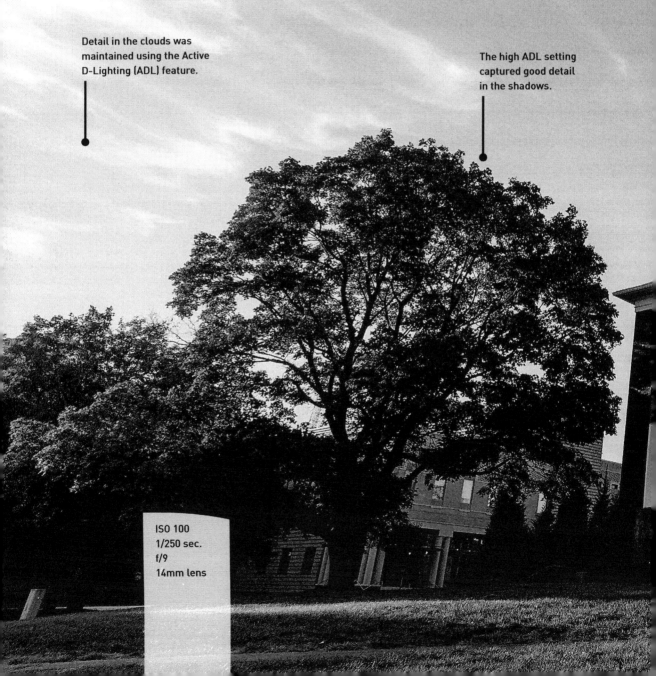

ISO 100
1/250 sec.
f/9
14mm lens

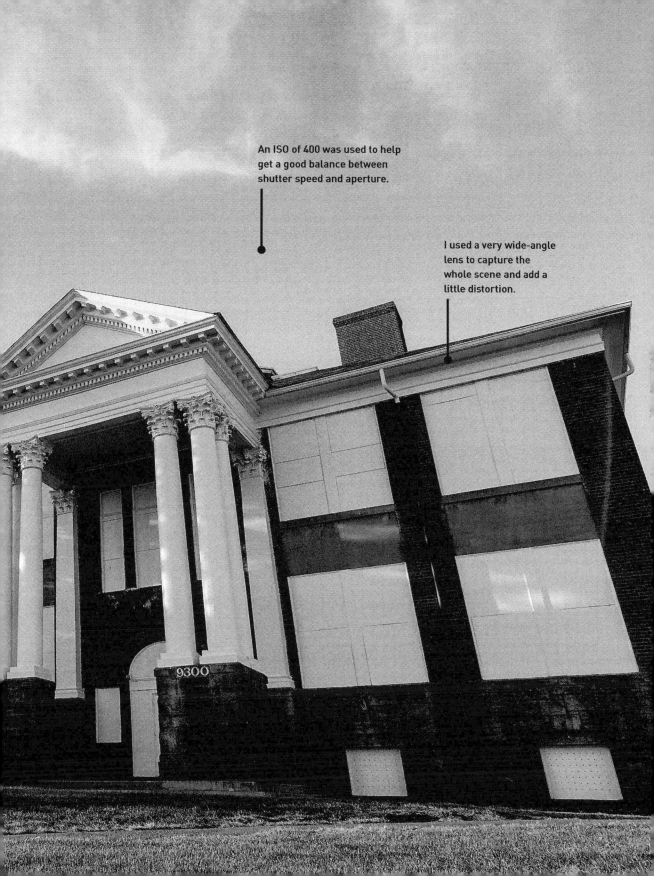

An ISO of 400 was used to help get a good balance between shutter speed and aperture.

I used a very wide-angle lens to capture the whole scene and add a little distortion.

9300

HDR REVISITED

Back in Chapter 7, I introduced you to the concept of high dynamic range, or HDR, photography. You might recall that the object of the HDR process is to shoot a series of photographs that best capture the dynamic range of a scene. This means that there will be at least one image for getting detailed shadows, one for the mid-tone values, and one or more frames for the highlight details. Once all the exposures are captured, the images are then processed in a program—like Adobe Photoshop or Photomatix Pro—that combines the best parts of each image to create a single photograph with good detail and information throughout the tonal range of the scene. The two keys to creating a great HDR image are having enough exposures to capture all the tonal values and using a tripod so that the images align correctly when they are combined.

That being said, I don't always have a tripod when confronted with a good HDR scene. In those situations, I make a few changes to how I normally shoot the bracketed exposures. Instead of using a low ISO, I raise the ISO to something that allows me to use fast shutter speeds. By combining the fast shutter speeds with the Continuous drive mode, I can hand-hold the camera while taking the bracketed exposures and then hope that my software can align the images. A little trick for this method is to find a good spot to place the focus point so that you can keep the camera positioned in the same spot during all the bracketed images (**Figure 9.1**).

USING THE IN-CAMERA HDR FUNCTION

If you aren't sure about combining bracketed photos in a software application but want the benefits of the HDR process, you can turn to the built-in HDR function. It's not as robust as the three-exposure method just discussed, but it can produce some great results, especially when working in high-contrast locations.

The HDR setting has a couple of limitations. First, unlike with traditional HDR imaging, which depends on using RAW images, you must have your camera's quality setting set on JPEG or TIFF. Also, the process uses only two exposures, so the amount of dynamic range captured between shadow and highlight is more limited.

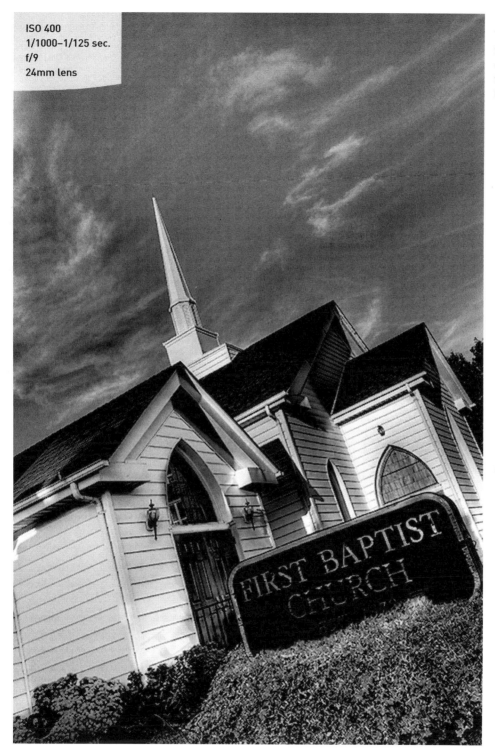

ISO 400
1/1000–1/125 sec.
f/9
24mm lens

FIGURE 9.1
The focus point was
fixed on the steeple
during shooting
to help align the
bracketed photos.

The benefit of using the in-camera HDR is that you can pretty much just shoot like you normally would without having to go through all the hoops of camera settings and tripods (although using a tripod is always a good thing when possible). Also, just because the HDR is happening in the camera doesn't mean you don't have some options for changing the look of your processed image. The menu options for HDR allow you to change the exposure variation between one and three stops and also change the amount of smoothing applied. Smoothing controls how the images are blended together and really controls the HDR look of your image (**Figure 9.2**).

FIGURE 9.2
A single exposure was not capable of capturing all the detail in the bright skies and the dark shadows. By setting the camera to HDR and using a 3 EV exposure variation, I was able to recover the missing details.

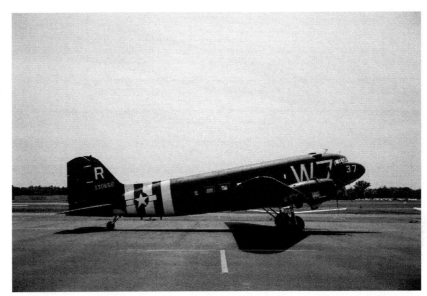

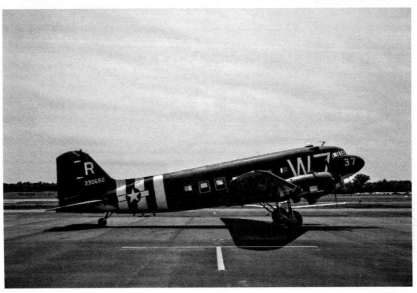

SETTING UP THE HDR FUNCTION

1. Set your camera to a quality setting of JPEG or TIFF (remember that TIFF images are not compressed and will take up a lot of room on your memory card).

2. Press the Menu button, navigate to the Shooting menu, highlight the HDR (high dynamic range) setting, and press OK (**A**).

3. Change the HDR mode from Off to either On (series) or On (single photo), and press OK. The series setting will continue to take HDR images until you turn the feature off, whereas the single setting will allow you to take one HDR shot and then the feature will be turned off automatically (**B**).

4. Select the amount of exposure differential. You can choose a setting from 1 EV (exposure value/stop) to 3 EV. The more contrast in the scene, the higher the value should be. The Auto setting will pick a setting based on what the Matrix meter determines to be appropriate (**C**).

5. The final option to set is the amount of smoothing. This is something you will need to experiment with to determine which effect you like the most. Just highlight smoothing, pick the option you want, and press the OK button (**D**).

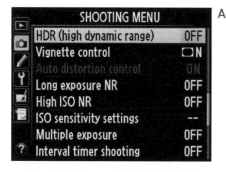
A

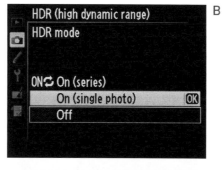
B

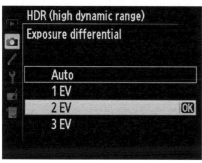
C

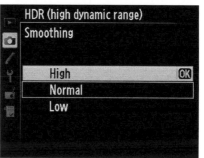
D

You can now exit the menu system, compose your shot, and take your HDR photo. You will not hear the camera shutter open and close twice like you normally would when taking two exposures. The camera will, however, take a little longer during the exposure process than you might be used to. Also, after the exposure is made, you will see the word "Job" and the HDR icon flashing in the control panel while the image is being processed. You won't be able to make any additional exposures until the camera has completed the HDR processing.

If your camera was set to single, you will now be back in regular shooting mode. If you selected series, you can continue shooting HDR images until the feature is turned off in the menu. If you can't remember which setting you picked, look for the HDR icon in the control panel. It will be displayed whenever the feature is active.

If you find that you are using the HDR feature a lot, you might want to customize the BKT button on your camera so that it turns on the feature and lets you change the exposure differential.

QUICK ACCESS TO HDR

1. To set HDR to the BKT button, press the Menu button, navigate to the Custom Setting menu, highlight f Controls, and press OK (**A**).

2. Highlight menu item f8 Assign BKT button, and press OK (**B**).

3. Change the function of the button from BKT to HDR, press OK, and then exit the menu (**C**).

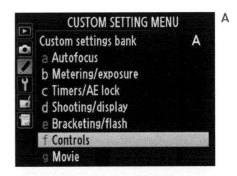

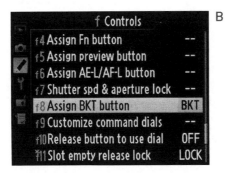

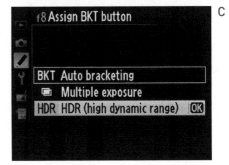

4. Press and hold the BKT button and then rotate the Sub-command dial to change the EV (you have the option of selecting 1 to 3 EV or Auto).

5. Use the Main Command dial to select between single and series. Rotating one click displays the HDR icon in the control panel and sets the camera to single mode. Rotating two clicks will add an L icon, which means you are operating in series mode.

ACTIVE D-LIGHTING

The other option for taming contrast in scenes is Active D-Lighting (ADL). This feature operates in a similar fashion to HDR except that it uses a single frame and makes adjustments to the light and dark areas of the images at the time of exposure. The main goal of Active D-Lighting is to help you retain details in the shadows and highlights. It does this by lowering the exposure in the highlight areas and amplifying the shadows (**Figure 9.3**).

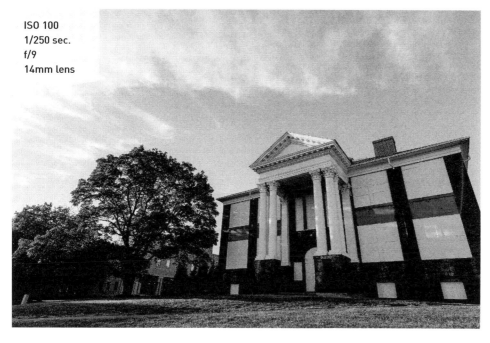

ISO 100
1/250 sec.
f/9
14mm lens

FIGURE 9.3
The Active
D-Lighting feature
can reduce the con-
trast and preserve
details in shadows
and highlights.

Active D-Lighting has five settings to choose from, ranging from Low to Extra High along with an Auto option. The key to using Active D-Lighting is to make sure you are using the Matrix metering mode. Another thing to consider when shooting with Active D-Lighting is the quality setting for the camera. If you are shooting in JPEG or TIFF mode, the effect will be applied to the image in the camera as part of the standard processing. If you are shooting in RAW mode, the effect will appear to be applied when looking at your LCD monitor but will not necessarily be displayed when you open your image in an image processing program. That's because RAW files, by definition, have no processing applied to them. You can, however, reapply the D-Lighting effect by opening your images in the Nikon ViewNX 2 software that came with your camera (**Figure 9.4**).

FIGURE 9.4
You can use the Nikon ViewNX 2 software to add D-Lighting to your RAW files.

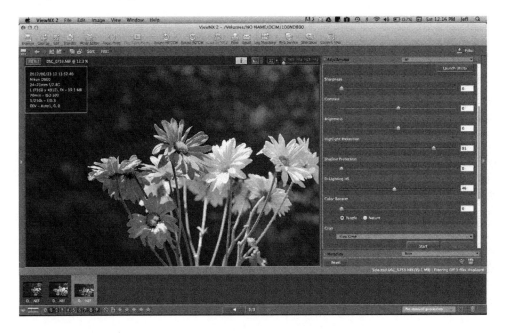

1. Press the Menu button and select Active D-Lighting in the Shooting menu. Press OK (**A**).

2. Select the desired amount of D-Lighting, and press OK (**B**).

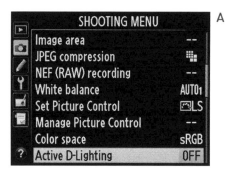
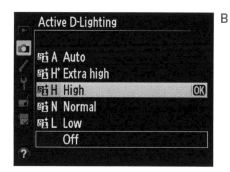

When ADL is selected in the menu, you should see the ADL icon in the control panel. This will stay active until you turn Active D-Lighting off in the menu.

ADL BRACKETING

If you aren't sure which ADL setting is right for the subject you are photographing, you can set up your camera to bracket the ADL settings. Bracketing will switch between the settings automatically so that you don't need to go back to the menu each time you want to try a different setting. You can also control how many settings you want to try in the bracketing by controlling the number of bracket exposures you take.

USING ADL BRACKETING

1. Press the Menu button, go to the Custom Setting menu, highlight the e Bracketing/flash option, and press OK (**A**).

2. Highlight item e5 Auto bracketing set, and press OK (**B**).

3. Change the setting to ADL bracketing, and press OK (**C**).

4. Once you exit the menu, press and hold the BKT button and rotate the Main Command dial to select the number of frames (from two to five) you want to shoot.

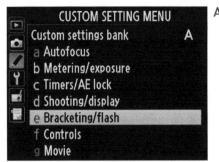

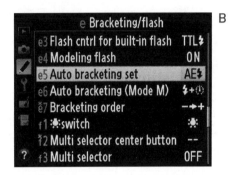

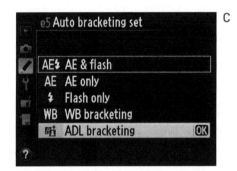

As you select the number of frames you want, the amount of ADL applied will increase, from Auto up to Extra High (five frames). If you want to use just two frames but want to compare different strengths of ADL, you can change the level of the ADL for the second shot by using the Sub-command dial.

Chapter 9 Assignments

Whether you are trying to tame extreme contrast or just interested in creating some unique exposures, the D800 gives you a lot of options for expanding your ability to capture a huge dynamic range and create great images. The best way to use them is to do a little experimenting to see which method will work best for a given situation.

Smooth out your HDR

The real key to HDR is figuring out how much smoothing to apply to your images. I prefer the more graphic look of the High setting, while some prefer a more realistic Low setting. Shoot some images and try applying different smoothing. Also, shoot some bracketed HDRs to see the difference between 1, 2, and 3 EV levels.

Tame the contrast with Active D-Lighting

This is one of the easiest ways available for you to capture a large dynamic range in a single click. I am often amazed at how well this setting can handle extremely contrasty scenes. But it can be overused in some scenarios, so it's important to know how the different levels of ADL work. The easiest way to do this is by using the ADL bracket setting. Follow the instructions earlier in the chapter to set up ADL bracketing, then take some five-shot brackets and compare the results in the LCD monitor.

Shoot HDR like a pro

If you really want to jump into the HDR pool, you will need to shoot multiple exposures and then download a program to process the photos. To start with, find an interesting subject, put your camera on a tripod, and frame your photo. Then set your ISO low, put your camera in Aperture Priority and select an aperture setting, and then set your camera to a five-shot bracket sequence that goes from two stops under to two stops over. Next, download a trial program like HDRsoft's Photomatix Pro (www.hdrsoft.com) and start getting creative with your HDR photography.

Share your results with the book's Flickr group!

Join the group here: www.flickr.com/groups/d800fromsnapshotstogreatshots

10

ISO 400
1/1000 sec.
f/2.8
120mm lens

Creative Compositions

IMPROVE YOUR PICTURES WITH SOUND COMPOSITIONAL ELEMENTS

Creating a great photograph takes more than just the right settings on your camera. To take your photography to the next level, you need to gain an understanding of how the elements within the frame come together to create a compositionally pleasing image. Composition is the culmination of light, shape, and, to borrow a word from the iconic photographer Jay Maisel, gesture. Composition is a way for you to pull your viewing audience into your image and guide them through the scene. Let's examine some common compositional elements you can use to add interest to your photos.

PORING OVER THE PICTURE

I call this my "brochure picture" because it reminds me of something you might see in a travel magazine. When my buddy Jeff Kelby and I ventured up to this rooftop pool, the sight of the huge umbrella, along with the blue water and sky, immediately struck me. But it wasn't until I walked around to the corner of the pool that I was able to find the angle that pulled all of the elements together into a balanced composition.

The repeating pattern of the deck chairs gives a sense of depth.

The strong blue sky adds stability to the scene below.

The wide-angle lens and fairly small aperture help keep all of the elements in focus.

The edge of the pool acts as a leading line to take the viewer up into the frame.

ISO 200
1/640 sec.
f/8.0
18mm lens

Wandering through the ruins of Angkor Wat, you see dozens of these lion and serpent statues. After photographing several of them, I started looking for a more interesting way to shoot them. I started circling around the area, moving farther and farther from them until I passed behind these trees. When I got between these two, I looked back at the statues and took note of the sloping trunks and how they were forming a curved frame for my subjects to appear in. Sometimes you just have to keep checking all the angles instead of shooting the obvious.

The trees vertically divide the frame into thirds.

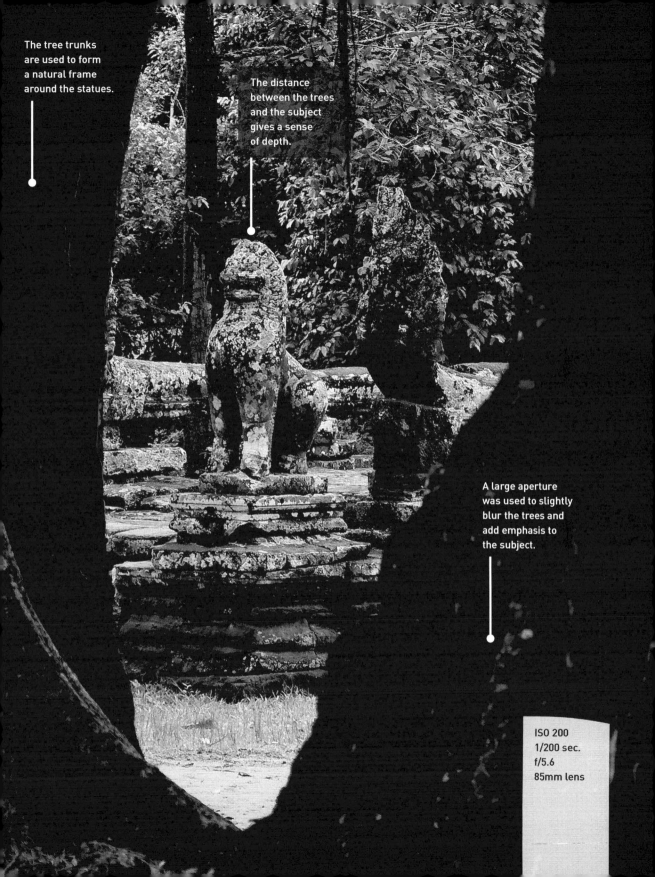

The tree trunks are used to form a natural frame around the statues.

The distance between the trees and the subject gives a sense of depth.

A large aperture was used to slightly blur the trees and add emphasis to the subject.

ISO 200
1/200 sec.
f/5.6
85mm lens

DEPTH OF FIELD

Long focal lengths and large apertures will allow you to isolate your subject from the chaos that surrounds it. I utilize Aperture Priority mode for the majority of my shooting. I also like to use a longer focal length lens to shrink the depth of field to a very narrow area (**Figure 10.1**).

The blurred background and foreground force the viewer's eye toward the sharper, in-focus areas, which gives greater emphasis to the subject.

Occasionally a greater depth of field is required to maintain a sharp focus across a greater distance. This might be due to the sheer depth of your subject, where you have objects that are near the camera but sharpness is desired at a greater distance as well (**Figure 10.2**).

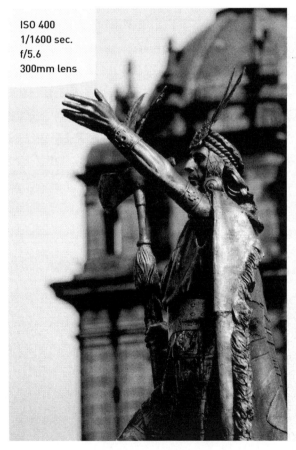

ISO 400
1/1600 sec.
f/5.6
300mm lens

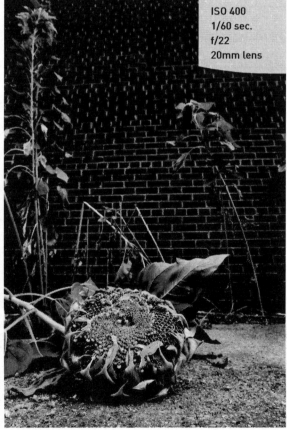

ISO 400
1/60 sec.
f/22
20mm lens

FIGURE 10.1
The combination of a telephoto lens and a large aperture can create a shallow depth of field to isolate the subject.

FIGURE 10.2
The closer you are to your subject, the smaller the aperture you will need to achieve a large depth of field.

Or perhaps you are photographing a reflection in a puddle. With a narrow depth of field, you would only be able get either the reflected object or the puddle in focus. By making the aperture smaller, you will be able to maintain acceptable sharpness in both areas (**Figure 10.3**).

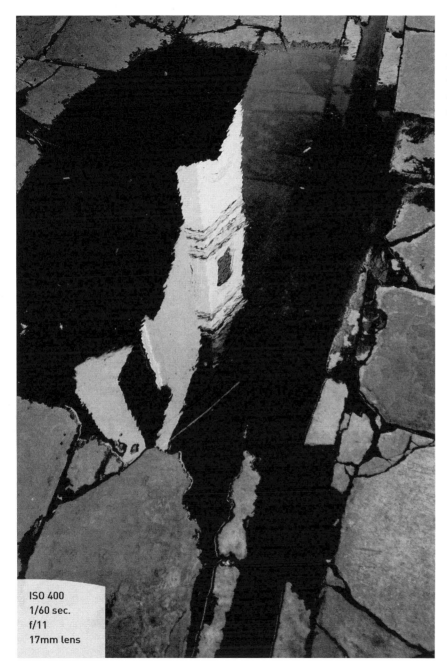

ISO 400
1/60 sec.
f/11
17mm lens

FIGURE 10.3
Getting a distant subject in focus in a reflection, along with the reflective surface, requires a small aperture.

PHOTOGRAPHING REFLECTIONS

A mirror is a two-dimensional surface, so why do I have to focus at a different distance for the image in the mirror? This was one of those questions that drove me crazy when I began to learn about photography. The answer is pretty simple, and it has to do with light. When you focus your lens, you are focusing the light being reflected off a surface onto your camera sensor. So if you wanted to focus on the mirror itself, it would be at one distance, but if you wanted to focus on the subject being reflected, you would have to take into account the distance that the object is from the mirror and then to you. Remember that the light from the subject has to travel all the way to the mirror and then to your lens. This is why a smaller aperture can be required when shooting reflected subjects. Sit in your car and take a few shots of objects in the side-view mirrors to see what I mean.

ANGLES

Having strong angular lines in your image can add to the composition, especially when they are juxtaposed with each other (**Figure 10.4**). This can create a tension that is different from the standard horizontal and vertical lines that we are so accustomed to seeing in photos.

FIGURE 10.4
The strong angular lines of the building create a dynamic composition.

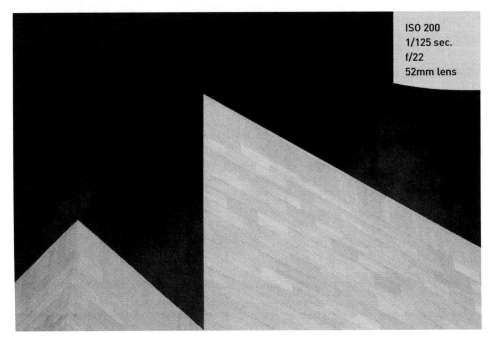

ISO 200
1/125 sec.
f/22
52mm lens

There are times when you can accentuate the angles in your images by tilting the camera, thus adding an unfamiliar angle to the subject, which draws the viewer's attention (**Figure 10.5**).

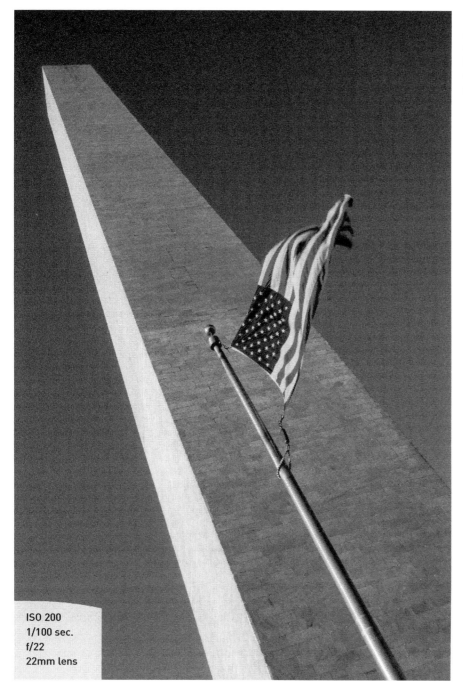

ISO 200
1/100 sec.
f/22
22mm lens

POINT OF VIEW

Sometimes the easiest way to influence your photographs is to simply change your perspective. Instead of always shooting from a standing position, try moving your camera to a place where you normally would not see your subject. Try getting down on your knees or even lying on the ground. This low angle can completely change how you view your subject and create a new interest in common subjects (**Figure 10.6**).

FIGURE 10.6
Put your camera into a position that presents an unfamiliar view of your subject.

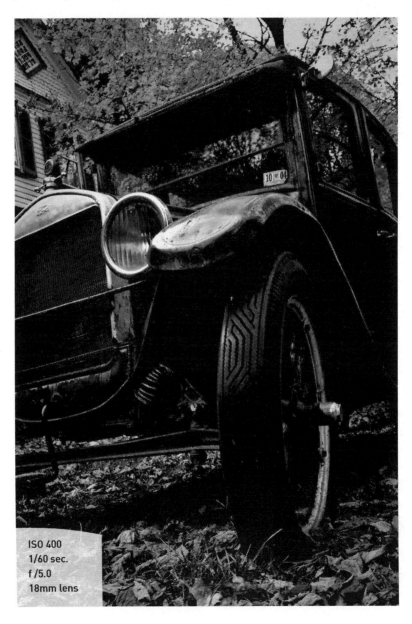

ISO 400
1/60 sec.
f /5.0
18mm lens

PATTERNS

Rhythm and balance can be added to your images by finding the patterns in everyday life and concentrating on the elements that rely on geometric influences. Try to find the balance and patterns that often go unnoticed (**Figure 10.7**).

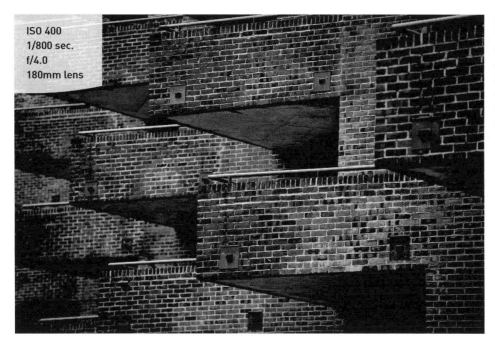

ISO 400
1/800 sec.
f/4.0
180mm lens

FIGURE 10.7
The patterns of these balconies, along with a shallow depth of field, create an almost three-dimensional effect.

COLOR

Color works well as a tool for composition when you have very saturated colors to work with. Some of the best colors are those within the primary palette. Reds, greens, and blues, along with their complementary colors (cyan, magenta, and yellow), can all be used to create visual tension (**Figure 10.8**). This tension between bright colors will add visual excitement, drama, and complexity to your images when combined with other compositional elements.

You can also use a color as a theme for your photography. One of the shots that I am known for is something that I call "the blue sky shot." If I am out shooting when the skies are blue, I can almost guarantee that I will try to use the sky as part of a background for some element of my image (**Figure 10.9**). The blue sky can act as a pleasing color contrast, giving visual interest and isolation to my subject.

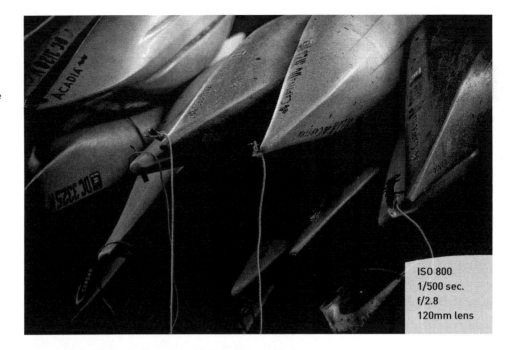

FIGURE 10.8
Cropping in tight on these kayaks allowed me to use color as the primary influence in the image.

ISO 800
1/500 sec.
f/2.8
120mm lens

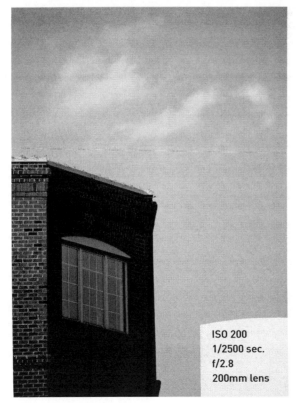

FIGURE 10.9
The predominance of the blue sky is balanced by the sky's reflection in the window.

ISO 200
1/2500 sec.
f/2.8
200mm lens

CONTRAST

We just saw that you can use color as a strong compositional tool. One of the most effective uses of color is to combine two contrasting colors that make the eye move back and forth across the image (**Figure 10.10**). There is no exact combination that will work best, but consider using dark and light colors, like red and yellow or blue and yellow, to provide the strongest contrasts.

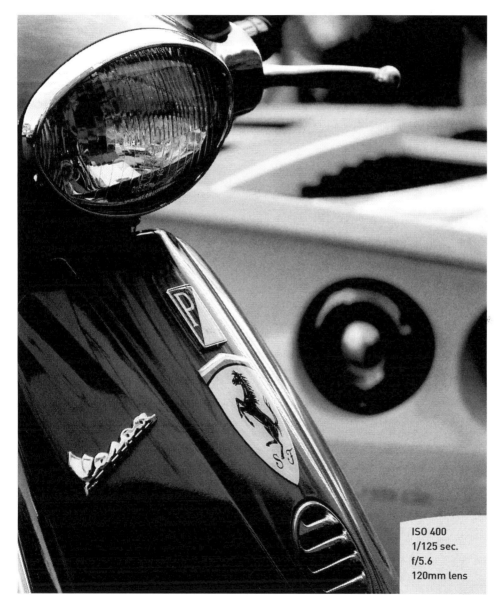

FIGURE 10.10
The contrasting colors complement each other and add balance to the scene.

ISO 400
1/125 sec.
f/5.6
120mm lens

You can also introduce contrast through different geometric shapes that battle (in a good way) for the attention of the viewer. You can combine circles and triangles, ovals and rectangles, curvy and straight, hard and soft, dark and light, and so many more (**Figure 10.11**). You aren't limited to just one contrasting element, either. Combining more than one element of contrast will add even more interest. Look for these contrasting combinations whenever you are out shooting, and then use them to shake up your compositions.

FIGURE 10.11
The angular lines of the building play against the curved lines of the sculpture, causing the eye to move back and forth across the image.

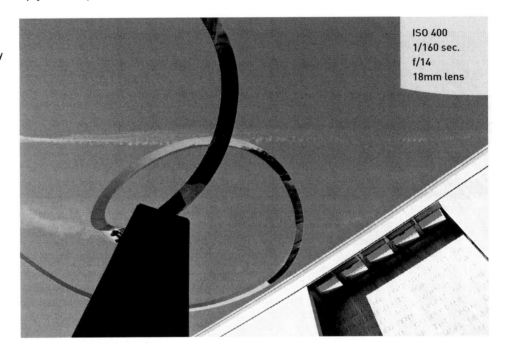

ISO 400
1/160 sec.
f/14
18mm lens

LEADING LINES

One way to pull a viewer into your image is to incorporate leading lines. These are elements that come from the edge of the frame and then lead into the image toward the main subject (**Figure 10.12**). This can be the result of vanishing perspective lines, an element such as a river, or some other feature used to move from the outer edge into the heart of the image.

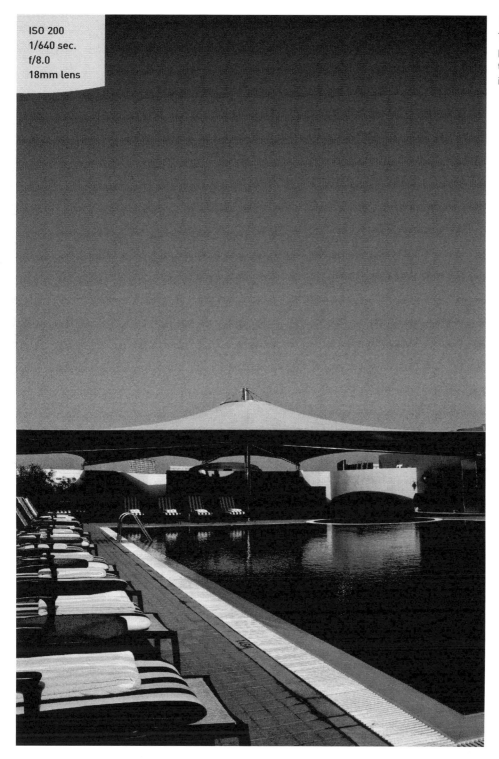

ISO 200
1/640 sec.
f/8.0
18mm lens

FIGURE 10.12
The edge of the
pool acts as a guide
to lead the eye up
into the frame.

SPLITTING THE FRAME

Generally speaking, splitting the frame right down the middle is not necessarily your best option. While it may seem more balanced, it can actually be pretty boring. When possible, you should utilize the rule of thirds when deciding how to divide your frame (**Figure 10.13**).

FIGURE 10.13
Not only did I place the tree line at the bottom third of the frame, I also moved the Capitol dome to the side instead of the middle. This adds more interest to the subject and allows the eyes to move across the image in a more pleasing way.

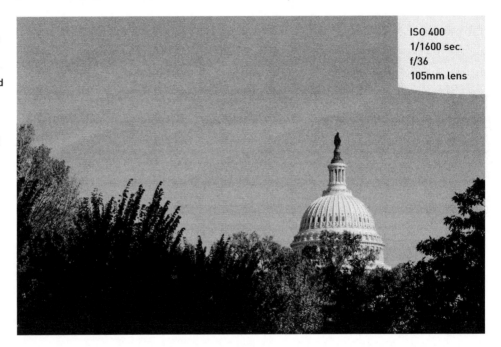

ISO 400
1/1600 sec.
f/36
105mm lens

With horizons, a low horizon will give a sense of stability to the image. Typically, this is done when the sky is more appealing than the landscape below. When the emphasis is to be placed on the landscape, the horizon line should be moved upward in the frame, leaving the bottom two-thirds to the subject below (**Figure 10.14**).

FRAMES WITHIN FRAMES

The outer edge of your photograph acts as a frame to hold all of the visual elements of the photograph. One way to add emphasis to your subject is through the use of internal frames (**Figure 10.15**). Depending on how the frame is used, it can create the illusion of a third dimension to your image, giving the photo a feeling of depth.

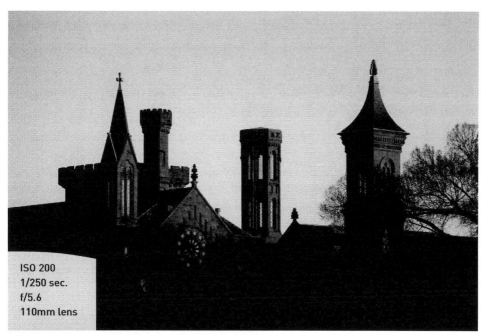

ISO 200
1/250 sec.
f/5.6
110mm lens

FIGURE 10.14
The warm glow of the Smithsonian Castle dominates the bottom two-thirds of the frame, leaving no doubt as to what the main subject is.

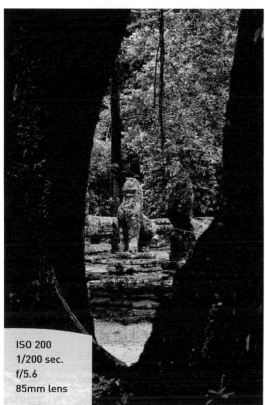

ISO 200
1/200 sec.
f/5.6
85mm lens

FIGURE 10.15
By positioning myself between the two tree trunks, I was able to use them as a frame to give emphasis to the statue in the middle.

Chapter 10 Assignments

Apply the shooting techniques and tools that you have learned in the previous chapters to these assignments, and you'll improve your ability to incorporate good composition into your photos. Make sure you experiment with all the different elements of composition, and see how you can combine them to add interest to your images.

Learning to see lines and patterns

Take your camera for a walk around your neighborhood, and look for patterns and angles. Don't worry so much about getting great shots as much as developing an eye for details.

The ABCs of composition

Here's a great exercise that was given to me by my friend Vincent Versace: shoot the alphabet. This will be a little more difficult, but with practice you will start to see beyond the obvious. Don't just find letters in street signs and the like. Instead, find objects that aren't really letters but that have the shape of letters.

Finding the square peg and the round hole

Circles, squares, and triangles. Spend a few sessions concentrating on shooting simple geometric shapes.

Using the aperture to focus attention

Depth of field plays an important role in defining your images and establishing depth and dimension. Practice shooting wide open, using your largest aperture for the narrowest depth of field. Then find a scene that would benefit from extended depth of field, using very small apertures to give sharpness throughout the scene.

Leading them into a frame

Look for scenes where you can use elements as leading lines, and then look for framing elements that you can use to isolate your subject and add both depth and dimension to your images.

Share your results with the book's Flickr group!

Join the group here: www.flickr.com/groups/d800fromsnapshotstogreatshots

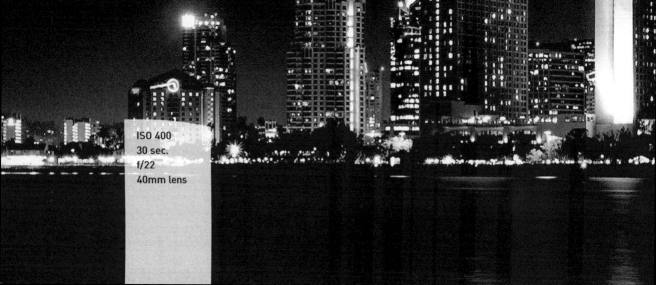

ISO 400
30 sec.
f/22
40mm lens

Advanced Techniques

IMPRESS YOUR FAMILY AND FRIENDS

We've covered a lot of ground in the previous chapters, especially on the general photographic concepts that apply to most of the shooting situations you might encounter. There are, however, some specific tools and techniques that will give you an added advantage in obtaining a great shot.

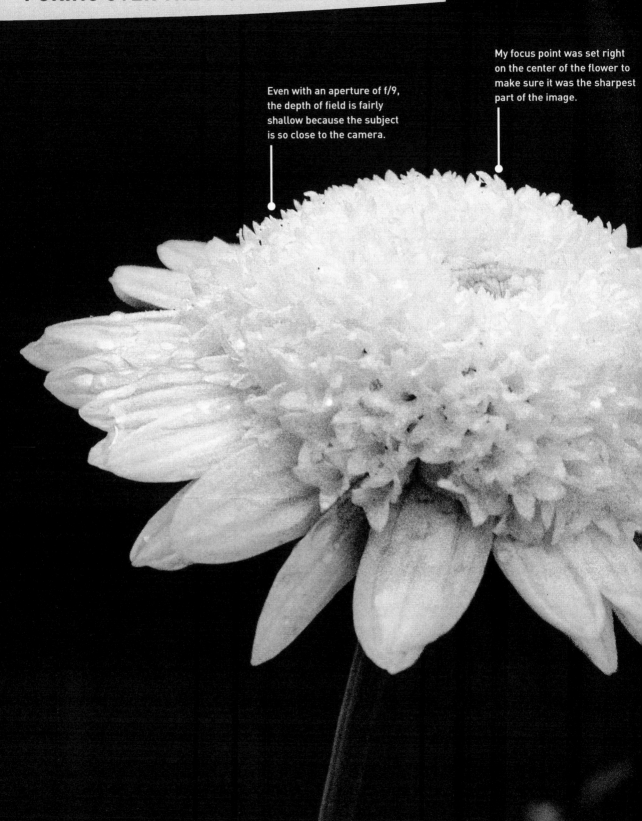

Even with an aperture of f/9, the depth of field is fairly shallow because the subject is so close to the camera.

My focus point was set right on the center of the flower to make sure it was the sharpest part of the image.

I much prefer to shoot live flowers rather than cut ones. Flower arrangement isn't really my strong suit, and I believe Mother Nature does a better job at it than anyone else. I also enjoy shooting close-up macro shots, because I think that much of the beauty in a flower lies in the little details. This particular shot was taken in a small garden in Peru just after sunrise. The garden was in shade, so I was able to get really soft details but still had enough light to shoot without a tripod.

The dark background helps move the viewer's eye toward the flower.

Diffused natural light made for soft shadows and saturated colors.

ISO 400
1/125 sec.
f/9
200mm lens

PORING OVER THE PICTURE

One of the things I enjoy about going on photowalks is the interaction I have with other photographers. Sometimes I learn new things, and sometimes I get to pass along something that I know. This image is the result of just such an instance, when I was teaching someone how to get better sunset shots. Luckily, the skies over Orlando were cooperating, and we got some nice shots.

The small aperture and wide-angle lens resulted in a large depth of field.

I chose to place the horizon at the bottom third of the screen, which put the emphasis on the buildings and sky.

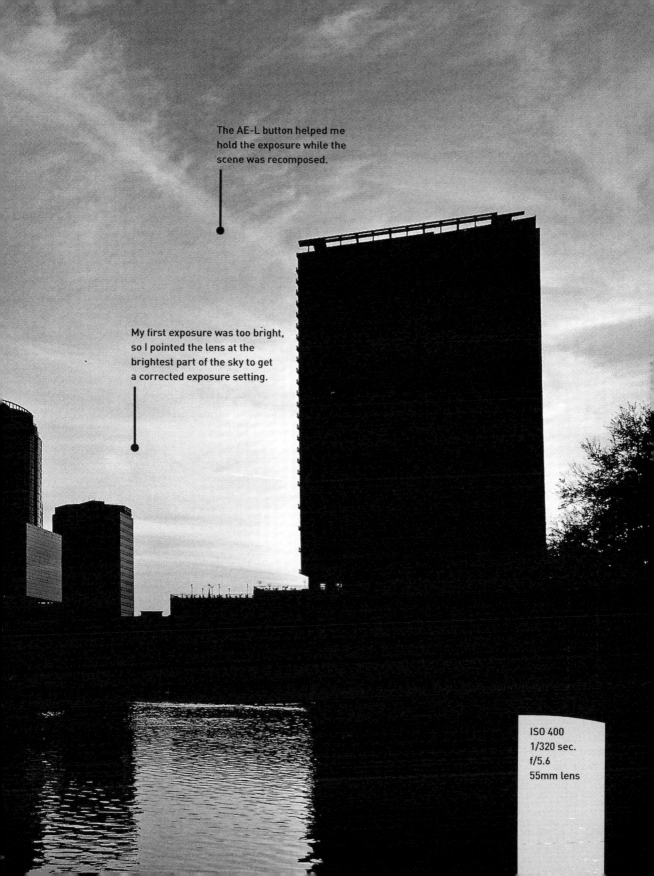

The AE–L button helped me hold the exposure while the scene was recomposed.

My first exposure was too bright, so I pointed the lens at the brightest part of the sky to get a corrected exposure setting.

ISO 400
1/320 sec.
f/5.6
55mm lens

METERING FOR SUNRISE OR SUNSET

Capturing a beautiful sunrise or sunset is all about the sky. If there is too much foreground in the viewfinder, the camera's meter will deliver an exposure setting that is accurate for the darker foreground areas but leaves the sky looking overexposed, undersaturated, and generally just not very interesting (**Figure 11.1**). To gain more emphasis on the colorful sky, point your camera at the brightest part of it and take your meter reading there. Use the AE Lock to meter for the brightest part of the sky, and then recompose. The result will be an exposure setting that underexposes the foreground but provides a darker, more dramatic sky (**Figure 11.2**).

FIGURE 11.1
By metering with all the information in the frame, you get bright skies and more detail in the foreground.

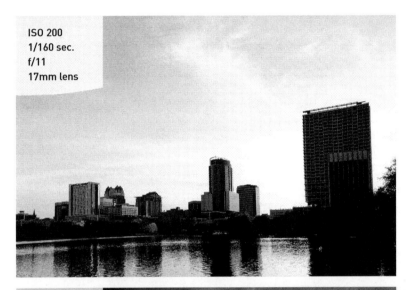

ISO 200
1/160 sec.
f/11
17mm lens

FIGURE 11.2
By taking the meter reading from the brightest part of the sky, you will get darker, more colorful sunsets.

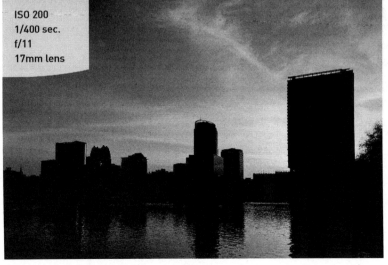

ISO 200
1/400 sec.
f/11
17mm lens

1. Point your camera toward a bright portion of the sky.

2. Press and hold the AE-L button with your thumb to activate the meter and lock the exposure.

3. While holding the button, recompose your photo, and then take the shot with the shutter release button. As long as you keep the AE-L button pressed, your exposure will not change.

MANUAL MODE

Probably one of the most advanced and yet most basic skills to master is shooting in Manual mode. With the power and utility of most of the semi-automatic modes, Manual mode almost never sees the light of day. I have to admit that I don't select it for use very often, but there are times when no other mode will do. One of the situations that works well with Manual is studio work with external flashes. I know that when I work with studio lights, my exposure will not change, so I use Manual to eliminate any automatic changes that might happen from shooting in Program, Shutter Priority, or Aperture Priority mode. In fact, every picture of the D800 camera in this book was taken using Manual mode.

Since you probably aren't too concerned with studio strobes at this point, I will concentrate on one of the ways in which you will want to use Manual mode for your photography: long nighttime exposures.

BULB PHOTOGRAPHY

If you want to work with long shutter speeds that don't quite fit into one of the selectable shutter speeds, you can select Bulb. This setting is only available in Manual mode, and its sole purpose is to open the shutter at your command and then close it again when you decide. I can think of four scenarios where this would come in handy: shooting fireworks, shooting lightning, shooting exposures that exceed 30 seconds, and painting with light.

If you are photographing fireworks, you could certainly use one of the longer shutter speeds available in Shutter Priority mode, since they are available for exposure times up to 30 seconds. That is fine, but sometimes you don't need 30 seconds' worth of exposure and sometimes you need more.

If you open the shutter and then see a great burst of fireworks, you might decide that that is all you want for that particular frame, so you click the button to end the exposure (**Figure 11.3**). Set the camera to 30 seconds and you might get too many bursts, but if you shorten it to 10 seconds, you might not get the one you want.

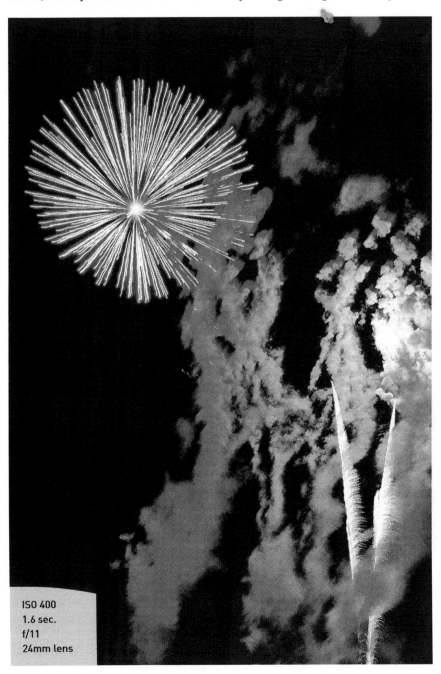

ISO 400
1.6 sec.
f/11
24mm lens

The same can be said for photographing a lightning storm. I have a friend who loves electrical storms, and he has some amazing shots that he captured using the Bulb setting. Lightning can be very tricky to capture, and using the Bulb setting to open and then close the shutter at will allows for more creativity, as well as more opportunity to get the shot.

Painting with light is a process where you set your camera to Bulb, open the shutter, and then use a light source to "paint" your subject with light. This can be done with a handheld flash or even a flashlight.

To select the Bulb setting, simply place your camera in Manual mode and then rotate the Command dial to the left until the shutter speed displays Bulb on the rear LCD screen.

When you're using the Bulb setting, the shutter will only stay open for the duration that you are holding down the shutter button. You should also be using a sturdy tripod or shooting surface to eliminate any self-induced vibration while using the Bulb setting.

I want to point out that using your finger on the shutter button for a bulb exposure will definitely increase the chances of getting some camera shake in your images. To get the most benefit from the Bulb setting, I suggest using the Nikon MC-30 remote cord (see the bonus chapter for more details). You'll also want to turn on the Long Exposure Noise Reduction.

BULB

If you are new to the world of photography, you might be wondering where in the world the *Bulb* shutter function got its name. After all, wouldn't it make more sense to call it the Manual Shutter setting? It probably would, but this is one of those terms that harkens back to the origins of photography. Way back when, the shutter was actually opened through the use of a bulb-shaped device that forced air through a tube, which, in turn, pushed a plunger down, activating the camera shutter. When the bulb was released, it pulled the plunger back, letting the shutter close and ending the exposure.

SHOOTING LIGHTNING

If you are going to photograph lightning strikes in a thunderstorm, please exercise extreme caution. Standing in the open with a tripod is like standing over a lightning rod. Work from indoors if at all possible.

AVOIDING LENS FLARE

Lens flare is one of the problems you will encounter when shooting in the bright sun. Lens flare will show itself as bright circles on the image (**Figure 11.4**). Often you will see multiple circles in a line leading from a very bright light source such as the sun. The flare is a result of the sun bouncing off the multiple pieces of optical glass in the lens and then being reflected back onto the sensor. You can avoid the problem using one of these methods:

- Try to shoot with the sun coming from over your shoulder, not in front of you or in your scene.

- Use a lens shade to block the unwanted light from striking the lens. You don't have to have the sun in your viewfinder for lens flare to be an issue. All it has to do is strike the front glass of the lens to make it happen.

- If you don't have a lens shade, just try using your hand or some other element to block the light.

FIGURE 11.4
The bright sun has created flare spots that are visible as colored circles radiating down the image.

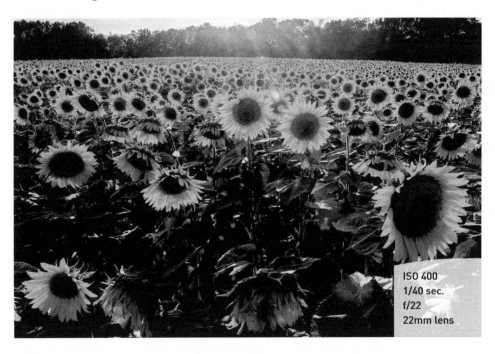

ISO 400
1/40 sec.
f/22
22mm lens

USING THE SUN CREATIVELY

Have you ever seen photographs where the sun is peeking through a small hole and it creates a very cool starburst effect? There is actually a little trick to pulling it off, and it's fairly easy. The real key is to be shooting at f/22 (or whatever your smallest aperture is). Then you need to have just a small bit of the sunlight in your frame, either peeking over an edge or through a small hole. The other thing you need to do is make sure you are properly exposing for the rest of your scene, not for the bright bit of sunlight that you are allowing in. With a little practice, you can really make some very cool shots (**Figure 11.5**).

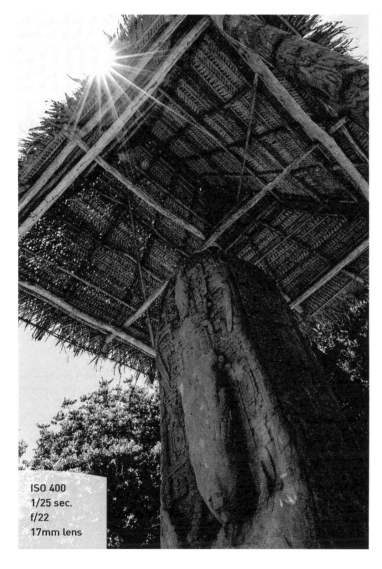

FIGURE 11.5
By letting the sun peek into my shot and using f/22, I was able to capture this starburst effect.

ISO 400
1/25 sec.
f/22
17mm lens

MACRO PHOTOGRAPHY

Put simply, macro photography is close-up photography. Depending on the lens or lenses that you got with your camera, you may have the perfect tool for macro work. Some lenses are made to shoot in a macro mode, but you don't have to feel left out if you don't have one of those. Check the spec sheet that came with your lens to see what the minimum focusing distance is for your lens.

If you have a zoom, you should work with the lens at its longest focal length. Also, work with a tripod, because hand-holding will make focusing difficult. The easiest way to make sure that your focus is precisely where you want it to be is to use Manual focus mode.

Since I am recommending a tripod for your macro work, I will also recommend using Aperture Priority mode so that you can achieve differing levels of depth of field. Long lenses at close range can make for some very shallow depth of field, so you will need to work with apertures that are probably much smaller than you might normally use. If you are shooting outside, try shading the subject from direct sunlight by using some sort of diffusion material, such as a white sheet or a diffusion panel (see the bonus chapter). By diffusing the light, you will see much greater detail because you will have a lower contrast ratio (softer shadows), and detail is often what macro photography is all about (**Figure 11.6**).

FIGURE 11.6
Flowers provide a great opportunity for moving in close and shooting macro shots.

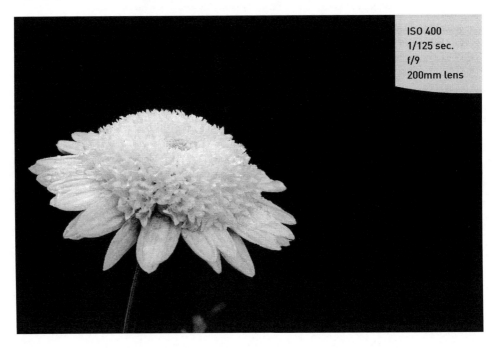

ISO 400
1/125 sec.
f/9
200mm lens

HANDS-FREE BRACKETING

Throughout the book, I have been preaching the use of a tripod and cable release. These two items are extremely helpful in the pursuit of sharp images. The cable release is especially helpful if you are trying to bracket your exposures, whether it's for an HDR shot or for an Active D-Lighting bracket series. That being said, it's not always possible to use these accessories all the time. I do have a neat little trick for the self-timer, though, that will let you fire off consecutive frames without having to have your hands on the camera.

Most often we think of the self-timer as something to be used for taking a group shot where you want to be included in the image. This is still true, but the D800 has a great feature that allows you to customize the self-timer to take multiple exposures and even determine the amount of time between each shot. Let's use the HDR scenario as our example.

When we set up a typical HDR bracket, we change the bracket sequence so that it shoots five frames with exposures from −2 stops to +2 stops. After setting that up, it's time to dive into the menu and customize the self-timer.

CUSTOMIZING THE SELF-TIMER

1. Press the Menu button, go to the Custom Setting menu, and select option c Timers/AE lock. Press OK (**A**).

2. Highlight item c3 Self-timer, and press OK (**B**).

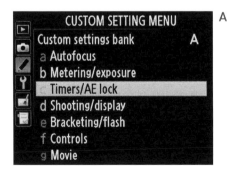 A

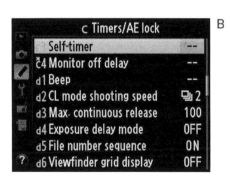 B

3. Change the delay for the self-timer to one of four different settings: 2, 5, 10, or 20 seconds. This delay will determine how long the camera waits after you press the shutter button before taking the first exposure. I usually go with 2 seconds so there is little change in the scene from the time I press it until it starts taking pictures (**C**).

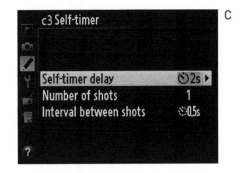

4. Set the number of shots to however many you need for your bracket sequence (**D**).

5. Finally, change the interval between each frame. There are four choices: 0.5, 1, 2, and 3 seconds. I usually stick with 0.5 seconds for an HDR sequence (**E**).

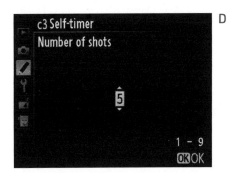
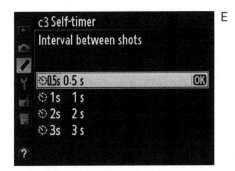

Once you have finished setting things up in the menu, all that is left is to turn the shooting mode dial to the self-timer setting, set the camera on a stable surface, and activate the camera by pressing the shutter release button.

If you are going to use the self-timer sequence for taking multiple shots using the flash, set the interval to 3 seconds. This will give the flash adequate time to recycle between photos.

CUSTOMIZE YOUR WHITE BALANCE

Previous chapters have addressed the issue of setting your white balance, but what if you are in a situation that doesn't really fall neatly into one of the existing categories like Daylight or Tungsten? You might want to consider creating a custom white balance. This is especially helpful if you are working in a mixed lighting scenario where you have more than one kind of light source shining on your subject. A perfect example might be inside with fluorescent lighting fixtures overhead and daylight coming in through a window. To ensure that you are getting the best possible results in a situation like this, you can perform a quick white balance customization by using the Preset Manual option. Don't worry, though; it's easier than you might think. All you really need is a white piece of paper and a few seconds in your camera menu.

SETTING UP A PRESET MANUAL WHITE BALANCE

1. Place a white piece of paper in your scene, or have your subject hold the paper so that it is being lit evenly by your light source.

2. Press the Menu button, navigate to the White balance option in the Shooting menu, and press OK (**A**).

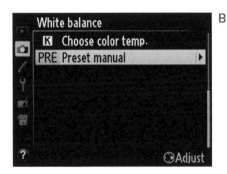

3. Scroll down to the Preset manual option, and press the right arrow on the Multi-selector (**B**).

4. Use the Multi-selector to pick one of the four preset destinations, and press the button in the middle of the Multi-selector (**C**).

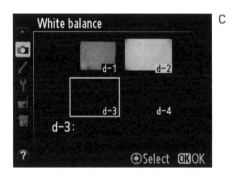

5. Exit the menu, and then hold down the WB button for about one and a half seconds until you see PRE blinking in your control panel.

6. While PRE is blinking, take a photo of the piece of paper so that the camera can measure the color temperature (be sure to fill the frame with the paper). If the white balance was recorded properly, you will see the word *Good* blinking in your control panel.

7. Now when you are shooting in that light, all you need to do is select that preset white balance to get accurate color in your images.

GETTING MORE REACH FROM YOUR ZOOM

The D800 has a lot of great features, but one that I really like is the ability to change the size of the image area being captured. There are a lot of reasons to do this, such as sizing the image for a traditional frame size. The 5:4 image size option on the D800 will crop the saved image to the same dimensions as an 8x10 photo. You could also go with the 1.2x setting for making 30x20 images.

The setting I like to use is DX. It crops my sensor to the same dimensions as my full-frame images but reduces the area covered, thereby reducing the angle of coverage. This gives me the same effect as using a lens that is one and a half times longer than what is on the camera. That means that if I am using a 300mm lens, I am getting an effective focal length of 450mm (**Figure 11.7**). That gets me a little tighter on the action, and because my D800 has 36MP of resolution, I am still getting an image in DX mode that is 17MP. That's still a lot of pixels to play with.

Another advantage to using the DX image size is that when the sensor is being cropped in, I am getting more coverage from my focal points. In fact, the 51 focus points cover more of the image area from side to side and top to bottom. That means there is less chance that my subject will not be covered by a focus point.

FIGURE 11.7
The DX image size
crops in to the
center of the image.

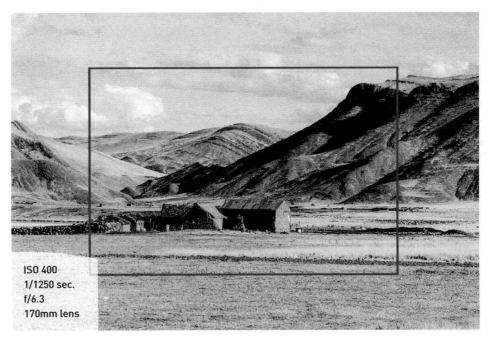

ISO 400
1/1250 sec.
f/6.3
170mm lens

CHANGING THE IMAGE SIZE

1. Press the Menu button, navigate to the Shooting menu, highlight Image area, and press OK (**A**).

2. Select Choose image area, and press OK (**B**).

3. Choose a new crop for your image, and press OK (**C**).

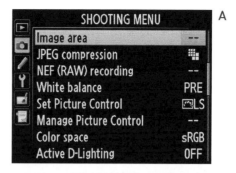

A

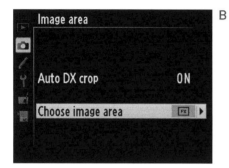

B

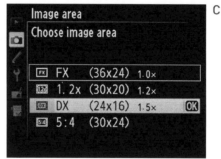

C

Now when you look through your viewfinder, you will see a rectangular box inside the normal view. This is the new crop for images, and anything on the outside of this crop box will not be recorded. The image size will stay in effect after the camera is turned off, so you will need to reset it to FX in the menu to return to full frame.

Chapter 11 Assignments

Many of the techniques covered in this chapter are specific to certain shooting situations that may not come about very often. This is even more reason to practice them so that when the situation does present itself, you will be ready.

Adding some drama to the end of the day

Most sunset photos don't reflect what the photographer saw, because the photographer didn't meter correctly for them. The next time you see a colorful sunset, pull out your camera and take a meter reading from the sky and then one without and see what a difference it makes.

Using the Bulb setting to capture the moment

This is definitely one of those settings that you won't use often, but it's pretty handy when you need it. If you have the opportunity to shoot a fireworks display or a distant storm, try setting the camera to Bulb and then play with some long exposures to capture just the moments that you want.

Moving in for a close-up

Macro photography is best practiced on stationary subjects, which is why I like flowers. If you have a zoom lens, check the minimum focusing distance and then try to get right to that spot to squeeze the most from your subject. Try using a diffuse light source as well to minimize shadows.

Add a little starburst for some flair

Next time you are shooting when the sun is high in the sky, look for some opportunities to use the sun as a creative element in your photos by capturing a starburst effect. Set your aperture to a small setting, and look for subjects that you can shoot where you can just let a glimpse of the sun come through. Try shooting through the canopy of a tree—you can usually get some good starbursts if the sun is peeking through the leaves.

Share your results with the book's Flickr group!

Join the group here: www.flickr.com/groups/d800fromsnapshotstogreatshots

12

ISO 400
1/2500 sec.
f/2.8
70mm lens

The Moving Picture

SHOOTING VIDEO WITH THE D800

Probably one of the reasons you purchased the D800 over competing cameras is its ability to capture video—and not just regular video, but high-definition video. As I discussed in the book's introduction, the focus of this book is on the photography aspects of the camera, but that doesn't mean I am going to skip the video functions. The fact is that the line between photography and video is getting blurrier each day, especially since the inclusion of video capture in DSLR cameras. In this chapter, we will address some of the basics of video capture with the D800 and also take a look at some of the creative things you can do with your video. First, though, let's take a look at why the video capture feature is such a big deal in a DSLR.

IT'S ALL ABOUT THE LENSES

Video cameras have been around for a long time, so why is it such a big deal that you can now use your DSLR camera to record video? The answer is simple: it's all about the lenses. If you have any experience using a video camcorder, you know that it always seems like everything is in focus. While this isn't always a bad thing, it can also be pretty boring. Using DSLR video allows you to use faster lenses (larger apertures), which can give you more shallow depth of field in your videos. This shallow depth of field can add a sense of dimension and depth that is normally lacking in most standard video cameras. The truth is that many videographers are turning their attention from video cameras costing tens of thousands of dollars to the much more affordable DSLR video cameras to produce similar professional, high-definition results.

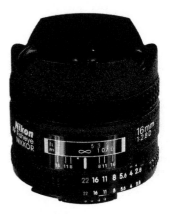

The D800 will not only allow you to capture video with a more shallow depth of field, it will also allow you the flexibility of using different lenses for different effects. While you may own only one lens right now, you have the ability to buy specialty lenses to enhance your video as well as your still capture. Any lens that you can use for still photography on your D800 can also be used for video, including an ultra-wide lens such as the AF Fisheye-Nikkor 16mm f/2.8 ED, the AF-S VR Zoom-Nikkor 70-300mm f/4.5-5.6G IF-ED, or even the AF Micro-Nikkor 105mm f/2.8D for getting extreme close-up videos (**Figure 12.1**).

FIGURE 12.1
Specialty lenses like this 16mm fisheye will add a unique look to your videos.

SETTING UP THE VIDEO FEATURES

While the actual act of shooting video is fairly simple, the key to getting the video results you want is to set up the camera. First, the video recording is a feature of the Live View capabilities of the camera. You have to put the camera into the active Live View mode to even begin to capture video. This is accomplished by rotating the Live View switch on the rear of the camera to the Movie position and then pressing the LV button (**Figure 12.2**). This activates the live video on the rear LCD monitor.

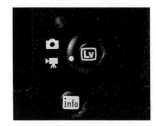

FIGURE 12.2
Turn the Live View switch to the Movie mode and press the LV button to activate.

Once Live View is active, place the focus box on the subject and press the shutter release button halfway—or press the AF-ON button—until the focus operation is complete and the rectangle turns green (**Figure 12.3**).

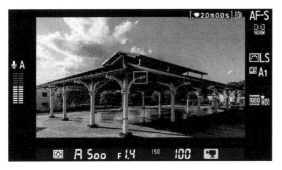

FIGURE 12.3
The camera will attempt to focus on whatever the focus point is covering.

CHANGING THE AF-AREA MODE

There are actually several focusing modes that you can use for your video recording. We just talked about the Normal-area AF, which uses the small rectangular focus point to lock focus on a subject. The focus point can be manually moved around the frame by using the Multi-selector. You can also quickly bring the focus point back to the center of the frame by pressing the center button on the Multi-selector.

If you are going to be shooting landscapes or other scenes without people, you might want to consider using the Wide-area AF mode. This provides a larger focus area and makes it a little easier to get a quick focus lock on general subjects.

If you are going to be recording people, you can use the Face-priority mode. This is pretty self-explanatory: it automatically detects and focuses on your subject's face. If there is more than one person, the camera will focus on the closest one, but you can change from one face to another by using the Multi-selector.

The final mode is used for tracking a moving subject, which is why it's called Subject-tracking AF. To use this mode, place the focus point over your subject and press the center button on the Multi-selector. The focus point will continue to track your subject until it leaves the frame or until you turn it off by pressing the button again.

1. To change the AF-area, activate Live View mode by pressing the LV button.

2. Press and hold the AF-mode button on the front of the camera.

3. Rotate the Sub-command dial until you see the icon for your desired area mode in the top of the Live View display.

CHANGING THE FOCUS MODE

Of course, these modes will focus only if you are pressing the shutter release button or the AF-ON button (and that includes Subject-tracking AF). If you want your camera to actively focus while you are recording, you will need to change the mode from AF-S to AF-F (Full-time servo AF). When you activate AF-F, the camera will continuously focus using the focus mode you have selected.

1. To change the focus mode, activate Live View mode by pressing the LV button.

2. Press and hold the AF-mode button on the front of the camera.

3. Rotate the Main Command dial until you see the icon for your desired focus mode in the top of the Live View display.

Once your subject is in focus, you can push the Record button on top of the camera to begin the recording process. When the camera begins recording, you will notice that much of the shooting information disappears and a few new icons show up on the LCD (**Figure 12.4**). In the top left will be a blinking red Record icon to let you know that the camera is in active record mode. In the upper right, you will notice a timer that is counting down your remaining recording time. This number is directly related to the quality you have selected for your video. To stop the video recording, simply press the Record button a second time. This will take you back to Live View mode. To turn off Live View, press the LV button once more or turn the camera off.

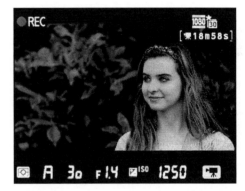

FIGURE 12.4
When recording is active, you will see a blinking red icon in the upper-left corner of the screen.

MANUALLY FOCUSING FOR MOVIES

While it's nice to use the autofocus for casual movie recording, if you really want to get serious you will probably want to manually focus your lens during recording. This is the way that the pros do it—and for good reason. The autofocus system in the camera is both slow and noisy. The noise comes from the internal focusing motors of the autofocus system. If you are using the built-in microphone, you will no doubt hear the autofocus system in your movies. This can be overcome by using an external mic, which is discussed in the bonus chapter. Because of the mechanics of the system, the slowness of the autofocus system is something that can't be helped. Typically what you will see when using the autofocus is that your subject will move in and out of focus while the camera tries to lock in a sharp focus. To combat this problem, most professionals manually focus their cameras as they shoot. This requires a lot of practice and sometimes some special gear, but when done right, it gives a more polished look to your video. To manually focus, just turn the AF-mode switch to M and use the focusing ring on your lens.

MOVIE SETTINGS

Now that we know the mechanics of recording a video, let's spend a little time looking at the settings you will use to dictate the quality of your video. First, we need to determine the size of the video that is recorded. The D800 records high-definition video, which is means that the video uses a 16x9 image format in two sizes. The two HD sizes available are 1280x720 and 1920x1080. Obviously the larger of the two will be higher quality, but it will also take up more recording space.

Along with selecting a size for your video, you will also need to pick a frame rate. Video is, after all, a series of still image frames that are displayed in rapid fashion to make what looks like a moving picture. The standard for most video is 30 frames per second. The European standard is 25 frames per second. There is also a setting of 24 frames per second, which is the frame rate used for movies shot on film. There are also additional choices for the 1280x720 sizes, which include 60 (U.S.A.) and 50 (Europe) frames per second. These faster frame rates are great if you intend to do some slow-motion edits of your videos since they contain twice as many frames per second. This means they can be played at half-speed and still look nice and smooth.

CHANGING THE MOVIE SETTINGS

1. To set the video size and frame rate, press the Menu button, navigate to the Movie settings option in the Shooting menu, and press OK (**A**).

2. Select the Frame size/frame rate option, and press OK (**B**).

3. Select one of the size/rate options, and press OK to return to the Movie Settings menu (**C**).

4. If you want to change the video quality, highlight the Movie quality option, press OK, and then select either High or Normal quality (**D**). This affects the quality of the video file, much like JPEG quality affects still image quality.

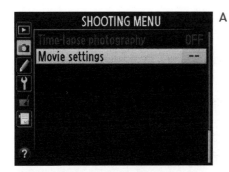
A

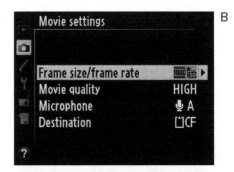
B

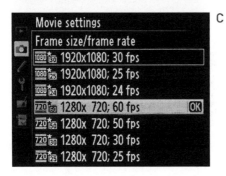
C

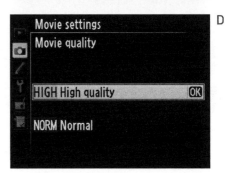
D

OTHER VIDEO OPTIONS

While you are in the Settings menu, you might want to go ahead and adjust some of the other options, like the microphone recording level and the movie destination. The D800's built-in microphone is monaural in nature, which means it records only a single channel of video. If you want to get stereo sound, you will need to use an external mic like the Nikon ME-1. You can also choose to just turn off the audio if you are going to add a soundtrack later during editing.

CHANGING THE AUDIO SETTINGS

1. To make adjustments to the audio settings, go back into the Movie Settings menu, select Microphone, and press OK.

2. To enable the camera to automatically adjust the audio levels, select Auto sensitivity, and press OK (**A**). If you want to adjust them yourself, highlight Manual sensitivity, and press OK.

3. You can select an audio level from 1 to 20 by using the Multi-selector (**B**). Just be careful to watch your audiometers to see that the audio level doesn't hit zero except during the loudest moments.

4. To turn off the microphone, highlight the Microphone off option in the menu, and press OK.

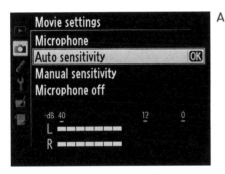 A

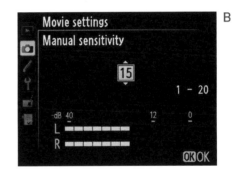 B

SELECTING A DESTINATION

The last option in the Movie Settings menu is called Destination, and it lets you pick which memory storage slot you want to use for your video files. This can be handy if you want to shoot both stills and video and have a CF and SD memory card in your camera. If you have only one card, the camera will automatically save your files there; if you have two, you can designate which one will hold the video files. To set it up, go into the Movie Settings menu, pick the Destination option, and select the card where you want the video to be saved (**C**).

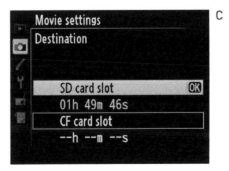 C

VIEW MODES

The Information On mode of Live View offers a lot of information for setting up your camera and lets you see things like the focus mode, the white balance, the frame size and rate, the selected picture control, and even the audiometer (**Figure 12.5**).

All of this is great stuff, but sometimes it can get in the way, which is why you have four other options available. For an uncluttered view, you can choose

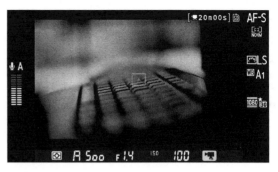

FIGURE 12.5
The Information On screen displays lots of video information.

to turn off all information (**Figure 12.6**). If you want to get a better idea of the exposure range that you are working with, you might want to enable the Histogram mode, which puts a histogram right in the preview (**Figure 12.7**); the histogram will be active only when recording is turned off, though the other two options are really helpful in composing your scene. The Framing Guides mode overlays a grid on the preview to help keep things squared up (**Figure 12.8**), and the Virtual Horizon mode puts an active level indicator right on your screen; this lets you know whether you are holding the camera straight and whether the lens is tipped forward or backward (**Figure 12.9**).

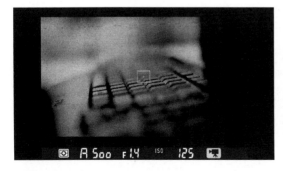

FIGURE 12.6
Use the Information Off mode for a clutter-free display.

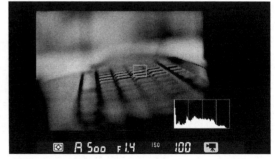

FIGURE 12.7
To get a live view of your exposure information, try using the Histogram mode.

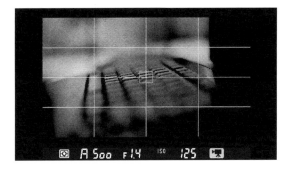

FIGURE 12.8
The Framing Guides mode helps with composition.

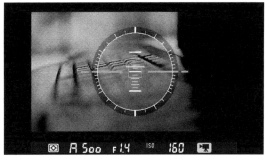

FIGURE 12.9
If your video always seems to be tilted, try using the Virtual Horizon mode.

ACCESSORIES

CLOSE-UP

In the bonus chapter, I discuss a lot of camera accessories, including a section on close-up accessories such as the Nikon close-up filter and extension tubes. Well, guess what? You can use those same accessories for getting great close-up video of tiny little subjects such as insects or flowers.

POLARIZING FILTERS

The polarizing filter will offer the same benefits to your videos as it does to your photographs. By utilizing this filter, you can eliminate the bluish color cast that can happen on those blue-sky days, bring accurate color and contrast to vegetation, reduce annoying reflections from water and glass, and darken your blue skies, giving them more depth and character.

NEUTRAL DENSITY FILTERS

Shooting in bright daylight conditions can sometimes overwhelm any attempts at using a larger aperture and achieving a shallow depth of field (see the section "Getting a Shallow Depth of Field" later in this chapter). To help combat this problem, you might want to employ the use of a neutral density filter to darken the scene. The filters come in varying densities or darkness values, so you will need to determine how much light you need to cut down to get the effect you desire. A great filter for this is the Singh-Ray Vari-ND filter, which lets you vary the amount of density by up to eight stops.

The problem with this filter is that it only comes in 77mm and 82mm sizes, and they are pretty expensive. You can create your own variable ND filter by purchasing a linear polarizing filter and a circular polarizer, which cost much less. Place the linear polarizer on your lens and then the circular on top of that. Then just rotate the circular polarizer and watch the scene get darker and darker. Dial in the amount of density you want and start recording.

TRIPODS

Another topic that is covered in the bonus chapter is the use of tripods to stabilize the camera for the purpose of achieving sharper images. The use of a tripod for video is not quite the same as for still image applications. When you are shooting video, you want to present a nice, smooth video scene that is fairly free of camera shake. One particular case for this is the pan shot. When you are following a subject from side to side, you will want the viewer's attention to be focused on the subject, not the shaky look of the video. To help in this effort, your preferred weapon of choice should be a tripod with a fluid head (**Figure 12.10**). A fluid head looks a little different than a standard tripod head in that it usually has one long handle for controlled

panning. To really make things smooth, the head uses a system of small fluid cartridges within the panning mechanisms so that your panning movements are nice and smooth. For around $130, you can get a nice fluid pan head that will mount on your existing tripod legs (if your existing tripod has a removable head).

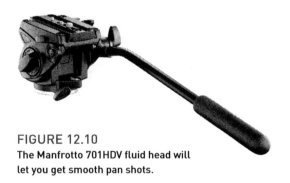

FIGURE 12.10
The Manfrotto 701HDV fluid head will let you get smooth pan shots.

CAMERA STABILIZERS

Aside from using a boom arm, there's really only one way to get jitter-free video on your camera while moving around: use a steady device. You have probably heard of SteadiCam rigs, but they can be cumbersome, expensive, and frankly a little bit of overkill for the normal video experience. But there are smaller, handheld rigs that provide the same benefit without the cost and bulk, like the ModoSteady from Manfrotto (**Figure 12.11**). One of the big advantages of this rig is that it has three different setups to choose from. The steady mode hangs a counterbalance under the camera to allow you to capture fluid-looking video movement. You can also move the balance arm to a different position and use it as a shoulder rig, much like the stock of a rifle. Finally, you can open the handle and turn it into a small tabletop tripod. That's a lot of functionality for under $100.

EASIER LCD VISION

I have one problem with shooting video on the D800 or any DSLR camera: I can't use the viewfinder as I record. Instead, I am forced to use the rear LCD screen, and while it is very large and sharp, my old eyes tend to make me hold the camera fairly far away from my body to see the screen. But there is another way, and it is perfect for old eyes like mine.

To really get a good look at what is happening in your LCD monitor, you should use a loupe like the Zacuto Z-Finder Pro 3X, which is made for 3.2" screens and attaches to the camera for hands-free operation (**Figure 12.12**). If you are going to be doing a lot of video recording, you will most certainly want to look into a device like this. Not only is it great for getting a better look at the LCD screen while recording, it also helps avoid glare on the screen while working outdoors.

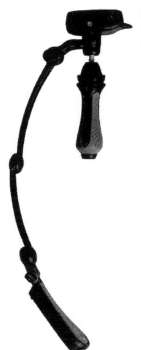

FIGURE 12.11
You can get smooth video movement by using a stabilizer like the ModoSteady.

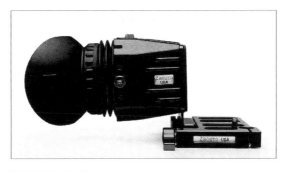

FIGURE 12.12
Using an attached loupe lets you get a better look at your LCD monitor.

GETTING A SHALLOW DEPTH OF FIELD

As I said earlier, getting the look of a production cinema camera means working with shallow depth of fields. The problem you might encounter when trying to get a large aperture in your video will be that the camera wants to use an auto-exposure mode to establish the correct camera settings for recording video. To get the benefit of a large aperture, you will need to work in either Aperture Priority or Manual mode.

If you are shooting in Aperture Priority mode, the camera will automatically adjust the shutter speed and ISO so that you can use your desired aperture setting. As the shutter slows to 1/30 of a second, the ISO will begin to rise to maintain an acceptable shutter speed. Of course, if the scene is really bright, the shutter speed will increase all the way up to 1/8000 of a second. If you want to adjust the brightness or darkness of the scene, you can use the Exposure Compensation setting, which will fool the meter.

To really get control of your exposure, you will want to use the Manual mode. Manual will let you make the scene darker or lighter than will the other modes, which are striving for a perfectly metered scene. The problem is that sometimes you might want the scene to appear darker or lighter than it is, which is a great time to flip into Manual. There is no auto function in Manual, so you will need to adjust the aperture, ISO, and shutter speed. Just as in Aperture Priority, you won't be able to set a shutter speed below 1/30 of a second. But since Manual mode has no auto adjustments, the Exposure Compensation feature will not render any difference in the exposure.

GIVING A DIFFERENT LOOK TO YOUR VIDEOS

USING PICTURE CONTROLS

Something that a lot of people don't realize is that you can use the picture controls to give your video a completely different look. Sure, you can use the Standard control for everyday video, but why not add some punch by using the Vivid setting? Nothing says HD like bright, vivid colors. Or maybe you want to shoot a landscape scene. Go ahead and set the picture control to the Landscape setting to improve the look of skies and vegetation. If you really want to get creative, try using the Monochrome setting and shoot in black and white. The great thing about using the picture controls is that you will see the effect right on your LCD monitor as you record so you will know exactly what your video is going to look like. Want to take things up a notch? Try customizing the picture controls and do things like shoot sepia-colored video. Check out the "Classic Black and White Portraits" section of Chapter 6 to see how to customize the look of your Monochrome picture control.

WHITE BALANCE

Another great way to change the look of your video is to select a white balance that matches your scene for accurate color rendition—or better yet, choose one that doesn't match to give a different feel to your video. You can completely change the mood of the video by selecting a white balance setting that is different from the actual light source that you are working in. Don't be afraid to be creative and try out different looks for your video.

TIPS FOR BETTER VIDEO

SHOOT SHORT SEQUENCES

Even though your camera can record fairly long video sequences, you should probably limit your shooting time to short clips and then edit them together. Here's the deal: most professional videos shot today are actually made up of very short video sequences that are edited together. If you don't believe me, watch any TV show and see how long you actually see a continuous sequence. I am guessing that you won't see any clip that is longer than about 10 seconds in length. You can thank music videos for helping to shorten our attention spans, but the reality is that your videos will look much more professional if you shoot in shorter clips and then edit them together.

STAGE YOUR SHOTS

If you are trying to produce a good-looking video, take some time before you begin shooting to determine what you want to shoot and where you want to shoot it from. You can mark the floor with tape to give your "actors" a mark to hit. You can also use staging to figure out where your lens needs to be set for correct focus on these different scenes.

AVOID THE QUICK PAN

While recording video, your camera uses something called a rolling shutter, which, as the name implies, rolls from the top to the bottom of the frame. If you are panning quickly from one side to another, you will see your video start to jiggle like it is being shot through Jell-O. This is something that can't be overcome except by using a slower panning motion. If you are going to be shooting a fast subject, consider using a camera setting that utilizes a fast shutter speed. It won't eliminate the problem completely, but it should improve it a little.

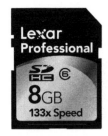

FIGURE 12.13
A fast memory card
will help prevent
dropped frames in
your video.

USE A FAST MEMORY CARD

Your video will be recording at up to 60 frames per second, and as it is recording it's placing the video into a buffer, or temporary holding spot, while the camera writes the frames to your memory card. If you are using a slower memory card, it might not be able to keep up with the flow of video—with the result being dropped frames. The camera will actually not record some frames because the buffer will fill up before the images have time to be written. This will be seen as small skips in the video when you watch it later. You can prevent this from happening by using an SD card that has a speed rating of class 6 or higher (**Figure 12.13**). These cards have faster writing speeds and will keep the video moving smoothly from the camera to the card.

VIDEO OVER TIME

SHOOTING TIME-LAPSE VIDEO

If you want to try something completely different from the standard video recording, you might want to explore time-lapse video, which allows you to take events that happen over long periods of time and speed them up so they can be watched in just a fraction of the time. This could be the blooming of a flower or maybe the setting of the sun on a colorful afternoon.

There are only two things you will need to capture time-lapse sequences. The first is a sturdy tripod. This is essential since the camera will be taking a lot of photos over a long period of time, and any movement in the camera will be distracting in the final video. The other thing you will need is something interesting to shoot. Some of my favorite subjects are clouds. I really like setting up my camera so that I can capture a nice landscape scene with clouds and then record several hundred frames over half an hour. The final videos are fairly short, but it's a lot of fun to watch the clouds quickly move across the sky.

SETTING UP THE TIME-LAPSE FEATURE

1. To shoot time-lapse, activate the camera menu, select the Time-lapse photography option in the Shooting menu, and press OK (**A**).

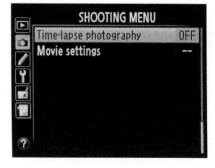

2. The feature will be set to Off, so press the right arrow on the Multi-selector to enter the next screen (**B**).

3. Set the interval for your shots. This is the amount of time you want between shots (**C**). You will need to experiment with this, but events that take place over a long period of time will have longer intervals. I set my cloud shots to about 30 seconds between shots.

4. Press the right arrow on the Multi-selector to get to the Shooting time settings, and set the time period that you want to capture (**D**). The maximum setting is 7 hours and 59 minutes but could be less depending on the size of your memory card.

5. Press the right arrow on the Multi-selector again to return to the start screen, highlight On, and press the OK button to begin the recording sequence (**E**).

6. The camera will begin shooting 3 seconds after you press the OK button. To end the sequence before the set time, push the OK button again. When the sequence is completed, you can press the preview button to watch your video.

B

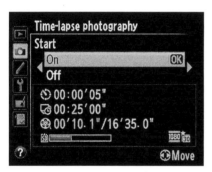

C

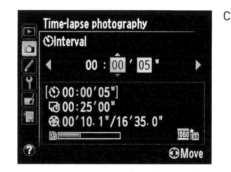

D

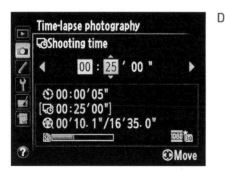

E

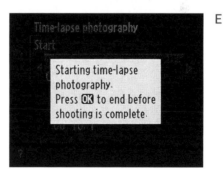

TIPS FOR TIME-LAPSE VIDEO

- Before activating the time-lapse feature, set your camera up on the tripod and compose your scene.

- Take a few test shots before starting your sequence so you know your exposure is correct.

- Use manual focus so that the camera isn't trying to focus before each shot.

- Use a fully charged battery so you are sure to have enough juice for long sequences.

- Turn off the auto-image review feature in the Display menu to save battery life.

- Use Manual mode if you are recording a sunset and want the scene to get darker as you go. A mode like Aperture Priority will always try to make the scene look normal.

- If you are shooting a night scene with long exposures, use an interval that is not only longer than your exposure time but also long enough to take the Long Exposure Noise Reduction into account.

- The time-lapse feature uses the video frame size to create the finished video sequence, so be sure to set this up in the Movie Settings menu before shooting your sequence.

- The length of your completed video will be displayed at the bottom of the main time-lapse menu screen. If you want a video that is a specific length, keep an eye on this information and adjust your settings accordingly.

A TIME-LAPSE ALTERNATIVE

The only problem with the time-lapse feature is that it creates the video but does not keep the individual frames, so you can't play with them later. If you would prefer to shoot a time-lapse sequence but create your own video file using a software solution, try using the Interval Timer Shooting feature. You can set similar options, such as interval time and number of total shots (up to 999 frames). Check out pages 201–206 in the user's manual for more info.

EXPANDING YOUR KNOWLEDGE

I have given you a couple of quick tips and suggestions in this chapter to get you started with your moviemaking, but if you really want to get serious there is a lot more you need to know. Videography can be a complex endeavor, and there is much to learn and know if you want to move beyond the simple video capture of the kids in the backyard or the trip to the amusement park. If you really want to explore all that your camera has to offer in the way of video moviemaking, then I suggest you read *Creating DSLR Video: From Snapshots to Great Shots* (**Figure 12.14**). It is written in the same easy-to-read style as this and all the Snapshots books, and it will give you a lot of information to help you step up to the next level.

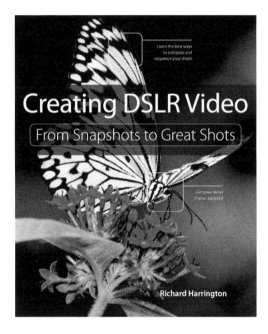

FIGURE 12.14
I highly recommend *Creating DSLR Video* for taking your video work to the next level.

Chapter 12 Assignments

Even if you don't think you will be shooting much video, it pays to know how to use it because you just never know when it will come in handy. The truth is that I used to turn up my nose at the video functions in DSLR cameras, but over time I have come to really appreciate the ability to create multimedia projects that offer expanded expression. Who knows, you just might be the next big indie director on the block.

Change your focus

There are several focus modes available for the movie/Live View mode, and you should give all of them a try before deciding which method works best for you. Try setting AF-S mode and focusing prior to shooting, and then shoot a sequence with AF-F mode to see if you prefer to have the camera autofocus continuously while you shoot.

Abandon AF

Once you are comfortable with the autofocus methods, go ahead and turn it off and go manual. The hardest part is getting used to which way the focus ring needs to turn for closer and farther focus points. Try this: put a piece of tape on the lens barrel and write N and F (for near and far) on it so you know which way to go. Now try to capture a moving subject while adjusting focus.

Go shallow

Remember that one of the big deals in using your D800 for video is the shallow depth of field you can achieve. If you don't have a lens with a particularly large aperture, try using it wide open and getting close to your subject. The closer you are, the narrower the depth of field will look.

Change the look of your video

The picture controls are a great creative tool for making movies. Check out all the options to see if you can add some pizzazz to your video. Want to preview a picture control's effect? Activate Live View, press the Picture Control/Lock button, and then use the Multi-selector to preview the different picture controls.

Speed up time

Even though it's not like real-time video making, I really enjoy making time-lapse sequences. The trick is to find a scene where something slowly changes over time. I mentioned that I like shooting cloudy-sky videos, but you could shoot an intersection, a sunset, or even slow boats moving in a harbor. Just pick a scene, set up on a sturdy tripod, and experiment. The only limit is your imagination.

Share your results with the book's Flickr group!

Join the group here: www.flickr.com/groups/d800fromsnapshotstogreatshots

INDEX

3D-tracking AF mode, using, 107
10-pin remote terminal, 2
24mm lenses, using, 40. *See also*
 lenses
35mm lenses, using, 41

A

A (Aperture Priority) mode. *See* Aperture Priority (A) mode
accessories
 camera stabilizers, 282–283
 neutral density filters, 281–282
 polarizing filters, 281
 tripods, 282
Accessory shoe, 4
action, freezing, 86
action shots. *See also* motion; sporting events
 3D-tracking AF mode, 107
 continuous shooting mode, 109–112
 direction of travel, 96–97, 115–116
 drive modes, 109
 fast-paced, 102
 focusing, 105–107
 ISO settings, 102
 lenses, 118
 subject placement, 114–115
 subject speed, 98
 subject-to-camera distance, 99
 tips, 114–117
 vantage points, 116–117
 watching buffer, 112
 zooming in, 100–101
additive color, 14
ADL (Active D-Lighting)
 bracketing, 229–230
 Matrix metering mode, 228
 seeing in Overview display mode, 17
 setting up for, 229
 settings, 228
 using, 227–229, 231
Adobe RGB color space, 14–15
AE-L (Auto Exposure Lock). *See also* exposures
 using, 130–131
 using for sunrise, 258–259
 using for sunset, 258–259
AF Assist, using in low light, 201

AF mode selector, 2
AF-area mode, changing for video, 275
AF-Assist/red-eye reduction lamp, 2
AF-C (Continuous-servo AF) mode
 Dynamic-area AF, 106–107
 features, 105
 selecting, 106
 shooting in, 106
 Single-Point AF, 106
AF-on button, 3
AF-S (Single-Servo AF) mode
 choosing center point, 133
 setting up, 132
 using, 131–133
Ambient brightness sensor, 3
angles, considering in compositions, 240–241
Aperture Priority (A) mode
 controlling depth of field with, 89
 depth of field, 79–81
 environmental portraits, 127
 features, 78
 isolating subjects, 103–104
 light availability, 81
 setting up, 82
 shooting in, 82
 versus Shutter Priority (S), 104
 sunny days, 104–105
 using, 79–81, 85–86, 126–127
apertures. *See also* f-stops
 function of, 49
 maximum, 81, 83
 role in exposure triangle, 44–45
 seeing in Overview display mode, 17
 settings, 49–50
 small versus larger, 81
 using to focus attention, 250
 wide, 126
audio settings, changing, 279
Auto Exposure Lock (AE-L). *See* AE-L (Auto Exposure Lock)
Auto ISO. *See also* ISO
 returning to shooting mode, 64
 sensitivity controls, 62–64
 turning on, 61
 using, 66
Auto-Area AF mode, setting, 64–65
autofocus. *See also* focus modes
 versus manual focus, 290
 overriding, 15–16
auto-off timers, setting, 7

B

back of camera
 AF-On Button, 3
 Ambient Brightness Sensor, 3
 Delete Image Button, 3
 Eyepiece Shutter Lever, 3
 Focus Selector Lock, 3
 Image Playback Button, 3
 Info Button, 3
 Live View Button, 3
 Main Command Dial, 3
 Menu Button, 3
 Meter Selector Dial/AE-L/AF-L Button, 3
 Monitor, 3
 Multi-Selector, 3
 Multi-Selector Button, 3
 OK Button, 3
 Playback Zoom In, 3
 Protect/Picture Control/Help Button, 3
 Release Mode Dial, 3
 Thumbnail/Playback Zoom Out, 3
backgrounds
 blurring, 126, 238
 considering in portraits, 143
battery
 charging, 5
 displaying current state of, 5
 keeping backup of, 5
 preserving, 106
black and white
 landscape photography, 164–166
 portraits, 133–134
"blinkies," appearance of, 87–88
"the blue sky shot," 243–244
bracketing
 ADL (Active D-Lighting), 229–230
 hands-free, 265–266
Bracketing button, 4
brightness, considering in composition, 173–174
buffer, watching, 112
built-in flash
 Manual power setting, 206
 metering modes, 205–206
 range, 204
 shutter speeds, 205
 testing limits of, 215
 TTL (Through the Lens) metering, 205–206
 using, 203–206

Printed in Great Britain
by Amazon